THE EVERYTHING®
Literary Crosswords Book

Dear Reader,

Books are beautiful. Even without reading them, books are just aesthetically pleasing. Take this book for example—turn it around in your hands, run your fingers through its pages, marvel at its construction. Why do we love books so much? Well, beauty is only skin deep and you can't judge a book by its cover. Of course, it's what's inside that really counts. Books are filled with ideas, knowledge, and stories communicated to you from someone a world or a lifetime away. Beautiful!

This book is a crossword puzzle celebration of books. More is required here than just reading. You will actually complete this book by filling in the puzzle grids. Think hard—each puzzle has a literary theme with related clues sprinkled into the grids. Clues from all sorts of books are included, nothing has been ruled out as too lowbrow or too highbrow.

So here is one more book added to the huge universe of published works. I hope that you find it entertaining!

Charles Timmerman

The EVERYTHING® Series

Editorial

Innovation Director	Paula Munier
Editorial Director	Laura M. Daly
Associate Copy Chief	Sheila Zwiebel
Acquisitions Editor	Lisa Laing
Production Editor	Casey Ebert

Production

Director of Manufacturing	Susan Beale
Production Project Manager	Michelle Roy Kelly
Prepress	Erick DaCosta Matt LeBlanc
Interior Layout	Heather Barrett Brewster Brownville Colleen Cunningham Jennifer Oliveira
Cover Design	Erin Alexander Stephanie Chrusz Frank Rivera

Visit the entire Everything® Series at *www.everything.com*

THE
EVERYTHING®
LITERARY
CROSSWORDS
BOOK

150 novel puzzles for book lovers

Charles Timmerman
Founder of Funster.com

Avon, Massachusetts

For my brother-in-law, Steve.

An Everything® Series Book.
Everything® and everything.com® are registered trademarks of F+W Publications, Inc.

Published by Adams Media, an F+W Publications Company
57 Littlefield Street, Avon, MA 02322 U.S.A.
www.adamsmedia.com

ISBN-10: 1-59869-339-5
ISBN-13: 978-1-59869-339-3

Printed in the United States of America.

J I H G F E D C B A

This book is available at quantity discounts for bulk purchases.
For information, please call 1-800-289-0963.

Contents

Acknowledgments

I would like to thank the more than half a million people who have visited my Web site, www.funster.com. You have shown me just how much fun words can be.

I'm happy to have the support and dedication of my agent, Jacky Sach. Thanks for keeping me so busy!

As always, it was a pleasure working with all of the nice people at Adams Media who made this book possible. In particular, Lisa Laing made my job easier.

Most of all, I'm grateful for the support and encouragement from my two reading buddies: Suzanne and Calla.

Introduction

▶ WHAT DO ROSA PARKS, Richard Nixon, Jesse Owens, and crossword puzzles all have in common? They were all born in the year 1913. In that year, a journalist named Arthur Wynne published a "word-cross" puzzle in the *New York World* Sunday newspaper. Though it was diamond-shaped, it had all of the features of crossword puzzles that we know and love today. The name evolved into *crossword* as the paper continued to publish the popular word puzzles.

It wasn't until 1924 that the first book of crossword puzzles was published. That was when the crossword craze really began. It joined other fads of the Roaring Twenties like goldfish eating, flagpole sitting, yo-yo's, and pogo sticks. Of course, not all of these fads survived (perhaps fortunately).

Besides crossword puzzles, some really beautiful things came out of the 1920s. In music, jazz surged in popularity and George Gershwin's *Rhapsody in Blue* was performed for the first time. In literature, F. Scott Fitzgerald published some of his most enduring novels including *The Great Gatsby*. In design, it was the beginning of Art Deco. That's how the world was when crossword puzzles came of age.

Crossword puzzles became popular in a time when entertainment required *active* participation. In those days, people actually played sports rather than watched them, told each other stories rather than turned on the television, and even sang songs rather than listened to an MP3. Like entertainment of yesteryear, crossword puzzles require your active participation. And this is a refreshing change for those of us who still enjoy a mental workout.

Today, nearly every major newspaper runs a crossword puzzle. Entire sections of bookstores are devoted to crossword puzzle books. (Thanks for choosing this one!) Indeed, crosswords are the most common word puzzle in the world.

Why do crossword puzzles continue to be so popular? Only you can answer that question since there are as many reasons to work a crossword puzzle as there are solvers. But perhaps it has something to do with the convenient marriage of fun and learning that crossword puzzles offer. Enjoy!

PUZZLES

Chapter 1: Romance

Jane Austen

Across

1. 50-and-over gp.
5. Antifur org.
9. Jane Austen novel named after the main character
13. Aaron Burr's daughter
14. Waterless
15. Song of praise
16. ___ Park, Jane Austen novel
18. Wearer of three stars: Abbr.
19. State in the SE United States
21. "God willing!"
24. Place of shelter
28. TV's Italian mouse ___ Gigio
29. Boat trailer
32. Kemo ___
33. Title of reverence for God
36. Can of worms, maybe
38. Eagle org.
39. Sense and ___, Jane Austen novel
42. One of the Cyclades
44. "Pay ___ mind"
45. Talisman
48. Made a web
50. WWW address starter
52. Teased
53. Metallic element
55. Disney World city
58. Clan leader
61. Blockbuster rental
64. Pride and ___, Jane Austen novel
68. Draconian
69. Baseball catcher Tony
70. ___ child

Solution on page 152

71. X-rated stuff
72. Adam's youngest
73. Rent

Down

1. Pressure unit equivalent to 760 torr: Abbr.
2. Solver's cry
3. Stimpy's TV pal
4. Defer
5. Hurts
6. Heretofore
7. Mah-jongg piece
8. Combines
9. They may be picky
10. Ryan of "When Harry Met Sally"
11. Sallie ___
12. Raggedy doll
15. "Give me another chance," e.g.
17. Honorarium
20. Young woman
21. "Make ___ double"
22. Coal carrier
23. Pogo, e.g.
25. Capital of the Chaldean empire
26. Observation
27. New Deal program: Abbr.
30. Head monk
31. Chiang ___-shek
34. "Gimme ___!" (start of an Iowa State cheer)
35. Panama and others
37. Lyricist Rice
40. Abbr. on a bank statement
41. 1926 La Scala premiere
42. Bar intro?
43. Mother of Jupiter
46. Principal's deg.
47. Auto racer Fabi
49. Like Miss Congeniality
51. Packing a wallop
54. "Oops!"
56. Prince of India
57. Lucy of "Charlie's Angels," 2000
59. "The Mod Squad" co-star, 1999
60. At liberty
61. Letters on tapes
62. "___ a Rock"
63. ___ Hill (Sisqo's old group)
65. Daughter of Cadmus
66. Not cloudy: Abbr.
67. Take a gander at

Bridget Jones's Diary

Across

1. Song popularized by Vincent Lopez
5. Lose one's cool
10. Legal costs
14. Lacking width and depth
15. Get away from
16. One of the deadly sins
17. Saltimbocca ingredient
18. Weighed down
19. Like some tea
20. "Bridget Jones: The ___ ___ ___," sequel to the first
23. Pacific nation since 1968
24. Remain alive
28. Sailor's yes
29. Fundraiser suffix
33. Situation comedy
34. Palestinian leader
36. Billions of years
37. "Bridget Jones's Diary" author
41. Broad bean
42. Yellowish-pink
43. Ancient city in S Egypt
46. Mao successor
47. Set
50. Capital of Venezuela
52. ___ Polo
54. Underground
58. Boxer's reach, e.g.
61. Beau
62. Mr. Uncool
63. Mislay
64. Chair man?
65. Inner: prefix
66. Length of time recorded in "Bridget Jones's Diary," one ___
67. Old hat
68. Noticed

Down

1. Multi-day devotion
2. At some point
3. Group
4. Harmonica virtuoso Larry
5. Money
6. Apple spray
7. Unclothed
8. Bright thoughts
9. Official count of population
10. Golden State Senator
11. SASE, e.g.
12. First lady?
13. Pink Floyd's Barrett
21. Weird
22. Geisha's sash
25. Religious image
26. Carol
27. Logos, e.g.: abbr.
30. A dynasty in China
31. Does in
32. Aquatic nymph
34. Variety of calcite
35. Prefix with type
37. More than a tee-hee
38. ___ and anon
39. K-O connection
40. Ism
41. Antitrust org.
44. Euro forerunner
45. Buffalo team
47. "The Power and the Glory" novelist
48. Game similar to euchre
49. Bridget Jones's city
51. Mink kin
53. Queen ___ lace
55. Madame Bovary's first name
56. Barn dance
57. Kennedy matriarch
58. Clever
59. Kicker?
60. High ___ kite

Solution on page 152

Wuthering Heights

Across

1. Adds
5. Twin sister of Ares
9. Bradley and Sharif
14. Established practice
16. Neighborhood
17. Pseudonym for "Wuthering Heights" author
18. Idealized concept of a loved one
19. Civil War initials
20. Ward of "Once and Again"
21. Park, for one
22. Reds and Cards
24. Nabokov novel
25. Walking
27. Simultaneously
31. "...who lived in ___"
32. Bake, as eggs
33. Vichy water
34. Rhîne's capital
35. Wet
36. Puts out, in a way
37. Allen wrench shape
38. Did not
39. Internet destinations
40. Dawn
42. One of the Beverly Hillbillies
43. Merry-go-round music
44. Theme
45. Detox centers
48. Main idea
49. Inc., in Britain
52. Little Boy or Fat Man
53. "Wuthering Heights" main female
55. Dynamite inventor
56. Delighting the senses
57. Voltaic cell component
58. Site of Jesus' first miracle
59. Aqua Velva competitor

Down

1. A writer may work on it
2. WWW addresses
3. Pensiveness
4. Poli ___
5. Stefan of tennis
6. Film units
7. 1985 film, To Live and Die ___
8. N.L. Central team inits.
9. Actor who played 28-Down
10. Instant
11. Open ___ of worms
12. Brand of sauce
13. ___ gin fizz
15. Early ascetic
21. Steamed
23. Animal with a mane
24. Sharp end
25. Lost color
26. Shelters
27. Muse
28. "Wuthering Heights" main male
29. Avid
30. ___-Japanese War
32. 1978 Peace Nobelist
35. Cambodian money
36. South American monkey
38. Trickle
39. Group of seven
41. Held responsible
42. Handel oratorio
44. Magnate
45. ___ fever (was sick)
46. Black, to a bard
47. Down-and-outer
48. Mother of the Titans
50. Wide-headed fastener
51. Boxer Oscar ___ Hoya
53. Blue Jays airer
54. Inlet

Solution on page 152

Danielle Steel

Across

1. Lettuce variety
5. Ltd., in Paris
8. Skye guy
12. "It's __ ever wanted"
13. Poison conduit
14. Crete's highest elev.
15. Spanish flowers?
16. "Render therefore ___ Caesar..."
17. Online marketing
18. "Toxic ___," Danielle Steel novel
20. Elvis ___ Presley
21. Monteverdi opera
22. __-Cat
23. Chiang Kai-shek's capital
26. Esteem
30. Simple shelter
31. High point
34. Home of Zeno
35. Running amok
37. Doctor
38. Bohemian, e.g.
39. Puff
40. Cast member
42. 1955 merger letters
43. Christian ___, Danielle Steel's denomination
45. Start of a Feiffer comedy
47. Knock
48. The ____ bin Laden in the news
50. Comic Sandler
52. Yellow flower
56. Short Internet message
57. Stick ___ in the water
58. Lytton heroine
59. Endured
60. Do banker's work
61. Turn over
62. Guam, e.g.: Abbr.
63. "___ you kidding?"
64. Number of times Danielle Steel has been married (as of 2006)

Down

1. Cutting remark
2. Hipbones
3. Political faction
4. Spiritual supervisor
5. Camp craft
6. Preface
7. Vanity cases?
8. "Sunset in ___ ___," Danielle Steel novel
9. "Later"
10. Aesir leader
11. 1960-61 world chess champ
13. Carry out
14. Stands for
19. Standing tall
22. Reason for an R rating
23. Melts
24. Containing gold
25. Formal response to "Who's there?"
26. Suggestive
27. Vote in
28. Agnes's uncle
29. Chevy SUV
32. Run in neutral
33. Extinct kiwi relative
36. Functor
38. Kind of wave
40. Narc's find
41. In seventh heaven
44. Pointed a finger at
46. Import or export duty
48. External
49. Backgammon piece
50. Upfront money
51. "Let's Make A Deal" choice
52. __ Cynwyd, Pa.
53. E. follower
54. Colgate, e.g.: Abbr.
55. ___ Le Pew
56. Repair shop fig.

Solution on page 152

Nora Roberts

Across

1. Motherless man
5. Port of ancient Rome
10. Recipe info: Abbr.
14. Italian bread
15. Les ___-Unis
16. Emperor of Rome 54-68
17. Disney president Robert
18. "___ Thoroughbred," Nora Roberts first book
19. Waxed
20. Two wheel vehicle
22. Field-hockey team
24. Novelist Calvino
25. Lacking a key
28. Aviator
30. Song of David
34. "Beats me"
37. Yr.-end holiday
39. Wish one hadn't
40. Saudi king
41. Fast delivery
43. Serene
44. ___ Simbel, Egypt
45. WW2 servicewoman
46. Give power to
48. California border lake
50. Cup holder
52. Nora Roberts pseudonym
54. Hot drink
58. Kay Thompson creation
61. Seaport on San Francisco Bay
63. Follower of Mary
64. The Sun, for example
67. __ dixit
68. Understood
69. "Go fly ___!"
70. Seasonal air
71. "Giant" author Ferber
72. African lake
73. Penny, perhaps

Down

1. Cover story
2. Toe*Finger
3. Asian palm
4. Nora Roberts home state
5. Trompe l'___
6. Flow
7. ___ chi
8. Tag antagonists
9. Wan
10. "___ Fall," Nora Roberts book
11. Ex-host Griffin
12. Genealogical record
13. Planted oats
21. Invent
23. Overtakes, in a way
26. Public passenger vehicle
27. Big sport's offer
29. Parks of civil rights fame
31. Sinai citizen
32. Quiet time
33. First-grader's attention-getter
34. "___ first..."
35. "Aba __ Honeymoon"
36. "No way!"
38. He played Obi-Wan
42. Part of UTEP
43. "___ Moon," Nora Roberts book
45. Puts together
47. Make out
49. Indian people of Canada
51. German subs
53. Daughter of Lear
55. Castrated cockerel
56. Start
57. Fred Astaire's sister
58. Berlin-born Sommer
59. Polaroid's inventor
60. Harbinger
62. Tract
65. "Montana ___," Nora Roberts book
66. Acapulco aunt

Solution on page 152

Chick Lit

Across

1. Quick
6. Madam
10. Rotate
14. Cacao powder
15. Wells race
16. Java is in it
17. Jennifer Weiner chick lit novel, made into a movie starring Cameron Diaz
19. Clothes lines
20. Discern
21. It's about a foot
22. Among
24. Advertiser's award
25. "This won't hurt ___!"
26. Chick lit author of "Bridget Jones's Diary"
31. This present day
32. Eins + zwei
33. Salesman's dest.
35. A corpse
36. Bridges in movies
38. Yucatán years
39. Star Wars inits.
40. __ Carlo Menotti
41. Cease being awake
42. Chick lit book by Candace Bushnell and a TV series
46. Temper
47. Katz of "Matinee"
48. Kind of blue
51. Highlands hillside
52. HBO competitor
55. Some greenbacks
56. Chick lit target audience
59. Pasture portion
60. Gofer
61. Like some suspects
62. Symbols of perfection
63. Once, long ago
64. Minor

Down

1. Biol. and chem.
2. Use a whetstone on
3. Pain
4. Beluga delicacy
5. Herb
6. Advantage
7. Bitter drug
8. Heartache
9. Handicapped
10. Bora Bora neighbor
11. Hand-me-down
12. Lens holders
13. Democratic donkey designer
18. Tibia
23. Late-60's fashion item
24. Ali, once
25. Unsubstantial
26. Gangsters
27. One of the Van Halens
28. Rare wedding response?
29. Largish combo
30. Viscid
31. The "Superstation"
34. Medicinal amt.
36. Typesetting machine
37. "Shane" star
38. Others, in Latin
40. London lockup
41. Foul-up
43. Short holidays?
44. Large stinging wasp
45. On-line periodical, for short
48. Jacket
49. Enough, for some
50. European capital
51. Insects
52. Censor's target
53. Miami basketball team
54. As recently as
57. Thole insert
58. Monosaccharide

Solution on page 152

Romantic Novels at the Movies

Across

1. Upper-crust
5. "___ Mountain," novel made into a movie
9. Blowout
13. Serve in the capacity of
15. Locale
16. Football's Karras
17. Puts back in
18. Swedish import
19. Title role for Peter Fonda
20. Novel by William Styron made into a movie starring Meryl Streep
23. NYSE debut
24. Fed. medical agency
25. Uncle Tom's wife
28. Roman goddess of wisdom
31. Narrative
33. Printemps time
34. Petition
35. Suffix with clown or brown
36. Isak Dinesen memoir made into a movie
40. Restroom, for short
42. One-eighty
43. ___-80 (old computer)
44. Wash
47. Hit the spot
51. Grimy
52. Biol., e.g.
53. Foot part
54. Colleen McCullough novel made into a mini-series
59. "The ___ of Living Dangerously," novel made into a movie
61. Hercules' love

62. Author Blyton and others
63. Nevada's second-largest county
64. "___ Story," novel made into a movie
65. Flood barrier
66. Plebeian
67. Barbara of "I Dream of Jeannie"
68. Sun. speeches

Down

1. Here and there
2. Squid relatives
3. Walk over
4. "Hell ___ no fury..."
5. Medicinal shrub
6. Spinachlike plant
7. Jacob's wife
8. Actress Maryam
9. South American cowboy
10. Word of praise
11. Attorney F. ___ Bailey
12. Bunyan's tool
14. Fed. stipend
21. Full of envy
22. Defunct Trucker Control Org.
26. Walk-___: bit parts
27. Afr. nation
29. Grounded bird
30. Stool pigeon
31. "___ Wiedersehen"
32. Confident
34. Pronounce
36. Pass

37. Payment
38. N.Y.C. subway line
39. Hit CBS drama
40. Calculator feature, briefly
41. Bard of boxing
45. Pulsating
46. Comic Louis
47. Hide
48. Make a big effort
49. Raw material
50. Approvals
52. Work out
55. Bit of mosaic
56. Engine cover
57. ___ canto (singing style)
58. Supermodel Sastre
59. "Sho 'nuff"
60. Angular shape

Solution on page 153

Jane Eyre

Across

1. Jumps rope
6. Emblems of power
10. Arborist's concern
14. Veranda
15. Pusher's pursuer
16. Fermented grape juice
17. Debate
18. Author of "Jane Eyre" (first name)
20. Beauty courted to make Jane Eyre jealous (first name)
22. Kind of salad
23. Billy the Kid portrayer Gulager
24. Sired
25. Jane Eyre's future husband
29. Pertaining to the nose
33. Gone
34. Its symbol is Sn
35. Mad wife who burned Thornfield Hall in "Jane Eyre"
36. Place to stay
37. Last: Abbr.
38. Multivolume ref.
39. Stretch of turbulent water
40. Colonize
42. Gee preceder
43. One in Weimar
44. Northern Indians
45. Take turns
47. Calendar sequence
49. Word with jam or roll
50. Say again
52. Poe poem

56. Position of Jane Eyre employed at Thornfield Hall
58. Librarian's device
59. "__ Death": Grieg work
60. Forensic concerns
61. Navel variety
62. Hair division
63. Env. info
64. Chicago's ___ Expressway

Down

1. Chunk
2. Auto pioneer Benz
3. Actress Swenson
4. Potbellied
5. Fin de ___
6. Years ago
7. Noise from a fan
8. Stiff drink
9. Rawboned animal
10. Like major generals
11. Singer Coolidge
12. __ 'acte: intermission
13. Shoebox letters
19. Inclined
21. Jostle
24. Film rat
25. Worker's reward
26. Dog tag datum
27. Last words of "Over the Rainbow"
28. Tiny bird
30. Narrow groove
31. "I can take ___!"

32. Oversight
35. Happened to
37. Loose overcoat
38. Frequently, in verse
41. Storm
42. Leprechaun
43. "Jane Eyre" country of origin
45. Go to
46. Band aide
48. Fish in a John Cleese film
50. Parks of civil rights fame
51. At any point
52. WWII power
53. Eclectic magazine
54. Chow ___
55. "__ Tu" (1974 hit)
56. Discontinuity
57. Down

Solution on page 153

The Scarlet Letter

Across

1. Newton or Stern
6. Radar's brand
10. Horse's hoof sound
14. Gnatlike insect
15. Yoked pair
16. Bigot's emotion
17. Flaxlike fiber
18. Ice melter
19. Numerical prefix
20. Let out
21. Rival
23. Island group near Fiji
25. Shrink back
26. Woman condemned in "The Scarlet Letter"
30. Songlike
31. Danube locale: Abbr.
32. Elevs.
35. Stravinsky and others
36. Econ. figure
37. Bow or Barton
39. Filmdom's Chaney
40. Pull
41. Watched
42. Planned in advance
45. Attempts
48. First Hebrew letter
49. Father of 13-Down
52. Watch chains
55. Go sprawling
56. Knicks great Monroe
57. "This way" sign
58. 1969 jazz album
59. Romance writer's award
60. Reed or Mills
61. Caustic alkalis
62. "Take it or leave it"
63. Deputy

Down

1. Hungary's Nagy
2. "The King and I" country
3. Entrance granted
4. Firebrand
5. Middle mark
6. "Uh-uh!"
7. Midterm, for one
8. SOS
9. Doctors
10. Selection
11. Milk: Prefix
12. 10th-cen. Holy Roman Emperor known as "the Great"
13. Daughter of 26-Across
21. Heart
22. Royal flush card
24. Boot camp fare
26. Some precipitation
27. Conclusion lead-in
28. Cowboy's home
29. "Uh-huh"
32. Author of "The Scarlet Letter"
33. Arbor Day planting
34. Prom-night safety gp.
36. Wrigley field?
37. Rouse to action
38. Jump over
40. Mosaic square
41. Reprehensible
42. Grassy plains of Argentina
43. Kvass ingredient
44. Trinity River city
45. Detroit dud
46. Nonsensical
47. Look happy
50. Place of honor
51. Intro drawing class
53. Former West German capital
54. Hostage situation acronym
57. Oklahoma town

Solution on page 153

Jackie Collins

Across

1. City south of West Palm
5. Entices
10. Short times, for short
14. Spanish eyes
15. Yet to be rented
16. ___ unto himself
17. Lucky ___, Jackie Collins character
19. Author of the children's book "If Roast Beef Could Fly"
20. Strike
21. Legal offense
23. Otherwise
25. "The World Is Full of ___ Men," Jackie Collins novel
26. City where Jackie Collins was born
28. Fake drake
29. "___ or lose it"
30. Babe and Baby
31. Fu ___ (legendary Chinese sage)
34. "The Mod Squad" role
35. Is bold
36. Jackie Collins' sister
37. "Saving Private Ryan" craft: Abbr.
38. Less offensive
39. Tablets
40. Abnormal body temperature
41. Do business with
42. Ancient Egyptian king
45. Grimy
46. To give in return
48. New Deal prog.
51. "Must be something ___"
52. Period in which flowering plants appeared
54. Dutch ___
55. Chemical compound
56. "The other white meat"
57. Spawning area of salmon
58. Loved ones
59. Fateful day

Down

1. "Hogwash!"
2. Sierra Madre valley
3. Land mass
4. Halifax clock setting: Abbr.
5. Enlargement of toe joint
6. Anguish
7. "___ Three Lives"
8. Common satellite function
9. Stands
10. Pay
11. Nicholas Gage book
12. Dugout, e.g.
13. Weapon
18. Playground retort
22. Greek love god
24. Money guarantor, for short
26. Break
27. Medical suffix
28. Engraver Albrecht
30. Horse bred for racing
31. "___ Wives," Jackie Collins novel
32. Highway department supply
33. Not __ many words
35. "The World Is Full of ___ Women," Jackie Collins novel
36. Cast aside
38. Certain tide
39. Georges who wrote "Life: A User's Manual"
40. Quaker
41. Indians play them
42. Ranking monastic
43. Throw with effort
44. Made a scene?
45. Librarian's gadget
47. Job legislation estab. in 1973
49. Unalloyed
50. Sets a price at
53. Prefix with dermal

Solution on page 153

Chapter 2: Mystery

Raymond Chandler

Across

1. "Rush!"
5. Bursae
9. Lith. and Ukr., once
13. Coolidge's veep
15. Where Pioneer Day is celebrated
16. High fidelity
17. Reddish yellow
18. A ___ bagatelle
19. Bookie's concern
20. Chandler's protagonist
23. Part of AT&T: Abbr.
24. Direct a gun
25. Italian scooter
28. Golfer Payne
31. Soon
33. Arab garment
34. John, to Paul
35. Regard
36. Chandler's first novel
40. "All-American Girl" star Margaret
42. Spike the director
43. Dershowitz's forte
44. Grades
47. Mother and father
51. Small stream
52. Many a delivery
53. Nosh
54. Chandler's only original screenplay
59. Online giggle
61. Awestruck
62. Attorney Melvin
63. Eye part
64. Perpetually
65. More artful
66. Ernie's Muppet pal
67. On one's guard
68. Docs prescribe them

Down

1. Takes as one's own
2. Small bag
3. For some time
4. Strip
5. Apex
6. Leading players
7. "The Alienist" author Caleb
8. Illustrator Silverstein
9. Fall of rain
10. Skirt
11. Mail abbr.
12. Family nickname
14. ___ Lankan
21. Short allegorical story
22. Ab ___ (from the beginning)
26. Work at
27. Word of assent
29. Guitar effect, when doubled
30. Actor Vigoda
31. "Help!"
32. The Netherlands
34. Shirt size: Abbr.
36. Simultaneously
37. Plural suffix
38. Stirrup's place
39. Yeanling producer
40. Dept. of Health and Human Services agency
41. Old what's-___-name
45. Nuke, maybe
46. __ out (just manage)
47. Poems
48. "South Pacific" heroine
49. Shadowed
50. Escalator alternative
52. A-one
55. Beer, informally
56. Volcanic flow
57. Pecs' partners
58. Skipper's post
59. Focal point
60. Apple of Adam's eye

Solution on page 154

Dashiell Hammett

Across

1. Semi parts
5. "The Maltese Falcon" star
10. Pulp
14. Storytelling dance
15. Like some milk
16. One on your side
17. News brief
18. Literary style of crime fiction pioneered by Dashiell Hammett
20. Marsh marigold
22. Slip
23. In heaps
25. Whiz
26. Fix
29. AFB to land a Space Shuttle
33. Plenty
34. Arrange in tiers
35. "What a surprise!"
37. Henry VIII's second or fourth
38. Yawning, maybe
39. Any of TV's Simpsons
40. Tape rec. jack
41. High building
42. Peter in 1941 Maltese Falcon
43. Nick and Nora's last name in Dashiell Hammett novel
45. Many Guinness listings
46. Save
47. Brusque
49. Water balloon sound
52. Wheels
56. Dashiell Hammett novel made into a film series
60. Stupefy
61. Assistant on the Hill
62. Seashore
63. Gumbo ingredient
64. Elated
65. Weeps
66. Honest-to-goodness

Down

1. Fashionable
2. Golf, for one
3. Squandered, as a lead
4. Main character in Hammett's "The Maltese Falcon"
5. How long one might stay
6. Physical condition
7. Craggy peak
8. Like the gray mare of song
9. Yankee's foe
10. Protective envelope
11. Sheryl Crow's "___ Wanna Do"
12. Musher's transport
13. Jekyll's counterpart
19. Actor's prize
21. Edges
24. Honey
25. Thunderstruck
26. Shut loudly
27. Pertaining to a cone
28. Dressing choice
30. Textile worker
31. Opportunities, so to speak
32. Two-reel movie
34. "Oxford Blues" star, 1984
36. Singles
38. Metal fastener
39. Bullfighter
41. It's a fact
42. Santa checks it twice
44. Lessened
45. Weatherman's lines
48. Demagnetize, as a tape
49. Without a date
50. "Murphy Brown" bar owner
51. Helen's mother
53. Help oneself to
54. Pound of literature
55. Tight closure
57. Former RR regulator
58. "___ iron bars a cage"
59. After April in Paris

Solution on page 154

Sherlock Holmes

The crossword grid (numbered 1–69).

Across

1. Lion, in Swahili
6. More than dislike
10. "Pogo" cartoonist Kelly
14. Eye layers
15. Word said before opening the eyes
16. Roman Eros
17. Type of glass carried by Sherlock Holmes
19. The O'Haras' home
20. Somewhat rashly
21. Severe
23. Stack role
25. Some is white
26. Food from the curds of milk
30. Unadorned
33. Meander
34. Holy one
35. Critic __ Louise Huxtable
38. First story to feature Sherlock Holmes
42. Range units: Abbr.
43. Sit in on
44. Ray of light
45. Varieties
46. Tapering mass of ice
48. Iraqi port
51. "Once I ___ secret love…"
53. Contrary to
56. Acacia-eating mammal
61. Tartan garb
62. "The Woman" to Holmes
64. Pollster Roper
65. Medical discovery
66. Marketing ploy
67. Jockey strap
68. Locksmith's stock
69. Old British guns

Down

1. Sport for heavyweights
2. ___ the Terrible
3. Start of something big?
4. "The Adventure of the Speckled ___" by Sherlock Holmes
5. Thais, e.g.
6. Garfield's predecessor
7. "What __, chopped liver?"
8. Watch
9. Tech sch. grad
10. Friend of Sherlock Holmes
11. Treasured violin
12. Large-eyed lemur
13. Slight amount
18. Gratis
22. Hill in 1991 news
24. Pert. to Spain
26. Study for finals
27. Multitude
28. Greasy spoon sign
29. Earthbound bird
31. Catalog
32. Mandela's org.
34. Faction
35. "Smart" one
36. "Agreed!"
37. "Don't look ___!"
39. Six-Day War hero
40. "Uh-huh"
41. Stat for a DH
45. Moon of Neptune
46. "Each Dawn __" (Cagney film)
47. Ring figures
48. Street where Sherlock Holmes resided
49. Like a gymnast
50. Game ragout
52. A de Mille
54. Ailing
55. "Can't argue with that"
57. Mine entrance
58. Absquatulate
59. Sinn ___
60. Coastal raptors
63. Trick ending

Solution on page 154

Agatha Christie

Across

1. Rotates
6. Some alerts, for short
10. Possesses
14. Happening
15. "Fame" singer
16. In good order
17. Spike Lee's "She's ___ Have It"
18. Bon mot
19. "Sweater Girl" Turner
20. Agatha Christie detective
23. Meteorologist's comfort meas.
24. Hither's partner
25. Moving stairway
31. Mountains
35. Narc's collar
36. They come and go
38. The Tigers, on scoreboards
39. "___ Under the Sun" by Agatha Christie
40. "The ___ Trap" play by Agatha Christie
42. "Death on the ___" by Agatha Christie
43. Adult males
44. Fertility goddess
45. Electronic music pioneer Edgard
47. Concerning
49. Device for triggering explosion
51. Fleur-de-___
53. Summer mo.
54. "Murder on the ___ ___" by Agatha Christie
61. Doll's cry

62. Part of a spread
63. Springs
66. RR schedule listings
67. Whale's location?
68. Dictionary listing
69. Smallville family name
70. Salty sauces
71. "Merry Company" artist

Down

1. Telephone ___
2. Pie in the sky?
3. Kind of IRA
4. Short letter
5. Catch off guard
6. Clear from a charge
7. One of the Fab Four
8. Cheese with a rind
9. Goofy
10. Connected to the Internet
11. It goes with wash
12. Second introduction?
13. PDQ, in the ICU
21. Magic spells
22. Exclamation of mild dismay
25. Plant swelling
26. Seas count
27. Queeg's vessel
28. Dumas motto word
29. Beneficial
30. Univ. dorm supervisors
32. Cutting down, after "on"
33. Horse of the Year, 1960-64
34. Range rover

37. Swallow
41. Human tail?
42. "We Do Our Part" org.
44. Pack ___
46. Los ___, CA
48. The N.Y. Mets' div.
50. Thin candles
52. Sports figures
54. City in SW Russia
55. Judge
56. One-named supermodel
57. Second time around?
58. Picture of health?
59. Off
60. Give a bellyful
64. Grand ___, Nova Scotia
65. Thesis introduction?

Solution on page 154

P. D. James

Across

1. __ room
4. Tabula __, a clean slate
8. Isn't timid
13. Folksy Guthrie
15. Laid up
16. Blessed ___
17. Winter air
18. Clinton's attorney general
19. In the worst way
20. Investigator/poet in many
    P. D. James novels
23. Mother ___
24. Historic beginning
25. Paranormal letters
28. First P. D. James novel
32. Test site
35. Rave in Spain
36. Teams
37. Goes awry
39. Wild guesses
42. Race that's about a quarter
    of a marathon
43. Be behind
45. Skier's way up
47. "Looker" actress
48. Wearing eyeglasses
52. Aliens, for short
53. Versailles agreement
54. Flybelt pest
58. "Death of an ___ ___," P.
    D. James novel
62. City SE of Milan
64. "You got that right!"
65. Droops
66. Prickly plant
67. Takeout order?
68. One-named artist
69. Pay out
70. Some pass catchers
71. Lottery letters

Down

1. Attacked, in a way
2. Sap
3. Calculator button
4. Rarity
5. Genesis shepherd
6. Hong Kong's Hang __
   Index
7. Newspaperman Ochs
8. Big name in diamonds
9. Gardner and others
10. Having red hair
11. Like a sgt. or cpl.
12. Pigs' digs
14. Ancient Mexican
21. Brit. decorations
22. E.U. member
26. Something to shoot
27. Like a gnat
29. Biblical suffix
30. Calf catcher
31. In good shape
32. Do not disturb
33. Stop, in St. Lô
34. Restaurant
38. Small drink
40. English network that
    televised many P. D.
    James novels
41. Soup crackers
44. Large spotted cat
46. Remainder
49. Nod, maybe
50. Philippic
51. Not too swift
55. Rips
56. Some NCOs
57. Slalom paths
59. Marvel superheroes
60. Capone's nemeses
61. Unite
62. American network that
    televised many P.D. James
    novels
63. Dada cofounder

Solution on page 154

Mickey Spillane

Across

1. Newsman Abel
5. Diamond protectors
10. Aladdin's find
14. ICBM type
15. Noted Chicago critic
16. Writer Seton
17. Detective in Mickey Spillane novels
19. Bank holding: Abbr.
20. Disney head
21. Roomy
23. Others, in Oaxaca
25. Test score range
26. Fixes
28. Nanki-___ of "The Mikado"
30z. Money guru Greenspan
31. Rubber tree
32. Serves the brewskis
34. Units
37. Egyptian ancient sun god
38. "___ Is Mine!," Mickey Spillane novel
40. Information Technology
41. Republic in S Arabia
43. Canonized pope
44. Altar constellation
45. "And giving ___, up the chimney…"
47. Verb ending
48. Attack time
49. One might be roasted
52. Extra
54. Water
56. "One ___ Night," Mickey Spillane novel
59. Cracked
60. Aust. Aboriginal instrument
62. Knockout
63. Long dists.
64. Become disenchanted
65. Chihuahua cheers
66. Toadies' replies
67. "The NeverEnding Story" writer

Down

1. One-named supermodel
2. Year Trajan was born
3. Annoying
4. Happenings
5. Unwrap in a hurry
6. 1972 treaty subj.
7. Radiation units
8. Gets ready
9. Shale features
10. Protect, in a way
11. Chemist Lavoisier
12. "___ ___ Is Quick," Mickey Spillane novel
13. Bel __ cheese
18. Part of H.M.S.
22. Spotted
24. Berlin output
26. "I, the ___," Mickey Spillane's first novel
27. Winglike parts
29. Start of some Keats titles
32. Barbershop quartet members
33. Some like it hot
35. Red giant in Cetus
36. Dog command
38. Poisonous
39. Unnecessary
42. Handcuff
44. Appended
46. "Kiss Me, ___," Mickey Spillane novel
48. Poet Levertov
49. Shout of exultation
50. Two-time batting champ Lefty
51. Cream
53. Côte-___, France
55. Popular ice cream
57. Like Hawaiian shirts
58. Past time
61. Coll. student's exam

Solution on page 154

Mystery Novels at the Movies

Across

1. Pops
4. Shorten, in a way
7. Objectives
11. Chase of "Now, Voyager"
13. Like some coincidences
15. Pesky biter
16. Polish partner
17. Watch over
18. Narrowly defeat
19. Raymond Chandler novel, first movie version with Bogie & Bacall
22. Writer LeShan
23. Otalgia
24. Warm-blooded vertebrate
26. Golf peg
27. Paradise
29. Like some stocks: Abbr.
32. Pal of Pythias
34. Longtime Susan Lucci role
37. Golden Triangle native
39. Designer Karan
41. Work with acid
42. Berlin output
44. Lion sounds
46. The dark side?
47. Physician
49. Coffee alternative
51. Stringed musical instrument
53. Sparkler
57. Sturm __ Drang
58. Dennis Lehane novel, film directed by Clint Eastwood
61. Writer Tarbell and others
63. Taj __
64. Wet, as morning grass
65. Baltic native
66. Rousseau classic
67. Director Kenton
68. Loser in war, usually
69. Helpful connections
70. Son of Odin

Down

1. Ski trail
2. Omega's opposite
3. Person who skis
4. North Sea tributary
5. Kind of hygiene
6. Telegram
7. Bronze __
8. "Double __," novella made into a film
9. A Gabor sister
10. Pilfer
12. Ready to swing
13. Brainiac
14. Tomato blight
20. Clinched
21. Make way?
25. "A __ formality"
27. "Prizzi's ___," novel made into a film
28. Sicilian resort
29. Bonus NFL periods
30. However, briefly
31. "The Manchurian ___," novel made into a film
33. Red Brigades victim Aldo
35. Third-century date
36. Philip of "Kung Fu"
38. "___ Rhythm"
40. Item
43. Ripoff
45. Affix a brand to
48. "I'm game!"
50. Kind of fertilizer
51. Culpability
52. Below
53. Clock faces
54. In the open
55. Recently
56. Clothesline alternative
59. Scandinavian native
60. "The ___ Man," novel made into a film
62. Hog heaven?

Solution on page 155

Edgar Allan Poe

Across

1. On __ with (equal to)
5. Mauna __
8. Unlikely to bite
12. Pathetic
13. Pillow covering
14. Rock of comedy
15. Long tale
16. NBA great Thurmond
17. "The Tell-Tale ___," short story by Edgar Allan Poe
18. Janitor
20. "The Mystery of ___ Vep" (Charles Ludlam play)
21. C. Auguste ___, detective in Edgar Allan Poe stories
22. Modern I.D. verifier
23. State positively
26. Ponderously
30. "Annabel ___," poem by Edgar Allan Poe
31. Edgar Allan Poe's birth city
34. Film director Petri
35. Link with
37. Department of eastern France
38. Crew alternative
39. Pharaoh's symbol
40. Fighting ___ (Big Ten team)
42. Randomizer
43. Save
45. Entrances
47. "Psst!"
48. Org. with the member magazine "Animal Watch"
50. "Hold on there!"
52. "___ ___ ___ the Pendulum," short story by Edgar Allan Poe
56. Capital of South Korea
57. Shout
58. Bavarian river
59. Deep cavity
60. Not too bright
61. Lubricate
62. Bone: Prefix
63. They make periodical changes: Abbr.
64. Play area

Down

1. Smart ___
2. Hemingway moniker
3. Islamic VIP
4. Withdraw
5. Uniform hue
6. Consumed
7. New World abbr.
8. Bird poem by Edgar Allan Poe
9. Ancient Syria
10. Paul Sorvino's daughter
11. Superlative finish
13. Stop daydreaming
14. Tableware
19. Supercharger
22. Thieves' place
23. Place to exchange vows
24. Paris bisector
25. Tries to find
26. ___ soit qui mal y pense
27. ___-France
28. Legal
29. Oxen joiners
32. Circular announcement
33. "Shop __ you drop"
36. "The Fall of ___ ___ of Usher" short story by Edgar Allan Poe
38. Leonardo da ___
40. Wall climber
41. Teat
44. Empire
46. In recent days
48. Coming up
49. Vends
50. Signs of disuse
51. Hall of Famer Wilhelm
52. Class
53. Water, in Oaxaca
54. S. Dakota neighbor
55. Scott in 1857 news
56. Start of many Brazilian city names

Solution on page 155

The Da Vinci Code

Across

1. "Punk'd" network
4. Unwholesomely gloomy
10. Sunblock letters
13. Architect Mies van der __
14. Historic Harlem theater
15. Coach Parseghian
16. The "E" of Q.E.D.
17. Remember
18. Swe. neighbor
19. Shape on dead man's stomach in "The Da Vinci Code"
21. Set afire
23. Inquired
24. Lunatic
27. Attention getters
28. Cockney residence
31. University where 35-Across is a professor in "The Da Vinci Code"
32. Board member
34. Chill
35. "The Da Vinci Code" main character
38. Prefix with sphere
39. Proclaim
40. Positions
42. "Star Wars" syst.
43. Winchester
46. Sequential
47. Black
49. Cable alternative
50. Jesus's dinnerware with magical properties, part of "The Da Vinci Code"
54. The Righteous Brothers, e.g.
56. Museum whose curator was murdered in "The Da Vinci Code"
58. Football legend Graham
59. Amiss
60. Root for
61. Suppose
62. Punch-in-the-stomach reaction
63. Rears
64. Aussie outlaw Kelly

Down

1. To a greater extent
2. "Much obliged!"
3. Sporty Chevy, informally
4. Helgenberger of "CSI"
5. Phone button
6. Portugal's Cape __
7. Exploding-cigar sound
8. Ailing
9. Kind of diplomacy
10. Capital of Chile
11. PGA player
12. "__ out!"
13. Satisfy, as a debt
20. Honor
22. Intrude upon
24. Frenzied woman
25. Give ___ for one's money
26. Alphabet trio
29. Unlawful killing
30. Dick's 1956 counterpart
31. Makes well
32. Steak house orders
33. RN's skill
35. Indian bread
36. Intermittently
37. "Peer Gynt" composer
38. Santa Catalina, e.g.: Abbr.
41. Hardened part of the skin
43. Beard
44. American rival
45. Hose material
48. "The Da Vinci Code" author
50. Massive
51. Exceeding
52. "Dianetics" author ___ Hubbard
53. Longs
54. Scooby-___ (cartoon dog)
55. Sky light?
57. Table scrap

Solution on page 155

Chapter 3: Poetry

Robert Frost

Across

1. Drought ender
5. Bar topic
8. Columnist read by 100+ million
12. Florentine flower
13. Key letter
14. Persona's opposite
15. LeBlanc of "Friends"
16. Alike: Fr.
17. Frost poem: "Stopping by Woods on a ___ Evening"
18. Frost's first book of poetry
20. Stumpers?
21. Growing outward
22. Little, in Lyon
23. Dynamo's pivot
26. President whose inauguration Frost recited "The Gift Outright"
30. Cap
31. Prior to
34. Montana native
35. Assists
37. Outback bounder
38. Sealy competitor
39. Bolt
40. Blanketlike cloak
42. Dinghy need
43. Frost's other occupation
45. Full-price payers
47. G.I. rank
48. Greek island
50. Baffin Bay sight
52. Home machine
56. Wavy pattern in fabric
57. Easy stride
58. Frost poem: "Nothing ___ Can Stay"
59. Of the ear
60. Golden
61. "Holy cats!"
62. Face-to-face exam
63. Hearty brew
64. Walkman maker

Down

1. "___ Lama Ding Dong" (1961 hit)
2. Watcher of the TV station Al-Jazeera
3. A big fan of
4. Procrastinator's reply
5. For real
6. "What __ your thoughts could tell": Lightfoot lyric
7. Frost poem: "Mending ___"
8. Make public
9. High school subj.
10. Yuppies' wheels
11. "Whoo-hoo!"
13. Be wary of
14. Quaker?
19. Social climbers
22. Second of April?
23. Employees
24. Indian drum
25. Muslim commander
26. McDonald's founder
27. Flynn of "Captain Blood"
28. Coup follower
29. Quite a while
32. Biology class staple
33. Suffix with ball or bass
36. Pertaining to time
38. "Ditto"
40. __ Park: Pirates' field
41. Small village
44. "___ Pretty" (song for Maria)
46. Conventions
48. Go bad
49. Frost poem: "After ___-Picking"
50. Number of Pulitzer Prizes Frost won
51. Milan money
52. Aquatic plant
53. Scrubbed
54. The Kennedys, e.g.
55. Water awhirl
56. Noted chairman

Solution on page 155

Poetic Words

Across

1. Spanish house
5. Post-Christmas event
9. "Cool it!"
13. Lover of Aphrodite
14. Pollex
16. Kind of bonding
17. Kittens' cries
18. A line of five metrical feet in poetry
20. Wide view of an extensive area
22. Bind morally
23. Entre ___ (confidentially)
24. Blind as ___
25. Little
27. Bikini parts
28. Mail place: Abbr.
31. In accord
32. A metrical foot used in various types of poetry
33. Spanish stew
34. Platters
35. British mil. honor
36. Reconnoiterer
37. Last word in a threat
38. It has a head and hops
39. Tiny particles
40. Marshal under Napoleon
41. Beer topper
42. Point a finger at
43. Scornful cries
44. Appear to be
45. Acid neutralizer
48. Apparel
52. Repetition of consonant sounds in poetry
54. Follow closely
55. Woody plant
56. Overshadow
57. Like a 911 call: Abbr.
58. Attends
59. Elite police unit
60. Bench's benchmates

Down

1. David, e.g.
2. WATS part
3. In stitches
4. Repetition of vowel sounds in poetry
5. One of the Twin Cities
6. Cries for attention
7. Large moth
8. First to respond, often: Abbr.
9. Refine
10. Mr. Hulot's creator
11. Vidov in "Wild Orchid"
12. A Dumas
15. Thick-trunked tree
19. CEOs' degrees
21. Play parts
24. Cause of knight sweats?
25. Subway entrance
26. Like some tree trunks
27. Headquartered
28. Dimness
29. Showy feather
30. They may be wild
31. Gulf of ___, off the coast of Yemen
32. Brainstorms
33. A line of eight metrical feet in poetry
36. "The Crucible" setting
38. At the rear of
41. Symbol of goodness
42. Deprived
43. Foundations
44. Pelvic bones
45. New Testament book
46. Erudition
47. Pants part
48. Nibble away
49. Christen
50. Not winning or losing
51. Some cameras, for short
53. Sympathetic sounds

Solution on page 155

Homer

Across

1. Convinced
5. "___ the night before…"
9. In
13. Old Olds
15. Walkaway
16. Scene of Jesus' first miracle
17. Poem by Homer about the Trojan War
18. Tom Joad, for one
19. Stadium shape
20. Pietà figure
22. Sincere
24. Nehi flavor
26. Homer's sequel to 17-Across
27. No mere dabbler
28. File folder features
31. Make a decision
32. ___ Vegas
33. Vegas lineup
35. Cut into cubes
39. Genre of Homer's poetry
41. Idiot
43. Whodunit board game
44. On top
46. Envelop in fog
48. Rover's remark
49. Mentalist Geller
51. Poker hand
52. Szechuan sauce source
53. Enactment
57. Children's doctor?
59. This present night
60. Surveys
61. Obsessed with
62. "Um, pardon me"
64. Press product
68. Place
69. Canadian coin
70. Opposition
71. Insured's report
72. Some are liberal
73. Collagist's need

Down

1. Biol., e.g.
2. Slick stuff
3. Muumuu accessory
4. Soap opera, e.g.
5. Legendary city in Homer's poetry
6. Large bowl-shaped pan
7. Pal
8. Big name in swimwear
9. Pert. to the sense of hearing
10. Song thrush
11. Vacuous
12. Big name in Chicago politics
14. Changes with the times
21. Domain
23. "___ Blue"
24. Spreadsheet menu selection
25. Former women's magazine
27. Court action
29. Simpleton
30. Throat bug
34. Davenport
36. Reunion group
37. Continental currency
38. Buck
40. Careful
42. Clamorous
45. Medicine
47. Ancient ___, Homer's world
50. Destination of the journey in 26-Across
53. Motionless
54. "Pagliacci" clown
55. Starts the poker pot
56. Old-time anesthetic
58. On drugs
60. CPR pros
63. "The Lord of the Rings" being
65. Oscar winner Benicio ___ Toro
66. Ostrich's cousin
67. Reuben base

Solution on page 155

Howl

Across

1. 20th letter of the Hebrew alphabet
5. Equal share, often
9. "Save me __"
14. Spanish pronoun
15. Type of gel
16. "When hell freezes over!"
17. List shortener
18. Musical symbol
19. "Honor is ___ scutcheon": Shak.
20. "Howl" publisher Lawrence
23. Sister of Venus
24. "Whazzat?"
25. Rubbish
28. Pronoun
31. Feminine
33. "Stay" singer Lisa
37. "Howl" line: "I saw the ___ ___ of my generation destroyed by madness"
39. "Howl" author, first name
41. Golfer's concern
42. Broadway backer
43. Light pastry shell
45. Prefix meaning "trillion"
46. "Aha!"
47. Locker room shower?
50. Gov. Pataki's place
51. It makes waves
53. Overseas
58. City where "Howl" was first performed
61. Tet observer
64. Ike's ex
65. Pest control brand
66. Melody
67. Dutch export
68. Yardage pickup
69. Give and take?
70. The scarlet letter
71. Soprano Berger

Down

1. Marine hazards
2. Perfume bottle name
3. Belle or Bart
4. Oscar-winning Berry
5. "The Human Condition" author Arendt
6. All excited
7. Plaster backing
8. Former FBI director Louis
9. Execration
10. Rest area sight
11. First family member
12. ___ Arann (Irish carrier)
13. Sei halved
21. Bank acct. benefit
22. Small clump of bushes
25. Where the buffalo roam
26. Like a big brother
27. 10 kilogauss
29. Suffix with flex
30. Saint-Germain's river
32. Money maker
33. "Alice" star
34. Branch of knowledge
35. They, in Tours
36. Howl is a work of the ___ Generation
38. Goes down
40. Annoying person
44. Powerful engine
48. Kind of hat
49. "The West Wing" network
52. Following
54. Crest
55. Grouchy Muppet
56. Decide at the flip of ___
57. Fashion's Karan
58. Uttered
59. Get on
60. Take out ___
61. Quantity: Abbr.
62. Big __, California
63. This ___ test

Solution on page 156

Roses Are Red

Across

1. Emeril catchword
4. Novel ID
8. Corp. section
12. Columbus discovery
13. Poi source
14. Greetings from Maui
16. Chief (rhymes with red)
17. Snow vehicle (rhymes with red)
18. Moolah (rhymes with red)
19. Inception
21. It may be critical
23. 1988 swimming gold medalist Kristin
24. Mystery writer
25. Crook
27. Harbor barge
29. Terrarium plant
30. Further
31. Workout site
34. Fine cord (rhymes with red)
37. Stay fresh
38. "Hollywood Squares" win
39. Golf club
40. Sleeping furniture (rhymes with red)
41. Important PC command
42. April initials
43. Demeanor
45. Stretch (rhymes with red)
47. No vote
48. Snoop
49. Make, as a CD
50. Cable network
51. Change places
52. Suffix for boy
55. Deeds
58. Campus locale
60. Mall binge
62. Fear (rhymes with red)
64. Lawn mower house (rhymes with red)
66. Metal (rhymes with red)
67. Wife of Homer S.
68. Sidle
69. Unique
70. "Tres __"
71. Radio feature
72. "Scream" director Craven

Down

1. Good, in Guadalajara
2. Put down
3. Put together
4. Sit, differently
5. Yellowish-pink
6. Smash
7. Signals approval
8. Bit of gel
9. N.F.L. Hall-of-Famer Hirsch
10. Pound, notably
11. What this isn't
12. A little lamb
15. Uproar
20. Heroine of Cather's "The Song of the Lark"
22. It's about a foot
26. Former California fort
28. Alley follower?
29. Gave food
30. Newsman Koppel
31. Left
32. Skywalker mentor
33. Emotional state
34. Kind of bed
35. Bar mitzvah dance
36. Optimistic
37. Understanding
40. Turkish governor
41. Ossuary
43. Army cops
44. Mideast hot spot
45. Explorer, e.g.
46. Chmn.'s cousin
49. Spanish grocery
50. Safire subject
51. Muslim messiah
52. "Goodnight" girl
53. Navy elite
54. Lamarr of film
55. Nav. officer
56. Constant complainer
57. Garr of "Young Frankenstein"
59. Put to work
61. Oxen's burden
63. Cubby hole?
65. Actor Benicio ___ Toro

Solution on page 156

Violets Are Blue

Across

1. Sound barrier?: Var.
4. Doubtable
8. Street
12. Footwear (rhymes with blue)
13. Ale (rhymes with blue)
14. Kind of space
16. Hard to pin down
17. Playwright Connelly
18. Earthenware pot
19. Soak
20. The Seminoles' sch.
21. "Alias" airer
23. Animal park (rhymes with blue)
24. Newly married woman
26. One of us
28. 1942-45 stat. disseminator
30. Rue Morgue perpetrator
32. Third degrees?
36. Liquid holder (rhymes with blue)
39. Casino game
41. Aretha's genre
42. Summer Games gp.
43. Spiral holder (rhymes with blue)
45. Handheld computer, briefly
46. Seize
48. Dead center?
49. Scene (rhymes with blue)
50. It's raised on a farm
51. NY-LA direction
52. Electric guitar hookup
54. Reporter's question
56. Donkeys
60. Petition (rhymes with blue)
63. Sheep (rhymes with blue)

65. A.E.C. successor
67. Gardner of Hollywood
68. Kind of ink
70. "...for __": "if you pay"
72. Munch (rhymes with blue)
73. Jordanian money
74. Heavy stick
75. Snobs put them on
76. Smooth, in a way
77. Primitive homes
78. Small ammo

Down

1. Like chiffon
2. Conductor Georg
3. "Get your hands off me!"
4. Some laptops
5. Haus wife
6. Chemin de ___

7. Blue Triangle org.
8. Danny Aiello's "Radio Days" role
9. "__ Town"
10. From __ (completely)
11. Like L.A.'s Argyle Hotel
12. Novi Sad resident
15. "Suspicion" studio
20. Small number (rhymes with blue)
22. "Later!"
25. Where the buck stops?
27. Bull markets
29. Contingencies
30. One-way sign
31. Composition in verse
33. Pueblo dweller
34. Person reared in a large city
35. Deli side
36. Jazz jobs
37. Singer in acting

38. Sch. with a Berkeley campus
40. Takes steps
44. Pugilists' org.
47. Submit
49. Corp. bigwigs
51. Blow away
53. Fella
55. Pricked up one's ears
57. Indian form of address
58. Tinker-Chance middleman
59. They need to go back and forth to work
60. Half-brother of Tom Sawyer
61. Colleges, to Aussies
62. Poet ___ St. Vincent Millay
64. A pop
65. Not masc. or fem.
66. Graycoats
69. Actor Holm
71. Grippe (rhymes with blue)
72. Pickup truck part

Solution on page 156

T. S. Eliot

Across

1. Tres y tres
5. Dungeons & Dragons game co.
8. Cream-filled pastry
14. Search thoroughly
15. Tic-tac-toe winner
16. From that place
17. Twice tetra-
18. Propel a boat
19. One behind the other
20. Influential T. S. Eliot poem
23. Short coming?
24. Holmes's creator
25. Candied
29. Tithing unit
31. Strive
33. Mary ___ cosmetics
34. Spanish Inquisition victim
38. Angler's hope
39. The "T. S." in T. S. Eliot
42. "___ Quartets," T. S. Eliot poems
43. Sink
44. "My mama done ___ me"
45. "___ durn tootin'!"
46. "If ___ you..."
50. Fright site?
52. Kind of acid
56. "___ Blu, Dipinto Di Blu": hit song
57. T. S. Eliot's "conversion poem"
60. Direction taken
63. Model Carangi
64. Golf targets
65. Kuwait's peninsula
66. BBC rival
67. It has bark, but no bite
68. Paraphrase
69. Definite article
70. "Billy Budd" captain

Down

1. Tried to bring down
2. Trick-taking card game
3. Apprentice
4. Lodge
5. Body of art
6. Like smokestacks
7. Spur
8. Sundance's girl
9. Alter
10. U.S. Open champ, 1985-87
11. So-so link
12. Assure
13. Sleep activity, for short
21. Leigh Hunt's "Abou Ben ___"
22. Housing developer William who has a Long Island town named after him
26. Closely related
27. Musical containing T. S. Eliot poems
28. Hook's partner
30. God of thunder
32. "Original Gangster" rapper
35. Tear down, in Dover
36. Deposit in trust
37. Nashville sch.
38. Suds
39. Bender
40. Storytelling dance
41. Carroll adventuress
42. Knox and Dix: Abbr.
45. Private line?
47. Stomach
48. Reaping machine
49. French president's residence
51. "Grand Hotel" star
53. Legitimate
54. Designer Head
55. Silly as a goose
58. Beer topper
59. Old show featuring the Schmenge Brothers polka band
60. Train unit
61. It's found in the ground
62. Detroit-based org.

Solution on page 156

The Raven

Across

1. Restrooms, informally
5. Crescent point
9. Transpire
14. March slogan word
15. Capri, for one
16. Old man
17. "Lohengrin" heroine
18. Nifty
19. Period
20. "Once upon a midnight dreary, while I pondered, ___ ___ ___," "The Raven"
23. Actress Lansbury
24. Cytoplasm stuff
25. Curved Alaskan knife
28. "___-haw!"
29. Come by
32. Heroic verse
33. Cybernote
34. Bit player
35. "The Raven" author
39. Elevator stop
40. "We ___ please"
41. General __ chicken
42. Joint heir
44. "Thar ___ blows!"
47. German article
48. Pelt
49. What to do with chips
51. "While I nodded, nearly napping, suddenly there ___ ___ ___," "The Raven"
54. Defendant's out
57. Lump
58. "Me, myself ___"
59. Alley button
60. Stone of many Libras
61. W.W. II weapon
62. Gift of the Magi
63. Goose egg
64. "Only this, and nothing ___," "The Raven"

Down

1. Wiggle room
2. Actress Dahl
3. Countenance
4. Reptile
5. Vermilion
6. Pre-owned
7. Side dish
8. "Great" czar
9. La Scala offering
10. Reproduction
11. Navy noncom
12. Merchandise ID
13. Pep rally yell
21. Baseball's Roberto
22. Darrow of "King Kong"
25. __ no good
26. "Over many a quaint and curious volume of forgotten ___," "The Raven"
27. TNT alternative
30. Overseas relative
31. God of the Koran
32. Really big show
33. Freudian topics
34. Bag
35. "So what ___ is new?"
36. "As of some one gently rapping, rapping at my chamber ___," "The Raven"
37. Tell it like it isn't
38. Friendly
39. Blooming business?
42. Diploma word
43. Where to find Eugene
44. Religion of Japan
45. Hamper
46. V-8, e.g.
48. Trust
50. Contraction
51. Handle holder?
52. Boxer's fare
53. Warty hopper
54. Shirt part
55. Pewter
56. 1949 UN entrant

Solution on page 156

Walt Whitman

Across

1. Blonde shade
4. IRA options
7. Spy guys
13. BART stop
14. White-spotted rodent
16. Medical fluids
17. American conflict during Whitman's time
19. Iron target
20. North African port
21. Mardi ___
23. Meadow mother
24. Bluefins
26. Poetry style of Walt Whitman
30. Feeling of pity
32. Code carrier, for short
33. Maryland emblem
34. Margin
35. Second sequel indicator
36. Dominion
37. Walt Whitman's collection of poems
41. Counseling, e.g.
42. Hosp. staffer
43. Alfred E. Neuman's magazine
44. Old greeting
45. Match a raise
46. Simpler
49. "O Captain! ___ ___!," poem by Walt Whitman
52. Toyota model
54. Datebook abbr.
55. Midleg
57. Cpls., e.g.
58. Fishing nets
61. Name of section added to 37-Across after the death of Lincoln
63. Put an end to
64. Fiend
65. Shar-___ (wrinkly dog)
66. Island in central Japan
67. Yonder
68. Vane dir.

Down

1. Fancy tie
2. Provoke
3. Capital of Cuba
4. PFC's superior
5. TV's "Deputy ___"
6. Gobbles (up)
7. Cool ___ cucumber
8. League of Nations seat
9. "Let's have a dance ___ are married": Shak.
10. Many
11. 1979 Pa. newsmaker
12. Govt. agency that has your number
15. Sandarac tree
18. Caught
22. Typeface embellishment
25. Hood's blade
27. Puzzle
28. Actor Mineo et al.
29. Stretch (out)
31. Brunch fare
35. Charge carrier
36. Glowing
37. Tax
38. End of a race
39. Command to Rover
40. Farrier's tool
41. Hardly an Oscar candidate
45. First Amendment concern
46. Zip
47. Fly the coop
48. Look into again, as a cold case
50. Em and Bee
51. Chinese leader?
53. Davis of "King"
56. Continental capital
58. Sound barrier?: Var.
59. Prefix with -cide
60. Moo ___ pork
62. Stag party attendees

Solution on page 156

William Faulkner

Across

1. Puss
4. Grants
9. Melody
14. It follows directions
15. Operative
16. Julio's opposite
17. Code-cracking org.
18. Faulkner's first novel
20. Oil derived from the resin of pine trees
22. Suffix with Caesar
23. Greeting in Grenoble
24. Drink of the gods
26. "As I ___ ___," Faulkner novel
30. Boot in geography class?
33. Tiny bit
34. Like some vbs.
36. Links prop
37. Wide area
40. Proximate
42. By means of
43. Prefix meaning "bad"
44. "Smooth Operator" singer
45. Love lots
47. ___ ___ consciousness, Faulkner literary device
51. Leatherneck
54. Network
55. Nero's lucky number?
56. Fulfill
60. Faulkner's home state
62. June honoree
63. Red as ___
64. Inventor Howe
65. Be in debt
66. Pitcher Martinez
67. Auto damage
68. Conflict

Down

1. Telepathic
2. Phoebe's sister on "Friends"
3. Gnarled
4. Perry Mason tale
5. Designer von Furstenberg
6. Shoulder muscle, informally
7. Termination
8. "Goosebumps" author R. L. ___
9. Nice sea
10. Vote out
11. Divide
12. OPEC nation
13. Evasive
19. Org. also known as the Common Market
21. Lecterns
25. Rant
27. Over there
28. Tiny, informally
29. Scottish refusals
31. ___ Cayes, Haiti
32. "Is it soup __?"
34. Think tank, perhaps: Abbr.
35. Keister
37. Clean air grp.
38. Marked, as a ballot
39. Pledged
41. Update the arsenal
46. Hiker
47. Geriatric
48. Field
49. Capital of Canada
50. Tributary
52. Robot add-on
53. Snooped (around)
55. Sensation, slangily
57. Quick drive
58. __ the crack of dawn
59. Overshoot, say
60. Atlas item
61. Lance of the bench

Solution on page 157

Tom Clancy

Across

1. Struck, old-style
5. Very profound
9. Music rights org.
14. Seaport in N Honduras
15. Violinist Leopold
16. Hollow rock
17. At first: Abbr.
18. Bond foe
19. Below
20. DVD player maker
21. U.S./Canada's __ Canals
22. "Clear and ___ Danger," Tom Clancy novel
24. Minor prophet
26. "The magic word"
28. Pitching style
30. "Nuns on the Run" star
34. Tom Clancy's most famous fictional character
37. Relief
38. Reheatable, maybe
39. Espoused
43. Skid row woe
44. "The Sum of ___ ___," Tom Clancy novel
45. Early sitcom name
47. 1000 times 1000
49. Drink up
51. Maj.'s superior
55. "___ Games," Tom Clancy novel
58. "The Hunt for ___ October," Tom Clancy novel
60. ET's ride
61. The ___ suspects
62. Border
64. "___ take arms against a sea of troubles": Hamlet
65. San __, Calif.
66. Catch red-handed
67. Exploits
68. Mature
69. Mil. awards
70. Russo in "Outbreak"

Down

1. "Red ___ Rising," Tom Clancy novel
2. Word of thanks
3. ___ artery
4. Make it
5. Pedestal part
6. Inhabitant of Europe
7. Hallow ending
8. Suitable
9. Chills
10. Karate instructor
11. Message symbols
12. "...__ of thieves" (Matt. 21:13)
13. Saucy
21. Jersey
23. St. Louis gridder
25. "__ silly question..."
27. PC-to-PC connection
29. Turn red, perhaps
31. "Star Trek" crewmember
32. One who waits
33. Byrnes and Hall
34. Actress Ashley
35. Penny, perhaps
36. British tax
39. Kind of reaction
40. Year in Justinian I's reign
41. Gone by
42. __ up (confined)
44. Dept. of mathematics
46. Republic in SW Asia
47. Bossy remark?
48. Have in view
50. Cockpit figure
52. Say "@#$%!"
53. When dogs want out
54. Unfettered
55. Mountain lion
56. "It's __ state of affairs!"
57. Layered skirt
59. Long fish
63. Russian assents
64. ABC's "On ___ Own"

Solution on page 157

Michael Crichton

Across

1. Woodstock gear
5. Bend
8. Winston Churchill's "___ Country"
12. "Run ___ Run" (1998 film)
13. It can be copped
14. Abrasive
15. Like some points
16. Gets older
17. Ease up
18. "The ___ Strain," Michael Crichton novel
20. McCartney and Jagger, for two
21. New York's __ Fisher Hall
22. Craps action
23. Good news
26. Michael Crichton's training, featured in his novels
30. Inclined
31. Mother of Joseph
34. "I'm ___ here!"
35. Respond to a stimulus
37. Toots
38. Drummer Fig of the CBS Orchestra
39. Country music's Dixie Chicks, e.g.
40. Overtakes
42. Omega
43. Michael Crichton's alma mater
45. Round lot's 100
47. Star quality?
48. Speed demon
50. Beginner
52. Animals in Michael Crichton's "Jurassic Park"
56. "The Great ___ Robbery," Michael Crichton novel
57. Past
58. Falklands War participant
59. Like undercooked eggs
60. Money for digs
61. Cuzco native
62. Burglar
63. Farm animal
64. Gray, in a way

Down

1. Diva Gluck
2. Earth's satellite
3. Slog
4. Small-time dictator
5. "Ragged Dick" author
6. Like a bassoon's sound
7. Spanish house
8. Aspiration
9. "State of ___," Michael Crichton novel
10. Newspaper section
11. Bar staple
13. Actress __ Sue Martin
14. Facilitated
19. Undisguised
22. ___ canto
23. Dana Carvey role
24. Musical drama
25. Flight segment
26. Department store department
27. More adorable
28. Make up
29. Makes a touchdown
32. Neighbor of Sudan
33. Sounds from Santa
36. Tegument
38. "Angela's ___"
40. Expert
41. Go along with
44. Prolonged pain
46. Kuwait's peninsula
48. Split radially
49. About
50. So
51. Yin's counterpart
52. Copperfield's bride
53. Coffee holders
54. Like cream pies
55. "Don't move!"
56. Take a crack at

Solution on page 157

Stephen King

Across

1. Sayings of Jesus
6. Big party
10. "The ___ Zone," novel by Stephen King
14. Maze word
15. In a dead heat
16. Ye follower
17. Novel by Stephen King, movie directed by Kubrick
19. Dapper
20. French seasoning
21. Fancy home
22. Peak
23. Coffee size
24. Communication
26. Novel by Stephen King, movie starring Tom Hanks
31. Equestrian's attire
32. Word from a pen pal?
33. Common article
36. Name of five Norwegian kings
37. Ad __ per aspera: Kansas motto
39. Connect
40. Cowboy Rogers
41. Heavy duty?
42. Direct
43. Car that Stephen King's "Christine" is about
46. A cartridge
49. Coll. figure
50. Oklahoma native
51. Vehement
54. Bio stat
57. Old-time actress Naldi
58. Deprived of reason
60. Old French coins
61. Fargo's state: Abbr.
62. Pending
63. Return mailer: Abbr.
64. It may be dominant
65. Stephen King's home state

Down

1. D-Day craft
2. "Top __ mornin'!"
3. Scottish Highlander
4. Treasury Dept. branch
5. Deep down
6. Kindly
7. Converse competitor
8. Pre-Easter season
9. Actress Jolie
10. Be generous
11. Chosen ones
12. "There Is Nothin' Like ___"
13. Dissuade
18. Getaway spot
23. Cry of relief
25. Hunter's quarry
26. Son of Odin
27. Angelic symbol
28. Bidding site
29. "Wrong!"
30. Russian space station
33. Vegan's protein source
34. Yesterday, to Yves
35. Professor Higgins, to Eliza
37. Any unnamed object
38. It may be tidy
39. Mutt's mate
41. Chihuahua cheer
42. Element used in electroplating
43. Request sweetener
44. Understanding
45. Old waste allowance
46. "Bag of ___," novel by Stephen King
47. New York city
48. Yoga position
52. "Das Lied von der ___"
53. Islands off Galway
54. No pro
55. Put on
56. Allure competitor
59. "Put ___ Happy Face"

Solution on page 157

John Grisham

Across

1. "Dragnet" org.
5. Strong criticism
9. Handwriting feature
14. 1975 Wimbledon champ
15. Move, in real estate jargon
16. Opposite of neo-
17. Capricious
19. Terrible
20. Stubbornness
22. Unleavened cake
25. "Rob Roy" star, 1995
29. Raise: Abbr.
30. Picnic spoiler
33. Sgt. Preston's org.
34. Presidential middle name
37. Freudian ___
39. Galley tool
40. John Grisham's first novel
43. Pierre's pal
45. Georgia ___
46. Lolling
49. "The ___," John Grisham novel made into a film starring Tom Cruise
51. Takes off
53. Hindu honorifics
54. Winter melon
56. Ancient Syrian
59. Little or Lesser Bear
62. Hot dog topping
65. "The ___," John Grisham novel made into a film starring Matt Damon
69. Recipient
70. Box office take
71. Go with
72. Treble clef lines
73. Hebrew measure
74. Spotted

Down

1. Bar topic
2. Fire residue
3. Key letter
4. John Grisham's party affiliation
5. Search, as a perp
6. Hannibal the Cannibal
7. Russian range
8. City on the Rhein
9. Elbowroom
10. John Grisham's other occupation
11. TV alien
12. Opposite of alt
13. "My mama done ___ me..."
18. Mom and pop store org.
21. Sorenstam of the LPGA
22. Lay low
23. Four quarters
24. Bakery buys
26. Hanks's "Bosom Buddies" co-star
27. Medical suffix
28. "Morning Edition" network
31. "___ Girls Go" (1948 musical)
32. 1969 Peace Prize gp.
35. Critic's pick?
36. Some Swiss watches
38. Indy area
41. Prefix with tourism
42. "A Study in Scarlet" inspector
43. Chargers' org.
44. War stat.
47. Convene
48. -speak
50. Roughed up
52. Certain Muslim
55. "The Pelican ___," John Grisham novel
57. Secret
58. Actor Arnold
60. Medea rode on it
61. Webb address?
62. Alphabetic trio
63. Biker's bike
64. Having five sharps
66. Mary ___ cosmetics
67. Warm days in Cannes
68. Part of Roy G. Biv

Solution on page 157

Virgina Woolf

Across

1. 1994 Jack Nicholson film
5. Principal
9. Actor Ray
13. Violinist Busch
15. "Cannery Row" character
16. Embarkation location
17. Toon rabbit
18. Bryce Canyon locale
19. Look up and down
20. Virginia Woolf novel popularized by "The Hours"
23. Comprises
24. Word in most of the Commandments
25. Like some retreats
27. Give the heave-ho
30. Bleach
32. Politician Bayh
33. Shopper stopper
35. "Ew-w-w!"
38. Group within a group
39. "___ ___ of One's Own," Virginia Woolf novel
41. Self-starter?
42. Preface
44. Long luxuriant hair
45. Exam for jrs.
46. Chicken serving
48. Gaiety
50. State of India
51. Top flier
52. Boxer's warning
53. Virginia Woolf novel about contrasts
60. Plunder
62. Frenchman
63. Brunch selection
64. Author Oz
65. Mezzo Borodina
66. Artist's stand
67. Slightly wet
68. Gets the point
69. Trace

Down

1. Friendly
2. Fish market feature
3. Records
4. Took off
5. X-rated
6. Printing process, for short
7. Stick in one's ___
8. "Very funny!"
9. Mil. mail drop
10. "To the ____," Virginia Woolf novel
11. Holdup
12. Minerals
14. Cameroon coin
21. "___ luck!"
22. Yin's complement
26. Spot for a Band-Aid
27. At any point
28. Virginia Woolf novel, a character study based on her brother
29. Logs in
30. Puff up
31. Author Uris
32. Paranormal letters
34. Weaponry
36. Phone button below the 7
37. Lush
40. Pilgrim's destination
43. Penny-pinching
47. Chiapas chums
49. From this moment on
50. Carnation emanation
51. World record?
52. Hefty competitor
54. Battering wind
55. Whopping
56. Tie
57. First name in 50's TV
58. Parrots
59. Canine cry
61. Sixth of a fl. oz.

Solution on page 157

Ayn Rand

Across

1. Buck
5. Drs. Zira and Zaius, e.g.
9. Losing power
14. Chihuahua child
15. ___ Alto, Calif.
16. Actress Taylor
17. Life lines?
18. Prudent foresight
20. Ayn Rand's first novel
22. One may be taken to the cleaners
23. Chair
24. Score
28. 451, in old Rome
30. Collection of books
32. Nile reptile
35. Lunch or dinner
37. Red dye
38. Ayn Rand novel about an idealistic young architect
42. "___ Theme" ("Doctor Zhivago" tune)
43. Bore
44. Atlanta-to-Tampa dir.
45. Star performers
48. Hindu land grant
50. "Keep it in"
51. Small plateau
53. Is mad about
57. Philosophy developed by Ayn Rand
59. Owner of a business
63. "Wishing won't make ___"
64. Edible pods
65. Moslem judge
66. Film director Mira

67. Main character in 38-Across
68. Be prolific
69. Kind of club

Down

1. Deceives, in slang
2. Lama's land
3. Loos
4. Medieval
5. Stove or washer: Abbr.
6. Resident of Paris
7. Student at the Sorbonne
8. Mixer
9. Medicine
10. Up to now
11. Kamoze of reggae
12. Prefix with orthodox
13. ___ X
19. Opponent
21. Last
24. David of "Rhoda"
25. Arid-area refuges
26. Met highlights
27. Old "Hollywood Squares" regular
29. Romanian coin
31. An Indic language
32. "___ Shrugged," Ayn Rand novel
33. Commandment verb
34. Socialite Mesta
36. Inc., in Ipswich
39. Observe Yom Kippur
40. Three before seven
41. "Society's Child" singer Janis
46. Prefix meaning "both"
47. Refuse to accept
49. Impelling
52. Stiff hairs
54. Indispensable
55. "Ah, Wilderness!" mother
56. Campfire treat
57. Ural River city
58. In great shape
59. ___ favor
60. "Suspicion" studio
61. Mouths, anatomically
62. Norm

Solution on page 158

John Updike

Across

1. Angel's instrument
5. Intellect
9. "Sesame Street" grouch
14. Under sail
15. Has power over
16. Platter player
17. John Updike character and alter-ego
19. "Rabbit ___," second in Updike series
20. Stopping place
21. Merriment
22. Sparks or Buntline
23. Safer associate
25. Just
28. Down
29. Bank no.
33. Eat like ___
34. Like some legal proceedings
36. Boris Badenov expression, "___ boy!"
37. "Rabbit, ___," first in Updike series
38. Express support
40. Chat room "I believe"
41. Pothook shape
42. Daybook
43. Share doubler
45. "I can _ church by daylight": Shak.
47. Not just any
48. "Rabbit ___ ___," third in Updike series
49. Starchy roots
51. Cobbler
52. Go to extremes
55. Seacoast
59. Japanese-American
60. "The ___ ___ Eastwick," Updike novel
62. Knock off
63. It's east of the Urals
64. Artless: Var.
65. Verdi aria
66. Ste. Jeanne ___
67. Times Square sign

Down

1. Cries of triumph
2. "I'd hate to break up ___"
3. Soap actress Sofer
4. Associate
5. No one
6. "The Virginian" author Wister
7. Pop's bro
8. Sound barrier?: Var.
9. Daytime TV staple
10. Young woman
11. It may be cracked by a spy
12. "Sometimes you feel like ___"
13. Popular theater name
18. Ceded
21. Man at the top of Microsoft
23. Spanish men
24. Hang around
25. Uncovers
26. Mistreat
27. Washer cycle
30. Hot dog topping
31. Humorous
32. Kind of fairy
34. Its license plates say "Famous Potatoes"
35. Delivery expert?
39. TNT part
44. Gift
46. "Rabbit ___ ___," fourth in Updike series
48. Drug for a poison victim, maybe
50. Gallic goodbye
52. Fairy tale beginning
53. Competitor
54. Morales in "Rapa Nui"
55. Slammer
56. "Out of Africa" author Dinesen
57. "I dare you!"
58. Two of fifty?
60. Lots of dough
61. "This ___ bust!"

Solution on page 158

Gone with the Wind

Across

1. "Gone with the Wind" state setting
8. Scarlett's nurse from birth in "Gone with the Wind"
13. Calm
14. Run
16. Throw loosely about
17. Roman goddess of wisdom
18. Promising
19. P.M. times
20. Elevator stop
23. "Gone with the Wind" author's last name
28. Prepare to drag
29. Pain
32. Great Lakes acronym
33. "___-haw!"
34. Stage plays
37. Tater
38. Scarlett's third husband in "Gone with the Wind"
41. Wash out
43. Actress North
44. Author LeShan
47. Brief advertisement
49. Totally absorbed
50. Early riser?
51. Winter racers
54. Torcher's misdeed
56. Code-breaking org.
57. Tex. neighbor
59. Cliff of "The McLaughlin Group"
63. Chooses formally
67. Eastern European variant of Catherine
68. Affinity
69. Elegance
70. Pittsburgh NFLer

Down

1. Neon, e.g.
2. Short list shortener
3. ___-Locka, Fla.
4. Back in?
5. Sidelines brand
6. Does in
7. Ethereal
8. Decent guy
9. Is for many?
10. Render imperfect
11. "Punk'd" network
12. "___, though I walk…"
14. Old Georgia arena
15. The Panthers of the Big East
20. Pan-broil
21. Traveller's rider
22. Late
23. Component parts
24. Nozzle site
25. Catherine the Great, e.g.
26. Romanian coin
27. '60s hallucinogenic
30. PC connections
31. Biblical verb
35. Subtle glow
36. Pace
39. Sage, for one
40. Not to mention
41. "The X-Files" org.
42. Lab abbr.
45. Pair
46. Abby's twin
48. Scarlett's daughter in "Gone with the Wind"
52. "…unto us ___ is given"
53. O'Hara plantation in "Gone with the Wind"
55. Put up
57. "Twelve ___," Wilkes plantation in "Gone with the Wind"
58. Jersey, e.g.
59. Ticker tape, briefly?
60. Choreographer Lubovitch
61. LAX posting
62. ___ welder
64. Stanley Cup org.
65. It gets under your collar
66. May time (abbr.)

Solution on page 158

John Irving

Across

1. Brewery need
5. Big East team
10. Overactors
14. Get ___ on the back
15. Give extreme unction to, old-style
16. Would-be MD's course
17. Parade honoree
18. Opposition
20. "The World ___ ___ ___," John Irving novel
22. Where the buck stops?
23. Lollapalooza
24. Sloppy digs
27. Undivided
29. ___ rasa (clean slate)
34. "A Prayer for ___ ___," John Irving novel
38. "The ___ New Hampshire," John Irving novel
39. Cover with wax
40. Cut's partner
42. Knife
43. Meat and vegetables on a skewer
45. Connecting flight?
47. Declares
49. Norma ___
50. Riddle-me-___
51. Sighs of relief
54. Indy 500 month
56. "The ___ ___ ___," John Irving novel and movie
64. Publicist
65. Morning haze
66. Augur
67. Peep show
68. Film rating org.
69. Equal
70. Goose genus
71. Part of BYOB

Down

1. "Very funny!"
2. Oil cartel acronym
3. Green spot in Paris
4. Prepared to sing the national anthem
5. Inveterate
6. "Dedicated to the ___ Love"
7. Kind of question
8. Bring into a line
9. Sonnet ender
10. Dutch name of The Hague
11. Oscar winner Paquin
12. Large, in combinations
13. Rung
19. Scroll in an ark
21. Scope
24. Punches
25. Bird word
26. ___ Buena (island in San Francisco Bay)
28. Drum sites
30. Anjou kin
31. ___ Pradesh (Indian state)
32. Contract
33. Pulitzer dramatist: 1994
35. Like some drinks
36. It may be picked
37. "A Widow for One ___," John Irving novel
41. Distance across a circle
44. "Setting Free the ___," John Irving novel
46. Posterior
48. Desert in N Africa
52. Hulk of wrestling
53. Court figures
55. Scrumptious
56. Navy noncoms
57. Role for Shirley
58. Judge
59. Crossword worker?
60. Large knife
61. T'ang dynasty poet
62. Jacob tricked him
63. *

Solution on page 158

Henry Miller

Across

1. Bowler's pickup
6. Book one of Henry Miller's Rosy Crucifixion
11. Some batteries
14. Spin doctor
15. Cast out
16. Philosopher Lao-___
17. Chambers
18. Elephantine
19. Before, informally
20. Stern rival
21. Little, in Leith
22. Henry Miller's second wife
23. "Ladders to Fire" writer
24. Govt. debt
27. Mixer
28. Standard setting at 0 degrees long.
29. Question from the unable
30. Beginning to exist
32. Ancient middle eastern ascetics
35. "All in the Family" spinoff
36. "Tropic of ___," Henry Miller novel
38. Tchaikovsky's first name
40. Remainder
43. Ball with four projecting spikes
45. Pen denizen
46. CAT's cousin
48. "Kate & ___"
49. Gibbons of TV
51. Lamb's lament
52. Grandmother, affectionately
53. Col.'s boss
54. Spare parts?
55. Alphabetic trio
56. Result of the 16th Amendment
58. Book three of Henry Miller's Rosy Crucifixion
59. Frozen Wasser
60. "A poem begins as ___ in the throat": Frost
61. Staggering
62. ER staffers
63. Snap course
64. Move laterally

Down

1. "Black ___," Henry Miller novel
2. Pledge
3. Quantities
4. St. Louis gridders
5. Printer's widths
6. Line part: Abbr.
7. Survive
8. Chinese island
9. Radius partner
10. Get hard
11. Got used (to)
12. Unintelligent
13. Prime
22. Cheerful
24. The Globe, for one
25. Amateur
26. One in the red
27. Catherine I, for one
31. "In the Land of Israel" author
33. Nova follower
34. Military address
37. Gospel singer Winans
38. Heroic champion
39. Ailment
41. Pure
42. Common temple name
43. "Tropic of ___," Henry Miller novel
44. Book two of Henry Miller's Rosy Crucifixion
47. Fight a b'ar, maybe
50. Opposition
53. Shindig
54. Gilpin of "Frasier"
56. Menlo Park initials
57. Where it's good to lose
58. Govt. advisory org.

Solution on page 158

Banned Novels

Across

1. Eat like ___
5. Omar of "Scream 2"
9. Sail holders
14. Luncheonette list
15. "Star Trek: T.N.G." counselor
16. Common sprain spot
17. Banned 1749 novel by John Cleland about a prostitute
19. Author of "Ulysses," banned in the U.S. until the 1930s
20. Widespread excitement
22. Cleansing preparation
25. Timber problem
29. Rikki-Tikki-___
30. Pay heed
33. Oliver's request
34. Snaps
37. Distribute cards
39. Entrepreneur-aiding org.
40. "Lady ___ Lover," novel banned in the U.S.
43. "___ job's worth doing…"
45. Brand of corn syrup
46. Flight of steps
49. Common mixer
51. Hirschfeld's girl
53. Genetic molecules
54. "___ of Cancer," novel banned in the U.S.
56. Banned 1759 novel by Voltaire, made into an operetta
59. Inflammation of the lungs
62. Spiked
65. Oddly
69. Part of a religious title
70. Lambs: Lat.
71. "What ___ is new?"
72. 1944 Preminger classic
73. Come clean, with "up"
74. Gull-like predatory bird

Down

1. Brunswick competitor
2. Legume
3. B & B
4. Person who makes firearms
5. Prefix with science
6. Place of confinement
7. Negri of silents
8. Riverbed deposit
9. Blair's predecessor
10. Assumed name
11. Blue-___ (unrealistic)
12. Nanny's asset
13. "Told ya!"
18. "You betcha"
21. Standards of perfection
22. "The racer's edge"
23. "Fat chance!"
24. Pear-shaped fruit
26. "Semiramide" composer
27. Symbol of sovereignty
28. Oolong, for one
31. Popular theater name
32. Artist Gerard ___ Borch
35. Furniture wood
36. Golf lesson topic
38. Replayed tennis shot
41. Part of TNT
42. Information found on tees
43. Novel ending
44. In lieu of
47. "Sweet!"
48. Memphis-to-Biloxi dir.
50. Show one's face
52. Squirrel's stash
55. Home to more than a billion
57. "Delta of Venus" author Nin
58. "Seduction of the Minotaur" author
60. Mil. fliers
61. Bank holding: Abbr.
62. Bad cholesterol letters
63. Penlight battery
64. Actor Gulager
66. North American deer
67. Fighting Tigers' sch.
68. Vote of support

Solution on page 158

Chapter 5: Classics

Moby-Dick

Across

1. Dip in liquid
4. Calamitous
10. Experiences
13. Himalayan goat
14. Freshen
15. Pizarro's prize
16. Intestinal sections
17. Admits
18. Blokes
19. Starting port in "Moby-Dick"
21. Jeanne d'Arc, for one (abbr.)
23. Our "mother"
24. Island off the SE coast of China
27. Youngest March sister
28. Get an ___ (ace)
31. Condiment
32. Republic in central Europe
34. Nutritional stds.
35. First line in "Moby-Dick"
38. "Moby-Dick" captain
39. Bony
40. China setting
42. Gridiron blockers: Abbr.
43. Trig. function
46. Unsteady gait
47. Sorbonne, e.g.
49. Tennessee athlete
50. Ill-humored
54. Tooth care org.
56. "Moby-Dick" ship
58. "What ___?"
59. That girl
60. Strict disciplinarian
61. Facial spasms
62. "Shoot!"
63. Author Fallaci
64. Compass point

Down

1. Bow
2. Porter's pen name
3. ___ & Whitney (airplane engine company)
4. Magnesium silicate
5. Raise a stink
6. "Laugh-In" first name
7. Frighten
8. "Lord, is ___?": Matthew
9. Official count of population
10. Domestic
11. "We ___ Family" (Sister Sledge hit)
12. Many a delivery
13. Skin problem
20. Ryder competitor
22. Aquarium fish
24. Edible clam
25. Kind of history
26. N.F.L. stat: Abbr.
29. Absorb gradually
30. Atoll order?
31. Cheap so-and-so
32. Percentage of light reflected by a planet
33. "___ for Rocket": Bradbury
35. ___ Phraya, Thai.
36. Large burrowing African mammal
37. Louvre, par exemple
38. Away from the bow
41. Among the league's best
43. Item the only survivor floats on before rescue in "Moby-Dick"
44. Water channel
45. Druids, e.g.
48. Benjamin
50. 640 acres: Abbr.
51. Aqua ___
52. Skilled diver
53. Ancient work including the Skalda
54. "Just as I thought!"
55. ___ Moines, Iowa
57. Audio receiver

Solution on page 159

The Grapes of Wrath

Across

1. Fleece
5. P.D. broadcast
8. Attacks
14. World's largest sultanate
15. Feathered stole
16. Monetary unit of Portugal
17. Polygonal recess
18. Dot on the Rhine
19. Conceit
20. Eldest Joad daughter in "The Grapes of Wrath"
23. Soft & ___ (Gillette product)
24. Mount with spirit
25. Seeps
29. Power source for Fulton
31. Awesome
33. WWII locale, in brief
34. Ammunition chest
38. Alphabet run
39. "The Grapes of Wrath" author
42. She played Julia on "Party of Five"
43. Is important
44. Comparing pair
45. CPO's group
46. Writer Asimov
50. Soviet forced-labor camp
52. Fiend
56. New Deal org.
57. Main character's earlier crime in "The Grapes of Wrath"
60. Presidential middle name
63. Architect Maya ___
64. "If it __ broke..."
65. Tater Tots maker
66. Ltd., in the U.S.
67. Driving force
68. Title role for Mia
69. Get the point
70. Lothario's look

Down

1. Planks
2. Foreign auto
3. Dog star
4. Baby bouncer
5. Behind
6. Aplomb
7. Get clean
8. Will of "Jeremiah Johnson"
9. Newsman Charles
10. __ Lodge (motel chain)
11. ___ generis
12. Computer pop-ups
13. "The Grapes of Wrath" main character
21. Ottoman Empire founder
22. Nimble
26. Galvanizing metal
27. Furry "Star Wars" creature
28. Dip in liquid
30. Long (for)
32. Last of the Stuarts
35. Precepts
36. Where fans may be found
37. Band performance
38. Hodgepodge
39. Proper name in Masses
40. Like some picture frames
41. To come with
42. Pick on
45. Where bananas are food
47. Clothes
48. Take vengeance for
49. Reagan's predecessor
51. At full speed, at sea
53. Island of immigrants
54. It's motto is "Dirigo"
55. Preventive measure?
58. Oldest Joad son in "The Grapes of Wrath"
59. Burglar's take
60. Homer Simpson exclamation
61. Prohibition ___
62. Spy novelist Deighton

Solution on page 159

The Great Gatsby

Across

1. Object of Gatsby's desire
6. Midmonth day
10. Union flouter
14. Informed
15. Right after
16. Descartes quote word
17. Novarro of silents
18. "___ yellow ribbon..."
19. __ Flynn Boyle
20. Actor Hardin et al.
21. It's definite
23. Jordan Baker's profession in "The Great Gatsby"
25. Late songstress Nyro
27. Anglers' hopes
28. Arthur Ashe's alma mater
31. Set (on)
32. "___-Tiki"
33. Nick's relation to Gatsby, initially
35. Fixed
39. They, in Tours
40. Wax producer
41. Bad-mouth
42. China's __-tse
43. Island off the SE coast of China
45. Myrtle Wilson's relation to 63-Down
47. Antiquity
48. ___ Kabibble
49. Tolkien creations
50. "__ of robins...": Kilmer
53. Periodic table listings: Abbr.
55. More than dislike
57. Collide with
58. Some rush-hour periods: Abbr.
61. "It's either you ___"
62. One of the Aleutians
65. Kind of room
67. Smoke combined with fog
68. Fabled fliers
69. Lofty
70. Was a fink
71. Porn
72. Panache

Down

1. Pub missile
2. Absent
3. Alpo alternative
4. B.O. sign
5. Rumormonger
6. Cabinet Department
7. Opus ___
8. Program file extension
9. Antlered animal
10. Marketing
11. Skill
12. Concur
13. Some tuskers
22. Married man
24. Double-reed player
25. Delay
26. From l. to r.
28. Condo
29. 1989 Literature Nobelist
30. "How to Murder Your Wife" star Virna
32. Hindu deity
34. Vitality
36. Secluded valley
37. Part of SEATO
38. Improvised bed
41. Doubt
44. Long Island location of Gatsby's house
45. Hamm of soccer
46. Home: abbr.
50. At __ (stumped)
51. Actress Shearer
52. Ireland's De Valera
54. Forebodings
56. Drum sites
58. "Dear" one
59. Gangster's gal
60. Popeye's ___ Pea
63. Husband of 1-Across
64. Horned Frogs' sch.
66. Great deal

Solution on page 159

The Catcher in the Rye

Across

1. Street fleet
5. Banks of note
9. Inquires
13. Sword handle
14. Recoils
15. Catch red-handed
16. Notion
17. Inflict, as havoc
18. Before mundi or regni
19. Holden's last name in "The Catcher in the Rye"
21. Leonine group
22. Effaced
23. Early Brit
24. Area with coin-operated games
27. Child who has lost both parents
29. One-named Spanish singer
30. Holden's dead younger brother in "The Catcher in the Rye"
32. Coffee order: Abbr.
34. Buoyant tune
35. Bear
36. Bleacher feature
37. Prefix with cycle or sex
38. Van Gogh's village
39. Unrefined
40. Place where business is conducted
42. Lacking skill
43. Alternative to acrylics
44. Intangible qualities
46. Early times
48. Age of the narrator in "The Catcher in the Rye"
52. Years in old Rome
53. ___ operandi
54. Not working
55. "You know how ___"
56. Some showdowns
57. Beaks
58. Wyle of "ER"
59. Res ___ loquitur
60. Little biter

Down

1. "Blondie" cartoonist Young
2. Verdi slave girl
3. Cordon ___
4. Steadfast partisan
5. Babe Ruth's number
6. Return on an investment
7. Admonish
8. Pop the question
9. Leader of a revolt
10. Institution where Holden is narrating "The Catcher in the Rye"
11. Sort
12. Shrub with plumlike fruits
14. Rip off
20. Pooch's name
21. Snowman prop
23. ___-dieu
24. Rights org. since 1920
25. Rhinoceros
26. State where Holden is narrating "The Catcher in the Rye"
27. Auto pioneer Ransom Eli ___
28. Cries out for
30. Skilled
31. Tell a whopper
33. Western writer Zane
35. Bows
36. Trustful
38. Is out of sorts
39. Family group
41. Complete
42. Salad green
44. Dangerous mosquito
45. Palate appendage
46. Large pipe
47. Wised up
48. Liquid food
49. Scene of a temptation
50. Seat of Coffee County, AL
51. Place that allows "eggs-tradition"?
53. Start of the 16th century

Solution on page 159

Lord of the Flies

Across

1. Po tributary
5. "Got it"
9. Elvis's swivelers
13. Half-moon tide
14. Common mixer
15. "The __ Love," R.E.M. hit
16. Reflected sound
17. Hubbard of Scientology fame
18. Solo
19. "Lord of the Flies" author, first name
21. "Lord of the Flies" author, last name
23. Possesses
24. L.A. hrs.
25. Sodium hydroxide
26. Very cold
29. Diligent worker
31. Hospital helpers
32. Actress Phillips
33. Lukas of "Witness"
37. "Choppers"
38. Break time, maybe
39. "Lord of the Flies" fat boy
40. Food for Morlocks
41. "Lord of the Flies" breakaway leader
42. Hydrolysis product
43. Slatted wooden box
45. Lays out
46. Look through a scope
49. Commercial prefix with vision
50. Explorer John and others
51. Fire starter in "Lord of the Flies"
53. Broadcast slot
57. Compass point
58. Tattled
60. Air freshener target
61. Suffix with fluor-
62. WWW facilitators
63. Zero
64. Plug up
65. Silver salmon
66. Antlered animals

Down

1. From the top
2. Metric prefix
3. "James and the Giant Peach" author
4. Regretful
5. "Lord of the Flies" setting
6. Campus digs
7. Nuptial agreement
8. Gangway
9. Grasp
10. How anchovies are packed
11. Small change
12. Word in two Steven Seagal movies
18. Der ___ (Adenauer)
20. "If only!"
22. Father of Balder
26. Destiny
27. Monetary unit of Cambodia
28. Logical start?
29. Chessman
30. Artificial gemstone
32. Numerical fact
34. Opposed to, hillbilly-style
35. "Yes, there is ___!"
36. Dict. offerings
39. A written document
41. Primer girl
44. Hustle
45. Declared
46. Infamous 1972 hurricane
47. Player's lament
48. Explorer Polo
50. "Lord of the Flies" initial leader
52. Put one's foot down?
54. Teen ___
55. Brother
56. "___ Tu" (1974 hit)
59. Granada grizzly

Solution on page 159

Animal Farm

Across

1. Lend a hand
5. Blue Jays airer
8. Art subject
12. Rent-___
13. __ mater: brain covering
14. Speedy
15. Karmann __
16. Giles or Jannings
17. Historical period
18. Political system illustrated by "Animal Farm"
20. Not a lick
21. Precious mettle?
22. TV diner owner
23. Iraqi terrorist act in 2004 news
26. "Animal Farm" author
29. Diminutive suffix
30. Doomsayer's recommendation
33. "Star Wars" dancing girl
35. Center
37. Here, in Le Havre
38. Chekhov
39. Hoops nickname
40. Milk and egg drink
42. Old cartoonist Hoff
43. Complete reversals
45. Dieters' lunches
47. Muslim holiday
48. Papa Doc ruled it
50. Name of several Norwegian kings
52. Final "Animal Farm" law: "All animals are equal but some are ___ ___ than others."
56. A hand tool
57. Songwriter Novello
58. Push
59. Match up
60. Meddle (with)
61. Had too much, briefly
62. Salon specialist
63. Source of heat
64. "tom thumb" star Tamblyn

Down

1. Caldron stirrers
2. Repeat
3. Secular
4. Pat on the back
5. Curry herb
6. Quick and active
7. Storm preceder
8. Name of character who becomes the undisputed tyrant in "Animal Farm"
9. "Once ___ a time..."
10. Backgammon equipment
11. Old English letter
13. Deceive
14. Take up again
19. Disassembled
22. '80s Peppard costar
23. Mooches
24. Yale of Yale University
25. Assailed
26. "Come ___!"
27. Mucho
28. Bridges in movies
31. Animals who rule in "Animal Farm"
32. ER test
34. Last-minute considerations
36. Minister of Propaganda in "Animal Farm"
38. Quartz marble
40. Sign off
41. Willows
44. Ransack
46. Whiskey
48. Hang like a hummingbird
49. Came to mind
50. Licentious revelry
51. Former Italian capital
52. Chevalier song
53. Indic language
54. Gets on
55. Watch readouts, briefly
56. Pop

Solution on page 159

The Three Musketeers

Across

1. Orbital point
6. City where the three musketeers are met
11. Jim Croce's "Time __ Bottle"
14. Conceited
15. Europe's "boot"
16. Fallen space station
17. Takes a stab at
18. One of three Ottoman sultans
19. Green legume
20. Salt Lake City students
21. Sterile places: Abbr.
22. Composed
23. "Kung Fu" actor Philip
24. "Don't ___ surprised!"
27. Martini's partner
28. Rapper Tone ___
29. ___-disant (self-proclaimed)
30. Dons clothes
32. Ocean condiment
35. Roswell crash victim, supposedly
36. "The Three Musketeers" protagonist
38. One of the Leeward Islands
40. Savings
43. Dangerous siren
45. Old World deer
46. Highly rated
48. Makes level
49. Emma of "Dynasty"
51. Psychedelic of the '60s
52. Splinter group
53. Down for the count
54. Part of P.R.

55. Club alternative
56. "The Three Musketeers" author
58. Crayola choice
59. Prefix meaning "ear"
60. Plant swelling
61. Coeur d'___, Idaho
62. Neighbor of Turk.
63. Explode
64. Bridges in movies

Down

1. De facto
2. Extroverted one of the three musketeers
3. Systematically arranged body of facts
4. Turner and Eisenhower
5. Lead-in for op
6. Actress Zadora
7. Oldest of the three musketeers
8. Strict disciplinarian
9. Seine sights
10. Old cartoonist Hoff
11. Deadlock
12. Big name in ratings
13. Musketeer who was brought up in a monastery
22. Triangular ratio
24. Besets
25. Unrefined
26. Knight fight
27. Tells
31. Kidnapper's demand
33. Coming

34. Catch some rays
37. Starting point
38. Newness
39. Kind of set
41. Classic Italian astronomer
42. Hometown of 36-Across
43. Sappho's home
44. Fraternal twin, in chemistry
47. Like an idol
50. Presidential name
53. African antelope
54. Somersault
56. She has a ball
57. Didn't play
58. James Dean's "East of Eden" role

Solution on page 160

A Tale of Two Cities

Across

1. Showed up
5. Approximately
10. Nickelodeon's "___ the Explorer"
14. "Family Ties" role
15. Kind of squash
16. The groundhog seeing its shadow, say
17. Roller coaster feature
18. Morocco's capital
19. Rejections
20. First five words in "A Tale of Two Cities"
23. It precedes one
24. Carry with effort
25. One of the two cities
28. Offered marriage
33. Little green man
34. Brownish gray
35. Nigerian people
36. Zest
37. Yes or no follower
38. Where to get off
39. Old greeting
40. Sensational
41. Wrap
42. Caddy rival
44. Charles ___, a main character in "A Tale of Two Cities"
45. Bacillus shape
46. Riled up
47. Last four words in "A Tale of Two Cities"
54. Sound
55. Diamond and others
56. Oz greeting
57. Mil. truant
58. Bank
59. Sea dogs
60. Japanese rice beer
61. It doubles your dough
62. Stevenson fiend

Down

1. Colombian city
2. Buckets
3. Kitty's comment
4. Enlarged
5. Sydney ___, a main character in "A Tale of Two Cities"
6. Corporate raider Carl
7. Choir attire
8. Constant complainer
9. Eland
10. "Please stay!"
11. Melville book
12. Sea hazard
13. Response: Abbr.
21. In a minute
22. Movie extra, in brief
25. Onetime NFLer
26. Greenish
27. Frisco footballer
28. One of the two cities
29. Felt sorry
30. Squelch
31. African virus
32. Inane
34. Inner tube surrounder
37. Abruptly
38. Physical power
40. 10th-century pope
41. One of the Channel Islands
43. Small bed for an infant
44. English Channel county
46. 1991-92 U.S. Open champ
47. Part of the Corn Belt
48. Crook
49. Very wide shoe spec
50. Exclamation of acclaim
51. Singer Anita
52. City district
53. Big Board letters
54. Krypton or radon

Solution on page 160

To Kill a Mockingbird

Across

1. Big drawer?
6. Gift ___
11. Here, in Juarez
14. Send on a PC
15. Sibling's daughter
16. R.N.'s forte
17. Black man on trial in "To Kill a Mockingbird"
19. Wren-___ (small brown bird)
20. Frozen carbonated drink brand
21. Hearts (abbr.)
22. "Editorially speaking," in cyber-shorthand
23. Sphere
25. Ghostlike
27. Cicatrix
28. Off base, perhaps
30. Nickname of daughter in "To Kill a Mockingbird"
32. Lofty lines
33. Actor ___ Cobb
35. Hillock
36. Author of "To Kill a Mockingbird"
39. Love, Spanish-style
41. Champagne name
42. Rep.'s opponent
45. "I wanna!"
47. Cut
49. Past tense of bid
50. Low point
53. Nickname of friend in "To Kill a Mockingbird"
54. Hoover's org.
55. Flight: Prefix
56. Map abbr.
58. Resinous stuff

Solution on page 160

59. Actor in movie "To Kill a Mockingbird"
63. Doctor's org.
64. "Say what?"
65. Ridge
66. 60's chess champ
67. Harplike instruments
68. Bacon piece

Down

1. New York ballplayer
2. First name in comedy
3. Dumas heroine
4. Ringlike formation
5. Cream ingredient
6. CIA's sea-going arm
7. Family name in "To Kill a Mockingbird"
8. Exploit
9. Squirrel's stash
10. Uncle ___
11. Lawyer in "To Kill a Mockingbird"
12. Weather conditions
13. One in a cast
18. Large amphibious rodent
23. Nickname of Arthur Radley in "To Kill a Mockingbird"
24. Furthermore
26. Permeate
27. French silk
29. Waker-upper
31. Where Minos ruled
34. Nickname of brother in "To Kill a Mockingbird"
36. Household
37. "Christ Stopped at Eboli" director
38. MacNeil's longtime partner
39. State setting for "To Kill a Mockingbird"
40. Curative
42. Chauffeurs
43. That's a moray
44. CCCX x V
46. Solar or geothermic
48. Experts
49. A neighbor
51. Toward the back
52. Herd orphan
55. "...___ in Kalamazoo"
57. Undergo lysis
60. Come-___ (marketing ploys)
61. The Company
62. Singer Starr

Greek Mythology

Across

1. Crimson Tide, briefly
5. Mariner's hdg.
8. Somewhat
12. B-boy link
13. Gillette product
14. $100 bill
15. Primate feature
16. Some deer
17. Greek underworld
18. Greek goddess of love
20. Harrow rival
21. Chosen ones
22. Exclamation of contempt
23. Designate
26. Greek goddess of the hunt
30. "___ will be done"
31. Greek goddess of wisdom
34. Business that makes little money
35. Diamond protectors
37. GPs' gp.
38. Co-conspirator of Brutus
39. Of the hipbone: Prefix
40. Classical lyric poet
42. __ Andreas Fault
43. What the college student took
45. Gofer's job
47. Consume
48. Threnody
50. Tel ___, Israel
52. Removal
56. Stage whisper
57. "As I Lay Dying" father
58. Wife and older sister of 60-Across
59. Got up
60. King of the Greek gods
61. Cockney cottages
62. Place for a firing
63. Dutch city
64. Mrs. Addams, to Gomez

Down

1. ___ Men ("Who Let the Dogs Out" band)
2. Pronto, in memos
3. Ho Chi __
4. Peace Nobelist Sakharov
5. Bite-the-bullet type
6. Quarterback Favre
7. Peace of mind
8. Object of loathing
9. Kind of list
10. "Got two fives for __?"
11. __ Moines
13. Fervent
14. Use crib notes
19. Gymnast Korbut and others
22. Suit top
23. Storage room
24. Will
25. Fertile Crescent land
26. Take ___ (doze)
27. ___ Solemnis
28. Atahualpa subject
29. Position
32. Lukas of "Witness"
33. Akihito, e.g.: Abbr.
36. Greek god of the sea
38. Welsh breed
40. Primed
41. Greek god of commerce and invention
44. Rescued
46. Did a double take?
48. Feasted
49. It's debatable
50. Wine spot
51. Bowed instrument
52. Fog
53. Interstate hauler
54. Greek god of war
55. Tie down
56. Pop the question

Solution on page 160

Roman Mythology

Across

1. Lowdown
5. Key of Beethoven's Symphony No. 7: Abbr.
9. Roman goddess of agriculture
14. L.A.-based oil company
15. No-no: Var.
16. Strictly accurate
17. Salt
18. Birdhouse dweller
19. River in Hades
20. His: Fr.
21. Nabisco cookies
23. Sound of a cat
24. Roman god of commerce
26. Akihito, e.g.: Abbr.
28. Octopus's defense
29. Supreme Roman god
33. Roman deities protecting the house and the family
36. ___ Kinte of "Roots"
37. Fire residue
39. Mother of Horus
40. Euro fractions
41. Mlle. from Madrid
42. Doctor
43. Keep an ___ the ground
44. Roman goddess of love and beauty
45. Roman goddess of luck
47. Batman after Michael
48. Coolers, briefly
49. Roman goddess of wisdom
53. Drop out
56. Gives forth
59. "Neato!"
60. Roman goddess of the hearth
62. Et __: and others
63. "Nothing ___!"
64. Poet Dickinson
65. Perform again
66. Suffix with differ
67. Actress Blakley
68. Ollie's chum
69. Big game

Down

1. Company with a blue globe logo
2. Pope's cape
3. Come to mind
4. Think tank output
5. On the job
6. Join in wedlock
7. Busy as ___
8. Roman goddess married to Jupiter
9. Animation unit
10. Free from an obligation
11. Pace
12. Bat's navigation aid
13. Slow-cook
22. School mos.
25. Young __ (tykes)
27. "Cara __"
29. Coup group
30. "Do ___ others…"
31. Make, as a living
32. Four before V
33. Something to flip
34. Since
35. Affluent, in Acapulco
36. Composer Jerome
38. Comprises
40. Bring about
41. Chosen
43. And so on: Abbr.
44. Furniture truck
46. Child's toy
47. Sight
49. Crete's highest elev.
50. TV exec Arledge
51. Communication medium
52. Adjust
53. Superior to
54. Note
55. "The fix ___"
57. Roman god of war
58. "__ a Song Go Out of My Heart"
61. Middy's assent

Solution on page 160

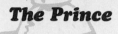

The Prince

Across

1. Caveman's weapon
5. Capts.' superiors
9. Some pears
14. Suffix with Lincoln
15. Thrust out the lips
16. Prepare to transplant
17. "benefits must be conferred ___," from "The Prince"
19. Took an oath
20. Gasteyer of "Saturday Night Live"
21. Big Band __
23. Outstanding
24. W.W. I soldier
27. "he who causes another to become ___ ruins himself," from "The Prince"
29. Lays to rest
32. They may be split
33. Beavis or Butt-head
34. Harlem theater
37. Author of "The Prince"
41. Predaceous insect
42. Reed in a pit
45. Tiny particle
47. Pressure lines
49. Commonplace
53. "___ is the most effective and efficient means to do something," from "The Prince"
54. Sound worked up
55. Consult
56. Clothier's concern
57. Birth country of 37-Across
59. "harm should be inflicted ___ ___ ___," from "The Prince"

64. Contemporary of Helena
65. Sixth-century date
66. Israel's Golda
67. Fertile soil
68. Flanders river
69. Wine datum

Down

1. Smoke, slangily
2. Choreographer Lubovitch
3. Acapulco article
4. Seaport near Barcelona
5. Film rating org.
6. Earthlink rival
7. Dixie drink
8. Commercial prefix with foam
9. "Speed" setting
10. Forward
11. Lampoons
12. Horn-shaped bone
13. Pittsburgh product
18. Word on a coin
22. Fearless
24. Favorite
25. Solitary
26. Couple
28. Compound with a hydroxyl group
30. Islands in W Atlantic Ocean
31. Political slant
35. Meal source
36. Roman 57
38. "Let's go!"

39. Surgical incision to sever nerves
40. Building beam
43. Dungeons & Dragons monster
44. Reverse of WNW
45. Congenitally attached
46. Names
48. "What ___?"
49. Bay window
50. 1969 Hoffman role
51. Prepared
52. Shouts
56. Worth a C, perhaps
58. Affirmative reply
60. Golf position
61. Once named
62. Bush Sr. once headed it
63. Goof up

Solution on page 160

Chapter 6: Biography & Memoirs

Presidential Autobiographies

Across

1. Bilko's rank: Abbr.
4. Way out
9. Entr'__
13. Sound of relief
14. Launch
15. Departments
17. Winter end
18. Kind of switch
19. Hospital figure
20. Author of "A Time to Heal"
23. Follower's suffix
24. Roughly
25. Corded cloth
26. __-Xers (boomers' kids)
27. Lays turf on
28. Bambino watcher
31. Smallville's Lang
32. Olympian's quest
33. Fenced areas
34. Author of "An Hour Before Daylight: Memoirs of a Rural Boyhood"
38. Scarlett's third
40. Covered
41. Listening devices
42. Like most newspapers
44. Rolling stone's lack
48. Caesar's hello
49. Garage stain
50. Declarer in bridge columns
51. Tourmaline, e.g.
52. Author of "My Life"
56. Pernod flavoring
58. Apple product
59. Forfeit or sum paid into the pool
60. __ Ark
61. Ground
62. Swellhead's trouble
63. You, once
64. Slip cover
65. "__War": '90s sci-fi series

Down

1. Steppes beasts
2. Summerhouse
3. Symbol of discipline
4. Like ___ from the blue
5. Furnish
6. Operatic prince
7. Son of Willy Loman
8. Disclose
9. Supermarket chain
10. French vineyard
11. "Mr. Mom" actress
12. Area of London
16. Regarded to be
21. Vienna's land: Abbr.
22. "The Crying Game" star
28. Soccer ___
29. One of the Khans
30. Start of the 18th century
31. New Guinea port
32. Clock std.
33. Pay stub abbr.
34. Book of the Bible
35. "___ true!"
36. Solely
37. Bit of hope
38. Author of "An American Life: The Autobiography"
39. An individual without wealth
42. Early sixth-century date
43. On the same side
44. Tues. preceder
45. Vent
46. Larry, for one
47. Dope
49. Beyond plump
50. Many Punjabis
53. Angle iron
54. McIntosh discard
55. Plenty
57. Naval pronoun

Solution on page 161

Basketball Biographies

Across

1. Ankles
6. Stone mound
11. Knock over
14. Great quantity
15. Prefix with -pathy
16. Brit. record label
17. "More Than A Game" biography subject
19. Capri or Corsica
20. Geologic time division
21. Spanish articles
22. Weapon
24. Lightweight boxing champ Edwin
26. ___ pole
28. "Bad As I Wanna Be" biography subject
32. Pre-entree course
35. Rough file
36. Band with the hit "Sweet Talkin' Woman"
37. Year-end formal
38. Illinois city
40. Football stats: Abbr.
41. Department of eastern France
42. What we have
43. Now
44. "My Life" biography subject
48. Following behind
49. Lift
53. 1980 DeLuise film
55. "___ Called Horse"
56. "Runaway" singer Shannon
57. Hosp. ward
58. "Life on the Run" biography subject
62. Pulled off
63. Actor Albert
64. Cooper role
65. Laudatory lines
66. Less common
67. Ham's place, perhaps

Down

1. Boozehound
2. Sneezing sound
3. Bridle attachments
4. "Do the Right Thing" pizzeria owner
5. Pained
6. Silkworm covering
7. Sets a price at
8. "___ not my problem"
9. Hupmobile contemporary
10. 24/7
11. Suggest as appropriate
12. Poet ___ Khayyám
13. "Drive: The Story of My Life" biography subject
18. Has ___: has connections
23. Joined
25. He raised Cain
26. Nicholas I or II
27. About
29. Dander
30. Canadian prov.
31. Snoopy
32. Junk e-mail
33. Operatic song
34. Meridian
38. Stephen King canine
39. Three-in-___
40. Inner Hebrides island
42. Tenth month of the year
43. Transport to Oz
45. Social connections
46. Quantity
47. Work with a pug
50. Goof-off
51. Flea-bitten
52. "Family Ties" mom
53. Pooch's name
54. Low-pH stuff
55. What George couldn't tell
59. "Esto perpetua" is its motto: Abbr.
60. CEO, e.g.
61. Cub Scout group

Solution on page 161

Baseball Biographies

Across

1. Give away
5. Grounded Atl. crossers
9. Get the lead out?
14. ___-Day vitamins
15. "I have ___ good authority"
16. Epileptic seizure
17. "When You Come To A Fork In The Road, Take It!" biography subject
19. Author Marsh
20. Singles bar
22. Determined
25. Theater district
29. North Carolina college
30. Crossword worker?
33. Stand in line, perhaps
34. Unprovoked
37. Sticky-tongued critter
39. It may elicit a call
40. "Juiced: Wild Times, Rampant 'Roids, Smash Hits, and How Baseball Got Big" biography subject
43. ___-Aztecan (language group)
45. NEA member
46. Asian capital
49. Triathlon leg
51. Six years, for a senator
53. "Able was ___..."
54. Nation in N North America
56. Republic in central Europe
59. An old person
62. "Our Gang" member
65. "Luckiest Man" biography subject
69. Concede
70. Confident
71. Swiss river
72. "Kisses on the Wind" singer Cherry
73. Stuttering actor Roscoe
74. Subsequently

Down

1. Miniature
2. Roxy Music co-founder
3. Trip segment
4. Attacked
5. Luis's lucky number
6. Take long steps
7. Undecided
8. Sweater problem
9. 1967 war locale
10. "Ya Gotta Believe!" biography subject, Tug ___
11. LAX guesstimate
12. French pronoun
13. General on Chinese menus
18. Mischievous
21. Chicken serving
22. Condensed moisture
23. Babb's girlfriend
24. Unite
26. Worker
27. Place for a tack
28. Giant who wore "4"
31. Belle or Bart
32. Security Council veto
35. Bone: Comb. form
36. Drink of the gods
38. Grade near failing
41. Compadre of Fidel
42. Gossip
43. Trojans' sch.
44. Former Pan Am rival
47. Jackie's O
48. School org.
50. "Close Shave" biography subject, Sal ___
52. Ripe
55. End of life
57. Hankerings
58. You, abroad
60. Rick's old flame
61. August, in Arles
62. Dapper one
63. Lime drink
64. Former White House inits.
66. Noise from a fan
67. Boiling blood
68. ___ X

Solution on page 161

Football Biographies

Across

1. Olympus neighbor
5. Small seed
8. Utterly senseless
14. Countrywide: Abbr.
15. Subj. for immigrants
16. Nephew of King Arthur
17. Nestling
18. Kung ___ shrimp
19. Keystone St. port
20. "Power, Money & Sex" biography subject
23. Boxer's warning
24. Social outcast
25. Elizabethan earl
29. School assignment
31. Appeared in print
33. Sharp feller
34. Disentangle
38. Some M.I.T. grads
39. "When Pride Still Mattered" biography subject
42. Yielding
43. Ceases
44. Wrestling win
45. MLK title
46. Do schoolwork?
50. French farewell
52. Montaigne work
56. Bud's bud
57. "When The Tuna Went Down To Texas" biography subject
60. Japanese robe
63. Boot one
64. Soften
65. Roomy dresses
66. Something to stroke
67. "I've Got ___ in Kalamazoo"
68. Big name in insurance
69. Drops on the ground
70. "Pretty Woman" actor

Down

1. Anxious
2. "I Am Third" biography subject, Gale ___
3. Flight of steps
4. "Not to mention…"
5. Coke competitor
6. Hayes of "South Park"
7. Cheap wine
8. "Let Us Now Praise Famous Men" author James
9. Sterile
10. They cut the cheese
11. Mideast fed.
12. Tombstone letters
13. Cloning basic
21. "No Strings Attached" pop group
22. Lettuce
26. Hourglass contents
27. Vet
28. Strikes out
30. Polly, to Tom Sawyer
32. Priests' vestments
35. Advise
36. Brit's exam
37. Columnist Marilyn ___ Savant
38. European language
39. Emptiness
40. Sidi ___ (Moroccan seaport)
41. Loft
42. Health resort
45. Undone
47. Contend
48. Worn around the neck
49. Jostle
51. Piano key material
53. Swiftness
54. Boot camp boss, informally
55. Shaft shot from a bow
58. Something that is lost
59. On-line periodical, for short
60. Intl. carrier to Seoul
61. Unwell
62. Italian possessive

Solution on page 161

Tennis Biographies

Across

1. Physique
6. Minnelli of "Cabaret"
10. One of the Bushes
13. 1935 Triple Crown winner
14. Like some keys
15. "Gang" preceder
16. "The Player" biography subject
18. "Oz" network
19. Deck material
20. Prenatal test, for short
22. Barely enough
26. Nameless
28. Embodiment
29. Calamitous
30. Jazz up
31. Critical
32. Outer: Prefix
35. Period
36. Like most newspapers
37. Pre-cable problem
38. Oklahoma county seat
39. Mythological trio
40. Paroxysm
41. Spanish constructions
43. Spicy cuisine
44. Allowance
46. Noisiest
47. A vital sign
48. Faults
49. Popular card game
50. "My Aces, My Faults" biography subject, Nick ___
57. King's title: Abbr.
58. Fancies
59. Puckish
60. Code-breaking gp.
61. Uptight
62. John of song

Down

1. Blubber
2. Med. ins. plan
3. Rhein feeder
4. Key letter
5. Photography pioneer
6. Overcome
7. It's kept in a pen
8. Pulitzer playwright Akins
9. Set up
10. "You Cannot Be Serious" biography subject
11. Jazzman Blake
12. Be bummed out
14. Repast
17. Endure
21. Printemps month
22. Mediterranean nation
23. Overgrown, in a way
24. "The Rivals: Chris Evert Vs. Martina ___"
25. Tabloid twosome
26. Europe/Asia divider
27. Blue shade
29. Takes a stab at
31. Like some communities
33. Loses heat
34. Bird word
36. Fix, in a way
37. Cast off
39. Comped thing
40. One on a board
42. Photo ___ (camera sessions)
43. Abbr. at the bottom of a page
44. Reject
45. Ditties
46. Fabrications
48. Do in
51. Uneven?
52. Race part
53. Unwell
54. Lizard, old-style
55. "Flying Down to ___"
56. Place to stay

Solution on page 161

Boxing Biographies

Across

1. Nile vipers
5. Pubmates
9. Symbols of hardness
14. Bible pronoun
15. Creme-filled cookie
16. One of the Keebler elves
17. Native of Hungary
19. Treasure map distances
20. "Golden Boy" biography subject
22. Sexologist Hite
23. Coup d'___ (takeover)
24. Nutritional inits.
27. Functional
31. Barbara, to friends
35. Treasury Dept. division
36. Entangle
37. Make larger
39. "Raging Bull: My Story" author, last name
41. Author Zora __ Hurston
42. Balloon filler
43. Breathing: Abbr.
44. "A Flame of Pure Fire" biography subject
48. Rub the wrong way
49. Swing a scythe
50. Manila hemp plant
55. "By George" biography subject
59. Rap duo Kris ___
61. Rearing of children
62. Like some alarms
63. Angered
64. "The African Queen" scriptwriter
65. Things to crack
66. Attendance figs., often
67. Wing it?

Down

1. Dumas adventurer
2. "Pipe down!"
3. Effeminate male
4. "Pound For Pound: A Biography of ___ Ray Robinson"
5. Lady's man
6. Auto racer Luyendyk
7. Traders
8. Handel bars?
9. Patronage based on family
10. "Knowledge can split ___ of light": Dickens
11. Personified
12. Fairway position
13. French pronoun
18. Mars: Prefix
21. Pillbox, e.g.
25. Indoor game
26. ___ of faith
28. Hog
29. It comes before long
30. __ close to schedule
31. Dog star?
32. Lend __: listen
33. 1924 Kentucky Derby winner or a 1947 Anthony Quinn drama
34. Polio vaccine developer
38. Kentucky Derby victory wreath
39. Fleur-de-___
40. "Right you ___!"
42. Becomes visible
45. Ballad's end?
46. Talkative person
47. Kitten's plaything
51. Test versions
52. Friend in a sombrero
53. City on Crete's coast
54. Tick off
56. Being, to Caesar
57. Worry
58. Big refs.
59. The Colonel's place, initially
60. 1990's Indian P.M.

Solution on page 161

Golf Biographies

Across

1. Jezebel's deity
5. One of the "Little Women"
9. Wind instrument
14. "Dancing Queen" pop group
15. "Dies __"
16. Cubist Fernand
17. Intimate
18. "__ the ump!"
19. Opposite one of two
20. "Golf & Life" biography subject
23. Prayer
24. "__ Town"
25. Controversial area under LBJ
28. Penthouse feature
31. Heavenly
33. Ring
37. "Every Shot I Take" biography subject
39. Big name in siding
41. Chicago transports
42. Acquired pattern of behavior
43. "Life Swings" biography subject
45. Oscar ___ Renta
46. Conflict
47. Chooses
50. Roll call response
51. Carbonium, e.g.
53. "Seinfeld" woman
58. "A Golfer's Life" biography subject
61. Reverie
64. Receipts
65. Cowardly Lion portrayer Bert
66. Dike, Eunomia, and Irene
67. Fish-eating eagle
68. Farming prefix
69. Position
70. "___ who?"
71. Prefix with -algia

Down

1. Musical instrument
2. Hungry as ___
3. Old adders
4. Songbirds
5. Annette wouldn't wear one
6. Playwright Bogosian
7. Confer
8. Pick-up line?
9. Thrive
10. Answer to "Shall we?"
11. "Bleah!"
12. Golfers mound
13. Misstep
21. Election time: Abbr.
22. TT Roadster maker
25. Mythical weeper
26. Blacksmith's block
27. "Gin a body ___ body": Burns
29. Pulitzer-winning biographer Leon
30. Ralph ___ Emerson
32. Prince who inspired "Dracula"
33. Violet variety
34. Choice group
35. Capital of Ghana
36. Norse god of discord
38. Brandy designation
40. 1978 Triple Crown winner
44. 1,000,000,000 years
48. Plain homes
49. Hearst kidnap grp.
52. Student's jottings
54. Detective Pinkerton
55. Publicist's concern
56. Jacket style
57. Clinker
58. Extremely narrow, as a shoe
59. Pasternak heroine
60. Fashion letters
61. Some AL batters
62. Make a stink?
63. Palindromic "before"

Solution on page 162

Biographies at the Movies

Across

1. Official records
5. Got a load of
8. "Ishtar" was one
12. Student at mixed school
13. Peppy
14. One who hears "You've got mail"
15. Notion
16. Mechanical teeth
17. Kahlo movie from the book
18. "Confessions of a ___ Mind," movie based on Chuck Barris's autobiography
20. Holiday ___
21. Actress Graff
22. Sandy's bark
23. King of pop
26. Everlasting
30. Honest ___
31. All-inclusive
34. Mark supplanter
35. Be in charge
37. ___ polloi
38. ___-Croatian
39. Second starter
40. Substitute kept in reserve
42. Kind of pad
43. The Sage of Concord
45. Harsh
47. Frigid
48. Dieter's device
50. Game divided into chukkers
52. "A ___ Mind," movie based on John Nash's biography
56. Distributed
57. Small islands
58. Role for Angelina
59. Dieter of rhyme
60. Peru native
61. Vortex
62. Hardy's "Pure Woman"
63. Book before Esther: Abbr.
64. Latin god

Down

1. Litmus reddener
2. Sonata finale
3. Freshman, probably
4. Slowly
5. Eating utensil
6. Debate
7. "The Swiss Family Robinson" author Johann
8. Joy Adamson's book made into a movie about the lioness Elsa
9. Lena of "Alias"
10. Docs prescribe them
11. It's uplifting
13. Coarse sieve
14. Lit
19. 1990's sitcom
22. Wolfed down
23. Chili con ___
24. Crosswise, on a ship
25. Marie Antoinette, e.g.
26. "CHiPs" star Estrada
27. Hospital figure
28. Ann ___, Mich.
29. Out of the yard
32. Part of a comparison
33. Summer Games gp.
36. "___ in the Mist," movie about Dian Fossey based on an article by Harold T.P. Hayes
38. Breadmaker's wheat
40. Baby in blue
41. Patriotic chant
44. Polar explorer
46. Hidden
48. English Channel feeder
49. "___ Me if You Can," movie based on the book
50. Toon Le Pew
51. Dinghy pair
52. Barbara of "Mission: Impossible"
53. Wash out
54. Language of Lahore
55. "Betcha can't eat just one" chips
56. It ends in Oct.

Solution on page 162

Famous Autobiographies

Across

1. Zilch
5. Singing style
9. Solid
13. ___ to one's ears
14. Shield border
15. Distant
17. Comrade
19. Debaucher
20. "The Story of My ___ with Truth," Gandhi autobiography
22. Tic-tac-toe victory
23. "Do I have to draw you ___?"
24. Call to arms
26. Country residence
29. Shakespeare's prankster
31. Land in la mer
32. Straight's partner
35. Counter offer
39. Russian-American writer with the autobiography: "Speak, Memory"
42. "This comes __ surprise"
43. Figure skater Zayak
44. Versailles ruler
45. Rather risky
47. Employee motivator
49. Polished
52. Ashe Stadium inits.
54. Common URL ender
55. Deafblind American with the autobiography: "The Story of My Life"
61. Gladiators' locale
63. Tailpiece
64. "___ in the Streets" (1950)
65. Scout's doing
66. Ticker tapes?
67. In __ land (spacy)
68. Burns and Allen: Abbr.
69. Egg container

Down

1. "Well done!"
2. Strong as ___
3. Let fall in a mass
4. Sex ___
5. Actress Braga
6. Hamper
7. Lotion additive
8. Next to N. Car.
9. Headache
10. __ carte
11. Copter part
12. "___ Want to Know a Secret?": Beatles
16. Booker T. Washington's autobiography: "Up ___ Slavery"
18. Cardin rival
21. Island off the SE coast of China
25. Not to mention
26. __ voce
27. Problems
28. Low-fat
29. Marshal
30. Rice-a-___
33. "Cocoon" co-star
34. Rub the wrong way
36. Creole vegetable
37. Way in
38. Dedicated
40. Dummy
41. Defeated
46. Cornell's home
48. Henry David Thoreau in the woods autobiography
49. Con
50. Virtuous
51. Last in a series
52. Let loose
53. Depot postings, informally
56. Young 'uns
57. Olympics event
58. Loch
59. Ova
60. Take a breather
62. Not a thing

Solution on page 162

Autobiographical Novels

Across

1. Maine's ___ Bay
6. Out of whack
11. Fly catcher
14. Astrologer Sydney
15. Silhouette
16. Pub brew
17. Louisa May Alcott's semiautobiographical novel
19. Zip
20. Hosp. area
21. Periods of note
22. Taillike
24. Skipper
26. Bishop's headdress
27. Publicity
28. Charles Bukowski's autobiographical novel
31. Arlene and Roald
34. "Eight Bells" painter Winslow
35. End for cash or court
36. "___ a man..."
37. Tabitha of MTV
38. Forensic concerns
39. It may be tidy
40. Jeweler's measure
41. Autobiographical work by Elie Wiesel
42. Nefarious
44. Noted chairman
45. Nick of "Cape Fear"
46. Eastern European variant of Catherine
50. Actress Lansbury
52. "Star Trek" helmsman
53. "__ blu, dipinto di..."
54. Down in the dumps
55. Author of the autobiographical novel "On the Road"
58. Extinct New Zealander
59. Shaq of the NBA
60. Musical with the song "Buenos Aires"
61. In the least
62. Crimean resort
63. Suppressed

Down

1. Baby's woe
2. Lady friend in Italy
3. Did a doggie trick
4. PC component
5. City liberated by Joan of Arc
6. City near Lake Nasser
7. Electrical units
8. Self expression?
9. Sample
10. Washington post
11. Roaming
12. Essayist's alias
13. "The ___ Jar," Sylvia Plath's semiautobiographical novel
18. Tenor in "The Flying Dutchman"
23. Niche filler
25. Joust
26. "Hoffa" screenwriter
28. Every 60 minutes
29. Popular rock 'n' roll refrain
30. While starter
31. Frisbee, e.g.
32. Asian river
33. Author of semiautobiographical "A Farewell to Arms"
34. Greek goddesses of the seasons
37. Hot wind
38. Sack dress creator
40. Wet blanket
41. Temperaments
43. A Stooge
44. Drone, e.g.
46. Fran's friend
47. Anorak wearer
48. "Peachy"
49. Old highway name
50. Soprano Gluck
51. When shadows are short
52. Three-handed game
56. Film frame
57. Gametes

Solution on page 162

Chapter 7: Best Sellers

Bestselling Novels in the 1900s

Across

1. "Hair" producer
5. Beanery handout
9. Dogie catcher
14. Voice of America org.
15. Onassis and namesakes
16. Paid to stay in
17. Upton Sinclair's bestselling novel of 1906
19. "The ___ of the Baskervilles," bestselling novel of 1902
20. Hard heads
21. Restricts
22. Vandalize
23. Gown material .
25. Capital of Canada
28. Twain
29. ___ II razor
33. Vice ___
34. Central nervous system
36. Blonde shade
37. ___ tree (trapped)
38. "___ of Sunnybrook Farm," bestselling novel of 1904
40. The Spartans' sch.
41. Box top
42. Outer limits
43. Construction girder
45. Genesis garden site
47. Eviscerate
48. Tabriz natives
49. Some tourneys
51. Presidents' Day, e.g.: Abbr.
52. "To Have and ___ ___," bestselling novel of 1900
55. Hot stuff

59. Habitation
60. "The ___," bestselling wild west novel of 1902
62. Author Cather
63. Manitoba Indian
64. Blue shade
65. Mount with spirit
66. They're caught at the shore
67. Maker of VAIO computers

Down

1. Short shot
2. Pallid
3. Slip site
4. Nightclothes
5. "Om," e.g.
6. Units of work
7. Nonexistent
8. Apply
9. Emmy winner Christine
10. Bless
11. Astound
12. Posted
13. Bookie's quote
18. Napping, so to speak
21. Stiff-upper-lip type
23. Avenue crossers
24. Military plane acronym
25. Fertilization site
26. Lukewarm
27. Deal between ball clubs
30. Japanese noodle soup
31. Very, to Verdi

32. Cronies
34. Dangerous toy
35. Capital of Kenya
39. Trenchant
44. Wildly enthusiastic
46. Noggin
48. Camera card contents
50. Say "not guilty," say
52. Shooting marbles
53. Final notice?
54. Financial predicament
55. Deuce topper
56. The ___-Japanese War of 1894-95
57. Genesis son
58. Kind of child
60. TV adjunct
61. Plan for later yrs.

Solution on page 163

Bestselling Novels in the 1920s

Across

1. Therewithal
5. Big name in jewelry
10. Cowpoke's pal
14. Han's love
15. Playground retort
16. Lo-cal spread
17. Booth ___, bestselling novelist in the 1920s
19. Zaire's Mobutu ___ Seko
20. Stat start
21. Aces
23. Rock bottom
26. Immediately following that
29. Raised
30. "Wait ___!"
31. "All Quiet on the Western ___," bestselling novel in 1929
32. Canton in N Switzerland
34. Griddle-baked Indian bread
36. "Gentlemen ___ ___," bestselling novel in 1926
41. Kind of market
42. Scale reading
44. "___ Gantry," bestselling novel in 1927
48. "Son of __!"
50. Literary conflict
51. Tea plantation
53. Headgear of a monarch
54. Fly-by-night?
55. Colombian metropolis
57. Kind of race
58. "The Bridge of ___ ___ ___," bestselling novel in 1928 by Thornton Wilder
64. Insect repellent
65. Venusian, e.g.
66. They poll with CNN
67. Actress Best

68. Something that causes ferment
69. Impudence

Down

1. High-pitched
2. Idyllic setting
3. Round Table address
4. Atomic research center
5. ___ Grey, bestselling novelist in the 1920s
6. Cants
7. Court do-over
8. That, in Tabasco
9. Submarine detector
10. Phony
11. Syrian city
12. Longtime NY Times columnist James
13. "Who ___?"
18. Her, in Hamburg
22. Specify
23. Org. for shooters
24. Not give ___
25. Writer Earl __ Biggers
27. Nonwoody vegetation
28. Environmental sci.
30. "The Clan of the Cave Bear" author Jean
33. Brawl
35. Burg
37. Part of ROM
38. Keepers of daily records

39. Frozen waffle brand
40. "___ Boat," bestselling novel in 1926
43. Basic cable channel
44. Online investors' company
45. Looked lecherously
46. Lunatics
47. Excrement
49. Family men
52. Iterate
53. Second-century date
56. Polly, to Tom Sawyer
59. Drink in a mug
60. Long of "Third Watch"
61. Wedge-shaped inlet
62. German river
63. "Indubitably"

Solution on page 163

Bestselling Novels in the 1930s

Across

1. Telephone button abbr.
5. Smooch
9. Civil rights org.
14. Allot
15. Supermodel Wek
16. Eyes
17. Greasy spoon sign
18. "Cleopatra" backdrop
19. Heads of Paris
20. "The ___ ___ ___," Steinbeck's bestselling novel in 1939
23. Election loser
24. One of the reeds
25. "One Mic" rapper
26. Chills
28. Defense advisory grp.
31. "Boola Boola" singers
34. "It's ___ of the times"
35. Ship rope
36. Bestselling novel in 1936 and 1937
40. Clock std.
41. Deal prerequisites
42. "Look!" to Livy
43. Jeanne d'Arc, e.g. (abbr.)
44. Victrolas, e.g.
45. Cloning basic
47. Fix up
49. Like some fishing
53. Author of "The Years," bestselling novel in 1937
56. Belief
58. Psychologist Jung
59. Nikita's negative
60. Star in Cygnus
61. Borgia in-law
62. Teen party
63. Cubic measure
64. Interstellar dist.
65. River in Belgium

Down

1. Last letter of the Greek alphabet
2. First name of "The Good Earth" author, bestselling novel in 1931 and 1932
3. Singers James and Jones
4. Rejoinder
5. Part of the Louisiana Purchase
6. Troy, as it's also known
7. Narcissist's love
8. Slant unfairly
9. Note well
10. Vinegar: Prefix
11. Genuine
12. French key
13. Gumshoes: Abbr.
21. Historic period
22. Coarse
26. Lenten symbol
27. Vamooses
29. In ___ (together)
30. Surrender
31. Diner menu section
32. "___ Horizon," bestselling novel in 1935
33. Mediate
34. Intro for boy or girl
37. Furniture for holding clothes
38. Disguised, informally
39. Weapons collectively
45. He'll give you a hand
46. Different
48. Pillow filler
49. Grimy
50. Some beans
51. Student at the Sorbonne
52. Following
54. Reykjavik's loc.
55. Political cartoonist Thomas
56. Some savings accts.
57. Collecting Soc. Sec.

Solution on page 163

Bestselling Novels in the 1940s

Across

1. "The ___ Edge," bestselling novel in 1944
7. Expectorate
11. Thrash
14. Eastern hospice
15. "Laugh-In" comedian Johnson
16. AAA suggestion
17. Katmandu native
18. Coward
19. E-mail address suffix
20. Author of "The Naked and the Dead," bestselling novel in 1948
23. Diver Louganis
26. Grain
27. Disney goldfish
28. Brush up on
31. Eye opener?
34. Hot time on the Riviera
35. It's found under a chapeau
37. Early cab
41. Author of "For Whom the Bell Tolls," bestselling novel in 1940
44. "Beats me"
45. Lee's uniform color
46. Anteceding
47. The villain in Othello
49. Fluid sac in animals
51. Closing
54. Kind of mask
56. Big refs.
57. "The Keys ___ ___ ___," bestselling novel in 1941
62. "Little" car of song
63. Delhi wrap
64. Even (with)
68. End for cash or court
69. Hairdo
70. Kook
71. Hue's partner
72. To be, in old Rome
73. "Don't bother"

Down

1. "Oysters ___ season"
2. Soul, in Savoie
3. Stun
4. Halloween hue
5. Move, to a realtor
6. Hoosegow
7. Yemen's capital
8. On the double
9. Twosome
10. Seaport in N Honduras
11. Fish, in a way
12. "___ ___ Grows In Brooklyn," bestselling novel in 1943
13. The "N" of U.N.C.F.
21. Ramadan, e.g.
22. Frosting
23. "How ___ Was My Valley," bestselling novel in 1940
24. In, again
25. Gage bestseller
29. On the ocean
30. Label anew
32. Medicine bottle
33. Roberts of "That '70s Show"
36. Head lines, for short
38. Ann-Margret, by birth
39. Paddled
40. Press Secretary DeeDee ___
42. Writer Wharton
43. Head honcho
48. Egyptian god
50. Realm
51. Reasoning
52. Following
53. Bedtime reading
55. Bowie's weapon
58. Suffix with fluor-
59. "Get Smart" villains
60. "The Moon Is ___," bestselling novel in 1942
61. ___ cat: ball game
65. Canada's Grand ___ National Historic Park
66. Gator's tail?
67. Staff

Solution on page 163

Bestselling Novels in the 1950s

Across

1. Stiffen
4. Still sleeping
9. Pound sounds
13. Metal container
14. ___ barrel
15. Salon stock
16. Bestselling novel in 1952 by John Steinbeck
18. "...to skin ___"
19. French soul
20. Long-jawed fishes
21. Industrial city of Germany
23. N.Y. engineering sch.
24. Inc., overseas
25. Panties with wide legs
27. Martial arts expert
29. Milo of "Barbarella"
31. Part of w.p.m.
32. Motor add-on
34. A Roach
35. Husband of Gudrun
36. "Lady ___ Lover," bestselling novel in 1959
39. Summons to prayer
41. Is suffering from
42. "Who ___ we kidding?"
43. Dien Bien ___
44. Summarize
46. Pianist Claudio
50. Cookie
52. Dawn deity
54. Joule part
55. Sleeveless garments
56. Jekyll's counterpart
57. Half of D
58. Find fault
59. "From Here ___ ___," bestselling novel in 1951
62. Exchange premium
63. Dunderhead
64. Log prefix
65. Meter man
66. Foot problems
67. Yr.-end month

Down

1. Seafood dish
2. Enter gradually
3. Blaster's letters
4. Yogurt type
5. Work too hard
6. "Bill & ___ Excellent Adventure"
7. Suffix with fail
8. Long, slender cigar
9. Visibly shocked
10. Income
11. "The Man in the Gray ___ Suit," bestselling novel in 1955
12. It no longer flies
16. Work for
17. Crazy Horse, for one
22. "The Old Man and the ___," bestselling novel in 1952
25. ___-Pei (wrinkly dog)
26. Asian honorific
28. Fourth Gospel
30. "___ Lady": Tom Jones song
33. Godless
35. Massachusetts town
36. Chat
37. Diplomatic trait
38. Error-correcting tool
39. Broadcast inits.
40. "Doctor ___," bestselling novel in 1959
44. Groove
45. "___ Place," bestselling novel in 1956
47. Prescription
48. Frigid
49. "The ___ American," bestselling novel in 1959
51. Hundred smackers
53. Playwright Clifford
56. Child of fortune?
58. Mortarboard
60. Prefix with meter
61. A Beatty

Solution on page 163

Bestselling Novels in the 1960s

Across

1. When Hamlet dies
5. Shirt label name
9. Three Gorges project
12. Coastal Brazilian state
14. Orbital point
15. Judicious
16. "____ by land..."
17. "The ___," bestselling novel in 1969 by Mario Puzo
19. Mex. neighbor
20. Baffin Bay sight
22. Leaning to the right
23. Culpable
25. Surefire
26. On board
28. Imply
29. Cave ___
30. What some stars stand for
32. Encouraging word
33. "Voila!"
34. Vibrato
37. Concert souvenir
39. Blood component
41. Grew really fast
43. Foiled
44. Warehouse user
45. Pay
47. Flower parts
48. Was indebted to
49. Evil spirit
52. "___ ___ ___ Staircase," bestselling novel in 1965
54. Roast host
56. Fizzles out
57. "Zip-__ Doo-Dah"
58. Genealogy
59. Winter weather, in Edinburgh
60. Sale site
61. In that case

Down

1. "___ Ben Adhem"
2. Lets go
3. "___ ___ and the Ecstasy," bestselling novel in 1961
4. "QB __"
5. Bar
6. "Franny and ___," bestselling novel in 1961
7. Like one
8. Precise
9. Showy perennial
10. Certain discriminator
11. Pharmaceutical giant
13. Uphold
15. Begins
18. Make up
21. Attorney's deg.
24. Abu Dhabi's fed.
26. Play a role
27. Watering hole
28. Mature male European red deer
30. "___ of Fools," bestselling novel in 1962
31. Prefix with centenary
33. Fifth day of the week
34. "___ ___ Cancer," bestselling novel in 1961
35. Bleed
36. "___ Mine" (Beatles song)
37. Sacred scrolls
38. Marker
39. Tom of "Tomorrow"
40. Part of some E-mail addresses
41. Intervene
42. Chinese restaurant freebie
43. Arles article
44. Taters
45. Strength
46. Held title to
50. Subway Series team
51. Mexican bread?
53. Sultana's chamber
55. "Who, me?"

Solution on page 163

Bestselling Novels in the 1970s

Across

1. Perjurers
6. Over, to Otto
10. Alehouses
14. Religion of the Muslims
15. Hair of the dog bee
16. __ the finish
17. "Remember the ___!"
18. "___ or Lonesome No More!," bestselling novel in 1976
20. "Rich ___, ___ Man," bestselling novel in 1970
22. Female demon in Semitic myth
23. Where to use a PIN
24. Free from
25. Pasta
29. Jam ingredients
33. Ashtabula waterfront
34. ___ gestae
35. If not
36. "The Winds of ___," bestselling novel in 1971
37. Mom-and-pop grp.
38. Monkey
39. Insurrectionist Turner
40. "The ___ File," bestselling novel in 1972
42. Lord's Prayer starter
43. ___-Seltzer
44. Opposite of sur
45. "Looking for ___ ___," bestselling novel in 1975
47. Hearsay
49. Early afternoon
50. Stiff
52. 1959 Ricky Nelson hit
56. "___ Gift," bestselling novel in 1975
58. Silas Marner's charge
59. "Gotcha!"
60. Hops-drying oven
61. "The ___ Birds," bestselling novel in 1977
62. IRS IDs
63. Bill and Louis
64. Factions

Down

1. Author O'Flaherty
2. Madonna's "La __ Bonita"
3. Deejay Freed
4. Storm
5. Peanut butter choice
6. SALT party
7. ___ canto
8. And others
9. Speedy
10. Evoking pity
11. Kind of pricing
12. Author of "Jonathan Livingston Seagull," bestselling novel in 1972 and 1973
13. Company shares: Abbr.
19. "Citizen Kane" actor Everett ___
21. Code of silence
24. ACLU concerns: Abbr.
25. Attach, in a way
26. Madrid museum
27. Broadcaster
28. Afternoon social
30. Potato sack wt., maybe
31. Expo '70 site.
32. Red giant
35. Pull out by the roots
37. Ersatz
38. Summer mo.
41. Disco fixtures
42. Bruins legend
43. University in Garden City, NY
45. Second day of the week
46. Geneses
48. Juicy gourd
50. Milquetoast
51. Foretoken
52. Believers at the end?
53. Footless animal
54. Spare change?
55. Poetic periods
56. Old what's-___-name
57. "The Waste Land" poet's monogram

Solution on page 164

Bestselling Novels in the 1980s

Across

1. Tams
5. Actress Merkel and others
9. Style
14. Multitude
15. Party giver
16. Have words
17. Former Bruin Phil, to fans
18. WWII ally
19. "___ Park," bestselling novel in 1981
20. "The ___ Protocol," bestselling novel in 1984
22. Suffix with law
24. Binds
25. Course
26. Come up with
28. Overseas article
30. "2010: Odyssey ___," bestselling novel in 1982
31. Part of EST
34. "Master of ___ ___," bestselling novel in 1982
38. Physician
40. Not nerdy
41. Aqua ___
43. Some votes
44. Worn around the neck
46. "The Prince ___ ___," bestselling novel in 1986
48. Wild blue yonder
49. Smidgen
51. Lucrative
52. In recent days
54. As a result
58. "...baked in ___"
61. Look over
62. "The ___ Identity," bestselling novel in 1980
64. First name of author of "Poland," bestselling novel in 1983
66. Exposed
68. Chief
69. "Wellaway!"
70. Campbell of "Party of Five"
71. Airing
72. Variety of coffee
73. Bore
74. Optimistic

Down

1. One who takes orders
2. Man of morals
3. ___ New Guinea
4. Wear
5. "Nah!"
6. Negatives
7. From Nineveh: Abbr.
8. Houston, e.g.
9. Flag
10. Dropped a line
11. Prefix with business
12. Zap in the microwave
13. Locksmith's stock
21. Ruffian
23. Unprocessed computer input
26. Was present
27. Further
29. Tell tales
31. Ocular woe
32. Bunion sites
33. A.M.A. members
34. Captured
35. Sacred
36. Allen wrench shape
37. Self-importance
39. Philanderer
40. Units in an ER
42. Up in the air
45. Orthodontists' org.
47. "What's ___ you?"
50. Surpassing
52. Hanger-on
53. Persona non grata
55. Wit
56. Heavens: Prefix
57. Piques
58. In __: stuck
59. ___ Alto, California
60. Apple variety
62. Blood type, for short
63. Covetousness
65. Reggae forerunner
67. Spacewalk, for NASA

Solution on page 164

Bestselling Novels in the 1990s

Across

1. Engaged in battle
6. Seville snack
10. Hamlet's soliloquy opener
14. Author Dahl
15. Maintain
16. Favorite
17. Plagiarizes
18. "The ___ Prophecy," bestselling novel in 1994
20. "___ boy!"
21. Number two
22. Top-40 DJ Casey
23. Corner map
25. Pub orders
26. Embryonic sac
28. Muscat native
30. Esteem
31. "___ Pete's sake!"
32. "___ Mountain," bestselling novel in 1997
36. Novel ending
37. "Politically Correct ___ Stories," bestselling novel in 1994
40. Toy magnate ___ Schwarz
41. Kind of prize
43. No-win situation?
44. Free from an obligation
46. When some take coffee breaks
48. Angel of the highest order
49. Temple of Zeus site
51. Confronted
52. Ratty place
53. Uppercut target
55. Drops in the air
58. "The Horse ___," bestselling novel in 1995
60. Smarter
61. "Comus" composer
62. ___ d'oeuvres
63. Backgammon piece
64. Insects
65. TV ad
66. "Peter Pan" heroine

Down

1. Ancient Spanish chest
2. It's no crime
3. "___ ___ Exhale," bestselling novel in 1992
4. Republic in S Europe
5. Map lines: Abbr.
6. Quietly understood
7. Tours with?
8. Fishing need
9. Blow away
10. April 1912 newsmaker
11. Horace, for one
12. "Bag of ___," bestselling novel in 1998
13. K-6: abbr.
19. It's got you covered
21. Private feud
24. Gather on a surface
25. Grated Italian cheese
26. Sterile
27. Middle: prefix
28. When dogs want out
29. "You don't mean me?!"
33. "The Bridges ___ ___ County," bestselling novel in 1993
34. Scandinavian
35. "How ___ the little crocodile": Carroll
38. It's spotted in casinos
39. Firm head
42. "The Ten Commandments" role
45. Recluse
47. Maryland athlete
49. Gandhi's father
50. "Dallas" family name
51. "To begin with."
52. Mop
53. Harvester's haul
54. Deli order
56. Satirize, with "up"
57. Good lowball card
59. Requests to speak up
60. Opposite of ENE

Solution on page 164

Bestselling Novels in the 2000s

Across

1. Jamaican exports
5. Place to crash
8. "Mary, ___," bestselling novel in 2005
12. Rat tail?
13. Mule's mom
14. Musical transition
15. Confront
16. Cookbook author Rombauer
17. Hangout
18. "___ ___ ___ Four," bestselling novel in 2004
20. Employs
21. Like some statesmen
22. Tough bug
23. Play opener
26. "The Nanny ___," bestselling novel in 2002
30. Tenor oboe
31. Stir
34. TV award
35. "The Mermaid ___," bestselling novel in 2005
37. Boundary: Abbr.
38. Quaker in a grove
39. Trotter stopper
40. "Angels & ___," bestselling novel in 2004
42. Brain test, for short
43. Heavy metal band whose name is a disease
45. Have ambitions
47. German article
48. "Our Gang" dog
50. McQueen in "Jimmy Hollywood"
52. "Skipping ___," bestselling novel in 2001
56. Courageous
57. Italy's ___ di Como
58. Hawaiian city
59. Wanders
60. "The heat ___!"
61. In the know about
62. "The Virginian" author Wister
63. Teacher's favorite
64. It's inert

Down

1. Large number
2. The Beehive State
3. Nutmeg-based spice
4. Dorm room staple
5. City in a Porter song title
6. Tanks and such
7. Heather Whitestone, e.g.
8. Gauges
9. Chills and fever
10. Baseball scores
11. Up to now
13. Basement problem
14. Longtime Dolphins coach
19. Of an arm bone
22. Half a sawbuck
23. Capital of Ghana
24. Canadian songwriter Leonard
25. Hair color, e.g.
26. Expo presentation
27. Kennedy Library architect
28. Arab leader
29. "The Playboy of the Western World" author
32. "Family Ties" son
33. Kipling novel
36. "The Five People You Meet ___ ___," bestselling novel in 2003
38. Dolts
40. Duryea or Dorfman
41. Country
44. Travels on
46. Constrictor
48. Aspect
49. Cereal killer
50. Black bird
51. Wealthy one
52. Illegal block
53. Go for the gold?
54. Glee club member
55. Any minute now
56. 'Hood salutation

Solution on page 164

Bestselling Nonfiction in the 1960s

Across

1. Bygone ruler
5. Malamute's burden
9. Lhasa __
13. Prefix with globin
14. "Are you calling me ___?"
15. Gunk
16. Door sign
17. Generic cow's name
18. "In ___ Blood," nonfiction bestseller in the 1960s
19. "Happiness Is a ___ ___," nonfiction bestseller in the 1960s by Charles M. Schulz
21. Groucho's "Duck Soup" role
22. Lightens up
23. So, in Sorrento
24. ___-Lorraine
27. Protect
29. Tough as ___
30. Fragile
32. M.I.T. grads
34. Weapons
35. "A Moveable ___," nonfiction bestseller in the 1960s
36. ___ were
37. Piece of work?
38. Kramden or Nader
39. "All My Children" role
40. All but
42. Doomed
43. The Orient
44. Mimic's skill
46. Scalawag
48. Author of "Travels with Charley," nonfiction bestseller in the 1960s

Solution on page 164

52. Elec. company, e.g.
53. Rag composer Joplin
54. Honest
55. Sped
56. Chief Justice, 1836-64
57. French weapon
58. Grasp
59. Over in Germany
60. Class

Down

1. Sullivan had a really big one
2. Numerical prefix
3. Islamic VIP
4. Mission offerings
5. Ski run
6. Speaks like Sylvester
7. "No problem!"
8. "Happiness Is a ___ Martini," nonfiction bestseller in the 1960s by Johnny Carson
9. Point the finger at
10. "___ ___ Courage," nonfiction bestseller in the 1960s
11. Helmsman of 1960s TV
12. Chances
14. Mistreat
20. D.C. fundraisers
21. Churn
23. Marker
24. Barney's nickname for his boss, the sheriff
25. Angelina played her in Tomb Raider (2001)
26. "Sex and the ___ ___," nonfiction bestseller in the 1960s
27. Obi
28. Free of ice
30. Sensed
31. Knock vigorously
33. African village
35. Speedy
36. Base kid
38. Wine choice
39. Make money
41. Roughed up
42. Nike, e.g.
44. Agreeing (with)
45. "The ___ Principle," nonfiction bestseller in the 1960s
46. Buzzi of "Laugh-In"
47. Scoreless tie
48. Healing sign
49. Haunted: Var.
50. David, for one
51. "Locksmith" painter
53. Alphabet trio

Bestselling Nonfiction in the 1970s

Across

1. Victory
4. It covers the Hill
9. Sports ___
12. "Bambi" doe
13. Finnish architect Alvar ___
14. Hitler's architect
16. Tempe sch.
17. It may be organized
18. Worry
19. "___: The Predictable Crises of Adult Life," nonfiction bestseller in the 1970s
21. Polynesian language
22. "...and __ grow on"
23. "The ___ Triangle," nonfiction bestseller in the 1970s
25. Within reach
26. "A Lesson From ___"
29. Society-page newcomer
30. Title bandit in a Verdi opera
32. Protection
34. "All the ___ ___," nonfiction bestseller in the 1970s
37. Masters and Jonson
38. Dracula portrayer Bela
39. Egyptian viper
40. Coke competitor
41. Grizzly's pad
45. "Pulling Your Own ___," nonfiction bestseller in the 1970s
48. Terra follower
49. Coins
50. "___ ___ ___ Sex," nonfiction bestseller in the 1970s

53. Bricklayer
54. Softly
55. One of "Them!"
56. Post
57. Lascivious man
58. Never, in Neuss
59. Toothpaste type
60. Syrian leader
61. Atlas abbr.

Down

1. Part of a Clue accusation
2. Certifiable
3. Sartre novel
4. Tree with pods
5. Puppeteer Tony
6. Ballerina's bend
7. Drive-thru bankers

8. S.F.'s ___ Valley
9. Reluctant to give
10. Be an inhabitant of
11. Knack
14. Coal-rich German region
15. __ Penh, Cambodia
20. Houston, e.g.
21. Autopsy performers: Abbr.
23. Entities
24. Situps strengthen them
26. Cuckoo bird
27. Spoons
28. Headed for overtime, maybe
31. Web feed letters
32. The law, to Mr. Bumble
33. Estevez of "Repo Man"
34. Follow in time
35. Retaliation
36. Vous, familiarly

37. ___ de deux
40. Some film ratings
42. Indo-Europeans
43. "Consider the job done"
44. Roof timber
46. "___ ___, You're O.K.," nonfiction bestseller in the 1970s
47. Endangered state bird
48. Long narrow arm of the sea
50. Argentinian aunts
51. Derbies
52. New Age singer
53. Cause of Chinese restaurant syndrome
54. Anti-drug ad, e.g.

Solution on page 164

Bestselling Nonfiction in the 1980s

Across

1. Indian author Santha Rama ___
4. Bar fare
9. Show concern
13. The bulk
14. Hippie's two-finger sign
15. Light greenish-blue
16. "___ ___ ___ Excellence," nonfiction bestseller in the 1980s
18. Baseball scores
19. Almost
20. Fact
22. Relinquish
23. History
25. 1952 Olympics site
27. Razzed
31. Tortilla
35. Start of a Web address
37. Dippy or dotty
38. Egyptian deity
39. Lout
41. Way off yonder
42. "A Brief History of ___," nonfiction bestseller in the 1980s
43. Lunar trench
44. Hawaii's state bird
45. Social instability
48. Insect nests
50. Blue dye
52. Prone
57. Public disgrace
60. Halogen element
61. Part of Mork's goodbye
62. "___: Ten New Directions Transforming Our Lives," nonfiction bestseller in the 1980s

Solution on page 165

65. Common contraction
66. Happen next
67. Plays a part
68. Friends' pronoun
69. Senate spots
70. Name of 13 popes

Down

1. Actress Blakley
2. Indian state
3. Sources of zygotes
4. Lively
5. Nuclear agcy. till 1975
6. "Well, ___-di-dah!"
7. Nut of an oak
8. Vanquish
9. Author of "Cosmos," nonfiction bestseller in the 1980s
10. Here, in Honduras
11. Shrimp
12. Start to come and go?
13. "The Closing of the American ___," nonfiction bestseller in the 1980s
17. Choir voice
21. Yard contents
23. Union locale
24. "___ Down," nonfiction bestseller in the 1980s
26. Skittish
28. Hotel convenience
29. Richard of "Love Me Tender"
30. Bell the cat
31. Toodle-oo
32. Exiled Ugandan
33. "Dream Along With Me" singer Perry
34. "The ___ ___ Manager," nonfiction bestseller in the 1980s

36. Poliomyelitis
40. "You're Only ___ Once," nonfiction bestseller in the 1980s
46. Mich. neighbor
47. Mingo player in "Daniel Boone"
49. Dr. Frankenstein's helper
51. Graff of "Mr. Belvedere"
53. Best
54. Coach Lombardi
55. Put an ___ (halt)
56. Headland
57. Hissy fit
58. Alternative to plastic
59. Charles' sister
60. Inhabitants: Suffix
63. Fed. property manager
64. Self: Prefix

Bestselling Nonfiction in the 1990s

Across

1. "Butterfield 8" author
6. Central points
10. Narrow margin
14. Capital on the Willamette River
15. Gov't. laboratory
16. Unusually excellent
17. Be rude in line
18. Baccarat accessory
19. Glacial ridges
20. "___ Ashes," nonfiction bestseller in the 1990s
22. "Bad As I ___ ___," nonfiction bestseller in the 1990s
24. Tune
25. Brazilian seaport
26. Large reddish kangaroo
30. Seafood dish
34. Addition column
35. MGM motto start
36. Massage
37. "Ben-Hur" studio
38. "The Seven Spiritual Laws of ___," nonfiction bestseller in the 1990s
41. _____ Lanka
42. Violinist Mischa
44. Frick collection
45. Poetic preposition
46. Vital
48. "The ___ Generation," nonfiction bestseller in the 1990s
50. Duck
52. Pitchfork-shaped letter
53. "Into ___ ___," nonfiction bestseller in the 1990s
56. Prayer book
60. "My ___!"
61. Fair to middling
63. "___: Her True Story," nonfiction bestseller in the 1990s
64. Parisian possessive
65. Fifty-fifty
66. Alchemist's mercury
67. Propend
68. Hot
69. Agreements

Down

1. Thessaly peak
2. Chemistry Nobelist Otto
3. Sleep like ___
4. Discloses
5. Flier Earhart
6. Moat
7. City in Kyrgyzstan
8. Best Actor of 2000
9. Paragons
10. Tough guy
11. Shuttle org.
12. Complain
13. "Take one!"
21. Pianist Claudio
23. Makes out
25. Thicket
26. "___ Who Run with the Wolves," nonfiction bestseller in the 1990s
27. Polygon's corner
28. "I wanna!"
29. Killer whale
31. Intermediate, in law
32. "Private ___," nonfiction bestseller in the 1990s
33. Chucklehead
38. 1983 Indy 500 winner Tom
39. Do the wrong thing
40. Paces
43. Growths in the upper throat
45. Put to use
47. Places for VIPs
49. "What is so rare ___ in June": Lowell
51. Herd
53. This partner
54. Blood pigment
55. Steel ingredient
56. Small liqueur glass
57. New Mexico art center
58. Being, in Barcelona
59. Cheerleaders' cheers
62. Madonna's nonfiction bestseller in 1992

Solution on page 165

Chapter 8: Fairy Tales

Cinderella

Across

1. "The Art of Love" poet
5. "Just ___ thought!"
8. Stud site
12. Wedding shower?
13. Dead-end jobs
14. Joy on "The View"
15. Feudal land
16. Type of exam
17. Boxer Ali
18. Structure tended by Cinderella
20. Matinee hero
21. Part of a tennis court
22. Serengeti sight
23. Colonel Sanders feature
26. Cinderella's lost item
30. Flight coordinators: Abbr.
31. Slowly, in music
34. Head of France?
35. First course, maybe
37. Gillespie, to fans
38. Coffee flavor
39. Syr Darya's outflow
40. "What fools these mortals be" writer
42. A hand
43. Cinderella's coach source
45. Cinderella's seeker
47. Presidential monogram
48. "___ the bag!"
50. Potatoes partner
52. Filibuster
56. Lion, in Swahili
57. Hawaii County's seat
58. Absent
59. Less hospitable
60. Fresh
61. Control

62. Paving stone
63. Cinderella's driver, originally
64. "Silent Running" star Bruce

Down

1. "Carmina Burana" composer
2. Henry ___
3. Bakery employee
4. Vanquish
5. Invisible vibes
6. Actor Keach
7. Ait
8. Precede
9. Wheeling's river
10. Event where Cinderella meets 45-Across
11. Paleozoic, for one
13. Like some oats
14. Russian pancakes
19. Say "not guilty," say
22. Mop & ___ (floor cleaner)
23. Fill the tank
24. Japanese port
25. Happy as ___
26. Giant economy ___
27. Pie nut
28. Guiding principles
29. Aptly named author
32. Yemeni port
33. Card player's cry
36. Kind of soup
38. One of the Osmonds
40. Be in session
41. "Strangers and Brothers" novelist
44. Relatively cool sun
46. Toward the inside
48. 1986 rock autobiography
49. Renter's sign
50. Cinderella's team of horses, before the spell
51. Send forth
52. ___-Pei (wrinkly dog)
53. ___ bit (slightly)
54. Animal house
55. Boston suburb
56. Sister

Solution on page 165

Snow White

Across

1. Dermal opening
5. Broke down
9. Much may follow it
13. Resell at inflated prices
15. ___-kiri
16. Booth
17. Not our
18. "War and Peace," e.g.
19. Ukrainian city
20. Indication
22. Dwarf's house type in "Snow White"
24. Ivories' place
26. Boston college
27. Evergreen tree
28. Unwakable state
31. Hole card
32. Egg: Comb. form
33. Huge, old-style
35. Glad
39. Looking up
41. Position
43. Sled dogs, as a group
44. Neighbor of Lucy and Ricky
46. Former enemy capital
48. Spasm
49. Fire preceder?
51. Comfy
52. "Falcon Crest" actress Alicia
53. Letter opener
57. Constructed
59. Sucker
60. Mikita of the NHL
61. Pro's rival
62. Sitar master Shankar
64. Sound of a horse
68. Botch
69. Norse Zeus
70. Poisoned in "Snow White"

71. Do a number
72. Clancy hero Jack
73. Daffy Duck or Donald Duck

Down

1. L.A. hours
2. Scottish "gee"
3. Arctic explorer John
4. "I Still See ___" ("Paint Your Wagon" tune)
5. A question of timing
6. Mystery monogram?
7. Cost
8. Puget Sound city
9. Maltreat

10. Old Chevys
11. Whiskey chaser?
12. Dwarf count in "Snow White"
14. Snow White's savior
21. Thugs
23. Georgia ___
24. Court position
25. Inhabitants of Ireland
27. Fairway warning
29. Cecropia
30. Locales
34. Director of "Marty"
36. Flower part
37. Coat material?
38. Disco standard
40. Longing
42. Uncertainty

45. Actress Kudrow
47. Large lizard
50. Truth-teller in "Snow White"
53. Loved ones
54. Blah feeling
55. Actor John
56. Not hesitant
58. All thumbs
60. ___ Fein
63. Using
65. New NYSE issue
66. Shine, in ads
67. Female lobster

Solution on page 165

Hans Christian Andersen

Across

1. Shock: Var.
6. "Amazing" magician
11. Pt. of a 1955 merger
14. Rhea's "Cheers" role
15. Happening
16. Sentimentality
17. "___ ___ New Clothes," by Hans Christian Andersen
19. Time of note
20. Bullfighter's need
21. Anthem start
22. Headed up
23. Horned goddess
25. Zapped, in a way
27. Jazz pianist Allison
28. Set up for use
30. Kicked off
32. Island in the Seine
33. Cardinal suffix
35. Yen
36. "The Little ___ ___," by Hans Christian Andersen
39. Abbr. at the bottom of a business letter
41. Curtain fabric
42. ASCAP counterpart
45. Exemplars
47. "The Little ___," by Hans Christian Andersen
49. Revealed identity in Hans Christian Andersen's "Ugly Duckling"
50. First of the minor prophets
53. Merle Haggard's "___ from Muskogee"
54. Hardy follower?
55. Cayuga or Keuka
56. Lass
58. Sei halved
59. "The ___ ___ the Pea," by Hans Christian Andersen
63. TV spots
64. Ninnies
65. Part of a voting machine
66. Queue before U
67. Money in the bank
68. Make rhapsodic

Down

1. Put-on
2. Tuba note?
3. Exact
4. The O's are in it
5. Desk accouterment
6. "Norma __"
7. Big dos
8. Western knot
9. El ___
10. Tiny, informally
11. Lasting for an age
12. Foreknow
13. Full
18. BB, for one
23. Sundial hour
24. Belushi's old show, briefly
26. Guinness
27. British blackbird
29. Whatsoever
31. Less adulterated
34. Art Ross Trophy org.
36. Big name in shoes
37. Hunter's prey
38. Cold era
39. AFB to land a Space Shuttle
40. Proximate
42. Greek pastry
43. DI doubled
44. Suffix with chlor- or fluor-
45. Babylonian love goddess
46. Round lot's 100
48. Bite
51. The Joads, e.g.
52. Just know
55. Se Ri Pak's org.
57. Castaway's locale
60. Trumpet's relative
61. Dogcatcher's need
62. Eminem's mentor

Solution on page 165

Three Little Pigs

Across

1. Once around the track
4. Newlyweds' car attachments
8. Knock one's socks off
13. "When I was ___..."
15. Actress Bonet
16. Doc
17. Balzac's "Le __ Goriot"
18. Bellicose deity
19. Daughter of Mnemosyne
20. Flimsy house material in "Three Little Pigs"
22. "not by the hair on my chinny ___ ___," from "Three Little Pigs"
24. Least arduous
26. In ___ (even)
27. Marshy inlet
29. "Sophie's Choice" star
33. Start of a Lawrence title
36. Representative
38. Home of the Mustangs
39. European car
40. Sturdy house material in "Three Little Pigs"
41. "Like that would ever happen!"
42. Hotfoot it
43. Beginning
44. Violinist Busch
45. Consisting of flowers
47. Return on an investment
49. Recedes, as the tide
51. Mice and men, e.g.
55. "I'll ___ ___ house in," from "Three Little Pigs"
59. Diner dish
60. Umbrella

61. Liquid food
63. Rating unit
64. Actress Garber
65. Nave's neighbor
66. Soft drink
67. Shooting sport
68. Essential
69. Opposite of NNE

Down

1. Come to an end
2. Prince Valiant's bride
3. Helen's abductor
4. Elegant
5. Cause of inflation?
6. Small fraction of a min.
7. Ice skater Cohen

8. Civility
9. "Moon River" lyricist Johnny
10. One of Esau's wives
11. Rigatoni relative
12. Supply-and-demand subj.
14. Acoustic power unit
21. New Jersey university
23. "Not to worry!"
25. "__ is human..."
28. Togetherness
30. "Put a tiger in your tank" company
31. Runner Zatopek
32. "I'll huff and I'll ___," from "Three Little Pigs"
33. "Three Little Pigs" bad animal
34. Silica gem
35. Office note

37. TV monitor?
40. "The Hobbit" hero Baggins
41. Formal speech
43. Tend
44. College grad
46. Install new wiring
48. Got hitched in a hurry
50. Writer Sontag
52. Choral section
53. Guides
54. Flimsy house material in "Three Little Pigs"
55. Belfry inhabitants
56. Onion's cousin
57. Folklore fiend
58. Hitchcock title
62. Waste not

Solution on page 166

Pinocchio

Across

1. Edible fruit
6. Relaxing spots
10. They may be checked
14. Assert as a fact
15. Rear end
16. Pizza place
17. Pinocchio puppet type
19. Pinocchio's grew
20. Suffix with insist or persist
21. Genghis Khan follower
22. Yahoo.com, e.g.
23. Process of combustion
24. Chief
26. "Pinocchio" author
31. Unsoiled
32. "Peanuts" girl
33. Woolly gal
36. Go for
37. Trail
39. TV's talking horse
40. Deposit
41. Destroy
42. Blue ___, Pinocchio's savior
43. Renditions
46. The land of promise
49. Counting-out bit
50. Latin conjugation word
51. Kennel sounds
54. Wrong
57. Swallowed Pinocchio and his father
58. Pinocchio's father's job
60. Outside: Prefix
61. Hillside shelter
62. Way to go
63. Simon ___
64. Bring forth young
65. Ant

Down

1. Peak
2. Strategem
3. Hair line
4. Flavius' 52
5. Expression of a strong feeling
6. Not mono
7. Last shot, usually
8. Film dog
9. Detective
10. Tiny tree
11. Steer clear of
12. "Beau ___"
13. Unkind look
18. Buster
23. Off-key, in a way
25. Ice cream maker Joseph
26. Soyuz rocket letters
27. Baseball family name
28. Musical pause
29. Grassy expanse
30. Jean-___ Godard
33. Explorer called "the Red"
34. "___ #1!"
35. Ice cream brand
37. Refuse admission to
38. Moroccan range
39. Numerous
41. Best Actor nominee of 1992
42. Trumpet flourish
43. Pity
44. Enter data
45. Grand Marquis, for short
46. Bistros
47. Lady friend in Italy
48. Beastly
52. After-bath wear
53. ___ song
54. Female gamete
55. Big celebration
56. Ukulele feature
59. CD follower

Solution on page 166

Beauty and the Beast

Across

1. Resell illegally
6. Puccini heroine
10. Big goon
13. Send to a mainframe
15. Auth. unknown
16. Word before and after "oh"
17. Beast's form, in the end
18. Beauty's father's position
20. Feast finale
22. German border river
23. Place in a bank account
26. Future jumper
28. Balanced
29. Neighbor of Bulg.
31. Napkin holder
32. Good, in street talk
33. Miles of Hollywood
34. "Well, I ___!"
38. Maxim
40. Tiny particle: Abbr.
42. Stretch
43. Chill
44. Beauty's requested item
46. "Every child. One voice." org.
47. Kind of center
49. Co. called "Big Blue"
50. Dorm denizen
51. Meeting plans
55. Odd
57. Gigantic
58. Capital of the Chaldean empire
60. Union agreed to at the end of "Beauty and the Beast"
62. Puzzle
66. 12/24 or 12/31
67. Pants part
68. Gainsays
69. CD-ROM alternative
70. Vittles
71. Possible punishment for Beauty's father's theft

Down

1. Have a late meal
2. E.M.T.'s skill
3. "Thrilla in Manila" boxer
4. Capital of United Kingdom
5. Steps off
6. Jerry Herman musical
7. Dead to the world
8. Subject to death
9. Business letters
10. Brazilian novelist Jorge
11. Finish the rec room
12. _____ nous
14. Hanker for
19. Hedda of Hollywood
21. Disturbance that causes Beauty's father to seek shelter
23. Prevent
24. Skirt
25. Bicycle part
27. Trip the light fantastic
30. New Zealander
33. Irritated
35. Mist
36. Sign on a door
37. "The Cloister and the Hearth" author
39. Win
41. Foyer
45. Obeyed the photographer
48. Place where changes are made
50. Poodle or pug
51. One of three Ottoman sultans
52. Jelly fruit
53. Wading bird
54. "Full House" costar
56. Spaced (out)
59. Flower fanciers
61. '50s slogan name
63. Supermodel Carangi
64. Confronted
65. Mountain tree

Solution on page 166

Charles Perrault

Across

1. Chew like a rat
5. "Huh?"
9. Spoiled child
13. Trevi Fountain locale
14. Interval of time
15. Abounding
16. Writer Seton
17. Tyrolean refrain
18. Harem quarters
19. Perrault's source for many stories
21. Garment worn by women
22. Short letters
23. "__ there, done that"
24. Swallow
27. Arboreal apes
29. Utter joy
30. High-quality cigar
32. Cry's partner
34. Storage spots
35. Perrault's hometown
36. Radiator part
37. Extremity
38. Fertile area in a desert
39. "Puss in ___," Perrault fairy tale
40. Hamilton in "Love at First Bite"
42. Firth of Tay port
43. Cartoonist Goldberg
44. Safe place
46. Writers of verse
48. Part 1 of Perrault fairy tale about a trip to Grandmother's
52. Break
53. Trig. function
54. Early Yucatán settler
55. Home of the Bruins
56. March marchers
57. Victim
58. "Pygmalion" dramatist
59. "Norma Rae" director
60. Hardy soul?

Down

1. Seles foe
2. Jaywalking, e.g.
3. ___ acetate (banana oil)
4. Feebleness
5. Intact
6. Conceals
7. Some are pale
8. ___ Aviv
9. Fragmented
10. Part 2 of Perrault fairy tale about a trip to Grandmother's
11. A long way off
12. Try out
14. Lawman Earp
20. Spinners
21. Dramatist O'Casey
23. They're uplifting
24. Cugat ex Lane
25. Stick
26. Perrault fairy tale with a pumpkin
27. Kimono sashes
28. Connected series of rooms
30. Lawyer's job
31. Swiss canton
33. In addition
35. Senate gofer
36. Scorn
38. Planets, to poets
39. Male of a bovine mammal
41. Lawless person
42. Pertaining to the Netherlands
44. Stop by
45. Alamogordo experiment
46. In addition
47. "Yow!"
48. Singer in acting
49. Extraordinary
50. Patch places
51. 24 hour periods
53. Geom. figure

Solution on page 166

Fairyland Creatures

Across

1. Esau's father
6. Small mischievous fairyland creature
9. Gangsters' guns
13. "The Gondoliers" flower girl
14. The East
15. ___ buco (veal dish)
16. Be of use to
17. E. Coast highway
18. Bingo call
19. Mischievous little Irish man in fairyland
21. "___ Smile Be Your Umbrella"
22. Dugout, for one
23. Need for liquid
25. Hindu wrap
29. Traveler's options: Abbr.
31. Nine: Prefix
32. Powerful serpent in fairyland
34. Autograph
36. Trysail
38. Fairyland creature in the sea
43. Sinai citizen
45. Of occult character
46. Scandinavian fairy tale creature
50. "How ___ to know?"
52. Author Morrison
53. Cap attachment
55. Respiratory organ
57. Singer Simone
58. Capable of being conceived
64. Shut with force
65. TV's warrior princess
66. Dental restoration
67. "I could ___ horse!"
68. Raise: Abbr.
69. "All in the Family" spinoff
70. Jeanne d'Arc et al.
71. Dutch city
72. Tools for duels

Down

1. Romance lang.
2. Golf's Ballesteros
3. "Quick!"
4. Region of Saudi Arabia
5. "The Alienist" author Carr
6. They may be taxed
7. In ___ of
8. Lacking brightness
9. Grotesque fairy tale creature
10. To the rear
11. Sleeping sickness carrier
12. Handel bars?
14. Nirvana attainer
20. Where two streets meet
24. Unit of inductance
25. '60s radical org.
26. Dada founder
27. Arctic explorer
28. Starter: Abbr.
30. Actor Alastair
33. Central Florida city
35. Third sign of the zodiac
37. Damp and chilly
39. Denver clock setting: Abbr.
40. From ___ Z
41. "Am __ your way?"
42. 601, in old Rome
44. Equilibrium
46. Present and future
47. Chew out
48. Baroque
49. Alpaca cousins
51. Sucrose
54. Playful sprite in fairyland
56. Underground creature in fairyland
59. Patch up
60. Take ___ (snooze)
61. Sky color
62. Put on
63. Looks at

Solution on page 166

Grimm's Fairy Tales

Across

1. Scandinavian native
5. Nicholas II was the last one
9. Cooked in oven
14. ___ Bator, Mongolia
15. 11,000-foot Italian peak
16. Minneapolis suburb
17. French film
18. 1982 Disney flick
19. Gee follower
20. Grimm's fairy tale with an eaten house
23. Shell team
24. Retail Employees Credit Union
25. Be unfaithful
28. Dinner jacket
32. It can precede or follow "to be"
33. "Tom ___," Grimm's fairy tale
36. "Little ___ Riding Hood," Grimm's fairy tale
37. "___ White," Grimm's fairy tale
38. Rub out with rubber
39. "The Fisherman and His ___," Grimm's fairy tale
40. Bone: Comb. form
41. Mirror ___
42. Forbidding words
43. Workshop of Hephaestus
45. Snares
46. Home to Columbus
48. Dispatch
49. Grimm's fairy tale, can you guess the name?
56. Walking ___
57. Sale labels
58. Start of a Melville title
59. Leonardo da ___
60. "Ignorance ___ excuse"
61. Busy as ___
62. Are
63. Part of Nasdaq: Abbr.
64. Vaccinator's call

Down

1. Of like kind
2. Others, to Ovid
3. "Buddenbrooks" author
4. Held by a third party
5. Lipton rival
6. Before boss or man
7. Pretty soon
8. Time off, briefly
9. Babe in the woods
10. Parting words
11. Singer Eartha
12. Suffix with refer or prefer
13. "James and the Giant Peach" author
21. Q.E.D. middle
22. "Understand?"
25. Kind of buddy
26. Artist Max
27. Govt. debt
29. Actress Gray and others
30. Friday's creator
31. "Awake and Sing!" playwright
33. Lilt syllable
34. Old crone
35. Milk, in a way
38. Screen letters
39. Lumberman
41. Receive by succession
42. "Cut it out!"
44. Themes
45. Wrestling hold
47. Old Roman port
48. Indications
49. Be itinerant
50. Computer operating system
51. Gershwin's "The ___ Love"
52. News agency of the USSR
53. Hoopster Bryant
54. Wild goat
55. Putin putoff

Solution on page 166

Chapter 9: Satire

Lewis Carroll

Across

1. Part of ACC
4. Kind of CRT
7. Spring
14. Lewis Carroll's real first name
16. Lewis Carroll's real last name
17. Spicy candies
18. On end
19. Saint-___ (Loire's capital)
20. Playboy
21. Lover of Aeneas
22. Spheroid
24. Trifling
28. Wine holder
30. Charge
33. Wade opponent
34. Stocking part
36. Good-looking
39. Lewis Carroll nonsense poem
41. Yardsticks
43. Sundial number
44. Norse goddess of death
45. Taking care of business
47. Scotland Yd. title
50. Runs in neutral
53. "...___ thousand times..."
55. Drawing card
57. Mussel genus
60. Flat
62. Lewis Carroll's home country
65. "Through the ___ -Glass" by Lewis Carroll
66. Penn State's football coach
67. Soul
68. Person who evades work
69. 1773 jetsam
70. Some Caltech grads

Down

1. Landed
2. Dogmatic
3. Pretentious
4. North Carolina school
5. "I Can't ___ Satisfaction": Stones hit
6. State positively
7. Linda of Broadway
8. Not stereo
9. Total
10. Monetary unit of Zambia
11. Comparison words
12. Slinky or yo-yo
13. Pair of nines?
15. Adjustable resistor
23. California's primary source of oil
25. City on the Hudson
26. Petty in music
27. "___-haw!"
29. Hoopster Bryant
31. Maxim
32. Fort ___ (gold site)
35. River through Aragon
37. Early seventh century date
38. Dermoid
39. Tumbler of rhyme
40. "Ich bin __ Berliner"
41. Phi follower
42. Dreaded ink color
46. Washroom
48. Flat on one's back
49. Son of the sovereign
51. Noted blind mathematician
52. "The Hunting of the ___" by Lewis Carroll
54. Win by ___
56. Narrowly defeats
58. Rest stop, in colonial times
59. Sneaker problem
61. Slugger Sammy
62. Some 45s, briefly
63. "I don't think so"
64. Volkswagen hatchback

Solution on page 167

Mark Twain

Across

1. Long-range weapon, for short
5. They may be picked
9. Do not disturb
14. Ethnic cuisine
15. Repeat verbatim
16. Run like ___
17. Popular Twain character
19. ___ de Mayo
20. Prom attendees: Abbr.
21. "___ Miniver," 1952 film
23. Clucking sounds
24. Cacao powder
27. One way to see
29. Distress
32. Orch. section
33. Voice-over: abbr.
34. Sun Bowl site
37. Twain's river
41. Attack
42. Key of Dvorák's Piano Quintet: Abbr.
45. Farm sight
47. Frito-Lay's parent
49. Russian Revolution participants
53. ___ crow flies
54. Man of Shangri-La
55. Patriotic org.
56. ___ mode
57. Caribbean resort
59. Craft Twain piloted
64. Drop off
65. "Hooray for me!"
66. Handed-down knowledge
67. ___ Yello (soft drink)
68. Spanish pronoun
69. Peel of "The Avengers"

Down

1. Cousin ___ of "The Addams Family"
2. "All-American Girl" star Margaret
3. Loud thud
4. State of USA
5. Bloomberg output
6. Inhospitable
7. Subject
8. Grieved
9. Resinous deposit
10. Perry White, e.g.
11. Present and future
12. ___ Thatcher, Twain character
13. Uneven
18. Kuwaiti, e.g.
22. Not freely moving
24. Cigarette pkg.
25. Mouths
26. Base of a crocus stem
28. Moonroof alternative
30. Teachings
31. Crimson rivals
35. Anti-drug ad, e.g.
36. "It can't be tasted in ___": Dickens
38. Room in a casa
39. Adequate
40. Not orig.
43. German gripe
44. Injun ___, Twain character
45. Mark Twain a.k.a. ___ Longhorne Clemens
46. Archer of fiction
48. Fortuneteller's reading material
49. Suffix with proto-
50. "Guitar Town" singer Steve
51. Flavor
52. Muchachas: Abbr.
56. Extremely narrow, as a shoe
58. G.I.'s mail drop
60. Summer hours in N.Y.
61. South Africa's ___ Paul Kruger
62. Elbow's site
63. 1773 jetsam

Solution on page 167

Satire Words

Across

1. Author Pirandello
6. Crumpled
10. Uttered
14. Fragrant compound
15. Level
16. Inactive
17. Hersey title town
18. Pulitzer winner Connelly
19. Shade of green
20. Mother and father
22. Satire that mocks and sneers
24. Polite address
25. Jackie's predecessor
26. Satire that humiliates
30. Satire that imitates
34. Cupid's counterpart
35. Kotter's org.?
36. ___ Haute, Ind.
37. Daddy-o
38. Pacific battle site
41. Stiller of "Meet the Fockers"
42. "There's ___ every crowd!"
44. Cause of unwanted points: Abbr.
45. Musical chairs goal
46. 2000 Olympics city
48. Double ___, a satirical device
50. Look from Snidely
52. La-la leader
53. Satire that spoofs
56. Indicator of illness
60. Here, in Honduras
61. Only
63. Capri, to a Capriote
64. Contented sound
65. "You can say that again!"
66. Like Fran Drescher's voice
67. Japanese rice beer
68. Det. Sipowicz's org.
69. ___ alcohol

Down

1. Spring
2. Meat-stamp letters
3. ___-Tass (Russian news agency)
4. First book of the Bible
5. Double-edged
6. Esteemed ones
7. The second Mrs. Sinatra
8. Vice ___
9. Bivouac
10. Undissembling
11. 1998 Sarah McLachlan hit
12. Pandora's boxful
13. Reckon
21. Main stem of a tree
23. Calf catcher
25. Ramble
26. Bank takebacks
27. Incongruous satirical device
28. Under sedation
29. Island greeting
31. Globular
32. Gloomy, in poetry
33. "Fiddler on the Roof" matchmaker
38. Bridge bid, briefly
39. Grass appendage
40. Clever and humorous satire
43. Fire up
45. Gets short with
47. Naval petty officer
49. Furrier's offering
51. Other side
53. Track circuits
54. Pool shade
55. Gloom
56. Fax, say
57. Nonsense
58. Oil of ___
59. Teen hangout
62. Corded cloth

Solution on page 167

Kurt Vonnegut

Across

1. Arab chief
6. They may provide relief
10. Goddess of youth
14. ___ incognita
15. Flooring calculation
16. Farm team
17. Whitewater VIP
18. Cabal
19. "Cleopatra" backdrop
20. City where Kurt Vonnegut was born
23. Achieve
25. At liberty
26. "___ ___ Champions," Kurt Vonnegut novel
30. Litter castoff, often
31. Burrito
36. Double-reed instrument
37. Expert
39. Defensive excavation
40. Chinese language
42. Orderly in "Nurses"
43. "God Bless You, ___ ___," Kurt Vonnegut novel
47. Therewithal
50. Of inferior quality
51. "Wampeters, Foma and ___," collected writings of Kurt Vonnegut
55. Apropos of
56. Use one's fingers, e.g.
57. "Same here"
61. "Slaughterhouse-___," Kurt Vonnegut novel
62. Tear down, in Dover
63. Olympic swimmer Janet
64. Drop from the eye
65. Frank
66. Doesn't play

Down

1. B'way crossers
2. Excited, with "up"
3. Victorian, for one
4. Vexed
5. Village in E Egypt
6. Boat basin
7. Operatic solo
8. Ivy League team
9. Narrative of heroic exploits
10. High public esteem
11. Deposed leader, perhaps
12. Misrepresent
13. Chemical endings
21. "What's the ___?"
22. Fizzling sound
23. Caribbean resort island
24. Mortise insert
26. ___ Bones (Sleepy Hollow bully)
27. Transcript preparer
28. Beat
29. Scrap for Rover
32. Unmoved
33. Disinclined
34. Cagney's TV partner
35. Suffix with comment
37. IAD posting
38. N, E, W or S
41. "I ___ the opinion."
44. Hot
45. Suffix with ranch
46. Roam
47. PGA great with an "army"
48. Stage between egg and pupa
49. Look of disdain
51. Present
52. Retro hairdo
53. Clear a hurdle
54. ___ majeste
58. Coll. aides
59. Bang maker
60. CIA forerunner

Solution on page 167

Joseph Heller

Across

1. Irish Rose's guy
5. "If it __ broke..."
9. Panhandle
12. Hollywood
15. "I ___ Kick Out of You"
16. Conflict in Joseph Heller's "Catch-22"
17. Iolani Palace locale
18. __ Friday's: restaurant
19. Festive occasion
20. Nearby
22. Is worthwhile
23. Like much fine wine
24. Kitchen gadgets
27. Theatrical
31. Soccer star Michelle
32. Early Tonight Show host
33. Sneaker, e.g.
34. "Closing ___," Joseph Heller's sequel to "Catch-22"
35. Kama ___
36. Clan
37. Jam-pack
38. Olive in a Caesar salad?
39. Water wheel
40. "Something ___," Joseph Heller's second novel
42. Beach resort near San Diego
43. Oodles
44. Poet
45. Sovereignty
48. Bull's target
49. Award bestowed by Queen Eliz.
52. Fish egg catcher?

53. Catch-22 situations are AKA ___ ___ or the egg problems
56. "If ___ be so bold..."
57. Previously owned
58. "___ Knows," Joseph Heller novel
59. Lacoste of tennis
60. Storm centers

Down

1. Periodic table abbr.
2. Bookstore sect.
3. Calvary letters
4. Subj. for U.S. newcomers
5. Continuously
6. Biased writing?: Abbr.
7. Role for Myrna
8. __-night double-header
9. Swain
10. People: Prefix
11. Showy trinket
13. Whodunit awards
14. Falls on the border
15. Joseph Heller novel about Jewishness
21. "Everybody Hurts" band
22. Imperative
23. Macaw
24. Quilt part
25. Director Kurosawa
26. Chart anew
27. Old hat
28. Unit of heat
29. Ancient land on the Aegean

30. Actor Romero
32. Whimpers
35. Shakespearean works
39. Moon of Neptune
41. Long period of time
42. Nymph of Greek myth
44. Breakfast strip
45. Math branch
46. __ sapiens
47. Scan
48. Gospel singer Winans
49. Give approval
50. Nota __
51. Cuts off
54. Part of HRH
55. Friend of Fidel

Solution on page 167

Dark Satire

Across

1. Basic skills
5. Make goo-goo eyes at
9. Some shirts
14. Theda of silents
15. In ___ of
16. Not out
17. "Three men in _____"
18. Allege
19. Holding a valid green card
20. Satirical novel by Evelyn Waugh about the funeral business in Los Angeles
23. Word part: Abbr.
24. Hunt in Hollywood
25. San Antonio cagers
27. Keyboard key
30. Calendar
34. "A Modest ___," satirical pamphlet by Jonathan Swift
39. Tragicomedy by Vladimir Nabokov
40. Rime
41. Skating event
43. Put ___ act
44. Acid neutralizer
46. Expecting
48. Do a museum job
50. Pou __: vantage point
51. Drawing
53. 1966 movie or song hit
58. Old Egyptian org.
61. "Fear ___ ___ in Las Vegas" by Hunter S. Thompson
64. Like some talk
66. Chits
67. Turkish leader
68. Ant
69. ___ care in the world
70. Like show horses
71. Grid great Grier
72. Hoover was one
73. Bar assn. members

Down

1. Take ___ (lose big)
2. Wash
3. Brutal
4. Black
5. Antarctica's Prince ___ Coast
6. "Had enough?"
7. City on the Aire
8. Moon of the planet Jupiter
9. Capital of Sicily
10. Be in debt to
11. Hangs back
12. Sanction
13. Auction off
21. Unfooled by
22. { }, to mathematicians
26. Drawing room
28. It's a relief
29. It's heard in a herd
31. One of a seagoing trio
32. ___ advantage
33. Pessimist's word
34. "___ Lap" (1983 film)
35. Stage part
36. Cork sources
37. Brooklyn's ___ Institute
38. Impudence
42. Four Monopoly properties: Abbr.
45. Faithfulness
47. Attack
49. Termination
52. Dimness
54. Dalai Lama's city
55. "___ Club," dark satirical novel by Chuck Palahniuk
56. ___ water
57. "Zounds!"
58. Laptop carrier
59. BB's and bullets
60. Trans World Dome team
62. "I'm ___ here!"
63. Simile center
65. Jeans brand

Solution on page 167

Shakespeare Comedies

Across

1. Palmtop organizers: Abbr.
5. Arch type
9. Kipling's wolf pack leader
14. Formerly
15. Cupola
16. Horizontal
17. Versatile bean
18. Diabolical
19. Bequeath
20. "The ___ ___ of Verona," Shakespeare comedy
23. Unwelcome obligations
24. Calendar square
25. "Friendly skies" flier: Abbr.
28. In case
31. Sharp pain
33. "Gunsmoke" bartender
36. "___ ___ of the Shrew," Shakespeare comedy
38. Island west of Maui
40. Help with the dishes
41. "Breaking Away" director
42. "The Merry Wives ___ ___," Shakespeare comedy
44. ___ amis
45. Occasion for dead reckoning?
46. Pre-release test phase
49. Dungeons & Dragons game co.
50. Diamond authority
52. Niece of Sir Toby Belch, in "Twelfth Night"
57. "Much Ado ___ ___," Shakespeare comedy
60. The second Mrs. Trump
63. Torture device
64. Are, in Avila
65. Flaw
66. Louver part
67. "Up and __!"
68. Charlotte ___ (cream-filled dessert)
69. Gateway Arch designer Saarinen
70. Red in the middle

Down

1. Green sauce
2. Destroy by immersion
3. "___ ___ Like It," Shakespeare comedy
4. Male deer
5. Danish city
6. Poli sci subj.
7. Disney's "___ and the Detectives"
8. Went sniggling
9. Passageway
10. Sharp
11. Stowe heroine
12. Monetary unit of Bulgaria
13. Pub offering
21. Slender fish
22. LeBlanc of "Friends"
25. Make one
26. De Mille of dance
27. Limbs
29. Criteria: Abbr.
30. Beat
32. Islamic holy man
33. Yeggs' targets
34. Menachem's co-Nobelist
35. Street name
37. Rochester's love
38. "Love's Labour's ___," Shakespeare comedy
39. Sit on, maybe
43. Expo presentation
47. Grew fond of
48. Supermodel Carol
51. Prize money
53. "Do __ a Waltz?"
54. Panoramic view
55. Lay to rest
56. "It's only ___!"
57. "___ Well That Ends Well," Shakespeare comedy
58. "The Winter's ___," Shakespeare comedy
59. Tarheel st.
60. Producer: Abbr.
61. Track-and-field org.
62. Lang. of Vladimir Putin

Solution on page 168

A Confederacy of Dunces

Across

1. Four gills
5. Vixen's master
10. Rise in the west
14. "Was ___ loud?"
15. Surpass
16. First name in fashion
17. "A Confederacy of Dunces" city setting
19. ___ Martin (cognac brand)
20. Obeyed the photographer
21. "Oklahoma!" girl
23. I's
25. Cub's club
26. JFK posting
29. Imitate
33. Thurman of "Henry & June"
36. ___ closet (where sheets are stored)
38. Zip
39. They Investigated the Columbia disaster in 2003 news
40. "A Confederacy of Dunces" main character
43. Musical chairs goal
44. Biblical preposition
45. Frasier's brother
46. Short trader?
47. Chuckle-evoking
49. Cen. parts
50. Place for a plug
52. Sushi wrapper
54. "A Confederacy of Dunces" prize won
59. Least furnished
63. Maintained
64. Wind speed measuring instrument
66. Epithet of Athena
67. Made mention of
68. Say ___ (deny)
69. Adult-to-be
70. Short literary composition
71. City of northern Oklahoma

Down

1. Spare parts?
2. News squib
3. Start of a prayer
4. "A Confederacy of Dunces" author's last name
5. Rarely
6. Feller
7. Org. with eligibility rules
8. Baby-sit
9. ___-ran
10. First name of "The Minx" in "A Confederacy of Dunces"
11. Ultimately
12. Teamster's rig
13. "___ sow, so shall…"
18. Governor
22. Figure to the right of Teddy on Mount Rushmore
24. Bush Sr.'s chief of staff
26. "I Still See ___" ("Paint Your Wagon" tune)
27. Large cat
28. Love poem of 1849
30. Goes the distance
31. Abut
32. Road crew's supply
34. Track specialist
35. Deep chasm
37. Corrode
39. 136% of LXXV
41. Elemental ending
42. Memory trace
47. Skill
48. No one
51. Quinn of "Benny & Joon"
53. Mother of 40-Across
54. Excellent, in modern slang
55. Congo river
56. Novelist Grey
57. Hazzard County deputy
58. Soaks, as flax
60. English public school
61. "The X-Files" org.
62. Crushed
65. "Cry ___ River"

Solution on page 168

P. G. Wodehouse

Across

1. Barber chair attachment
6. Processing time meas.
10. French protest phrase
14. "Star Trek" role
15. Height: prefix
16. French door part
17. Citadel student
18. Loafer, e.g.
19. Author Sarah ___ Jewett
20. British honor given to P. G. Wodehouse
22. Game often featured in P. G. Wodehouse novels
23. Potting need
24. Play openings
26. Cop's collar
30. Caribbean and others
32. VCR button
33. Valet in P. G. Wodehouse novels
35. Triathlon, e.g.
37. Colonised
39. Employer of 33-Across
44. Nice notion
46. Incompetent
47. Spring up
51. Lose it
53. Like many a cellar
54. Blandings ___, location in P. G. Wodehouse novels
56. Glimpse
58. Flooring option
59. Pensiveness
65. "This ___ outrage!"
66. "___ corny..."
67. Andrea Doria's domain
68. Chianti, e.g.
69. Sausage unit
70. 1961 Heston role
71. Pulls the plug on
72. Mother of the Valkyries
73. "Maria __": 1940s song

Down

1. Draw by suction
2. Comparison word
3. Fashion pioneer Gernreich
4. Salem's st.
5. Trajectories
6. Five iron
7. Student
8. Switch suffix
9. Some students
10. Highest point
11. Peerage members
12. Founder of the Shakers in America
13. Deem necessary
21. Like some salads
25. Antigone's cruel uncle
26. Bedwear, briefly
27. Wide spec.
28. Soak
29. Lowest army rank: Abbr.
31. Maxim
34. First name in architecture
36. Ticket
38. French surname start
40. Sorrowful
41. As yet unscheduled: Abbr.
42. Street of nightmares
43. Workout unit
45. P. G. Wodehouse birth country
47. Lively
48. Kind of bread
49. Cuba, e.g.
50. They serve dictators
52. Where Denali National Park is
55. Writer Zola
57. John D. MacDonald sleuth Travis ___
60. Kuwaiti bigwig
61. Hades
62. First word in a fairy tale
63. Cut of beef
64. When tripled, a "Seinfeld" catch phrase

Solution on page 168

Garrison Keillor

Across

1. Republic in the Caribbean
5. "___ ain't broke..."
9. Marina sights
14. Letters on a B-52
15. Central point
16. Game needs
17. Very, in Vienna
18. Change from one state to another
20. "A ___ ___ Companion," Garrison Keillor's radio show
22. Hockey milieu
23. Isolated
24. Jewelry designer Peretti
28. Lock opener?
30. Official sitting
32. Pompous person
35. Salinger orphan
37. "___ big deal"
38. Garrison Keillor's bestselling novel in 1985
42. Serengeti family
43. Gambler's need
44. Freelancer's encl.
45. Abject
48. Deposited
50. Opening wager
51. Hamilton-Burr affair
53. V.P. under G.R.F.
55. Garrison Keillor 1990 book, taken from 20-Across monologues
59. Capital of Suriname
63. California's San ___ Dam
64. Friendship 7 astronaut
65. Seventh-century date
66. "This ___ my day!"
67. "You know as well ___..."
68. Suffix with old
69. ___ point (never)

Down

1. Pointed end
2. PC operator
3. Faith that arose in Persia
4. Continent
5. Monetary unit of Peru
6. Front limb of an animal
7. Hells Canyon locale
8. Mortise insertions
9. Cheese with a rind
10. Away
11. Ring master?
12. Auto racer Fabi
13. Fig. in identity theft
19. Hook's helper
21. Renovated
24. Founded: Abbr.
25. Old Apple computers
26. "Crime and Punishment" heroine
27. Win by ___
29. General's name on a chicken dish
31. Submerging
32. Beginning
33. Wrap choice
34. Penniless
36. Sniggler's prey
39. Beat by a whisker
40. Credulous
41. South American tuber
46. Ancient Greek concert halls
47. Protects
49. Showy perennial
52. Throw out
54. Awaken rudely
55. K-P connection
56. "The Adventures of Guy ___, Private Eye," Garrison Keillor creation
57. Garrison Keillor home state (abbr.)
58. "Salus populi suprema lex ___" (Missouri's motto)
59. Tiger's org.
60. Capone and Capp
61. Old Portuguese coin
62. In addition

Solution on page 168

Erma Bombeck

Across

1. Meathead
5. Thick-soled shoe
9. Invites
13. Shots, for short
14. White with age
15. Search
16. Picnic hamperer
17. Comedic Ole
18. Full of pep
19. "If Life Is a Bowl of Cherries–What Am I Doing ___ ___ ___?," Erma Bombeck book
21. Adorable one
22. Kilns
23. Scandinavian native
24. Battered
27. Language communication
29. Sunday singers
30. "Say what?"
32. Haul
34. Apportion
35. Sow
36. Chutist, briefly
37. Tuba sound
38. System of shorthand
39. Art able to
40. Actor Quaid
42. Woven container
43. Quantity of paper
44. No-see-ums
46. "Balderdash!"
48. Carry
52. Jeer
53. Construction site sight
54. Fish market feature
55. "American ___"
56. Platters
57. San ___
58. Gentlewoman
59. "Aunt Erma's ___ Book," Erma Bombeck book
60. Breakfast-in-bed item

Down

1. Adriatic port
2. Mideast land
3. Fail to mention
4. Geniality
5. Gen. Powell
6. Holds up
7. Lode contents
8. Dr. for women
9. Suppose
10. "The Grass Is Always Greener over the ___ ___" Erma Bombeck book
11. "Felicity" star Russell
12. Terrier type
14. Crossed one's fingers
20. By any chance
21. City near Le Havre
23. Rod at a pig roast
24. Dudley Do-Right's org.
25. Leading
26. "___: The Second Oldest Profession," Erma Bombeck book
27. Squealed
28. Gymnastics apparatus
30. Brewpub fare
31. "Family: The Ties That Bind ... and ___!," Erma Bombeck book
33. Light bulb unit
35. Schoolmarmish
36. "When You Look Like Your ___ Photo, It's Time to Go Home," Erma Bombeck book
38. Chew on
39. Felines
41. Tidily
42. Spoilers
44. Clutch
45. Effeminate male
46. Ochs of folk
47. Scotch companion
48. Peter, Paul and Mary, e.g.
49. Wroclaw's river
50. Colosseo site
51. Helen of ___
53. Gp. concerned with bioterrorism

Solution on page 168

Chapter 10: Science Fiction

H. G. Wells

Across

1. Viva-voce
5. Bara of the silents
10. Bag brand
14. Actress Moore
15. Swift
16. Painter Bonheur
17. "Amscray!"
18. "He's ___ nowhere man" (Beatles lyric)
19. Like the Negev
20. H. G. Well's fourth dimension novel
23. Campaigned
24. Keogh kin
25. Like draft beer
28. Hootchy-___
31. Amherst inst.
35. Rockefeller Center muralist
36. Villain
38. "Give ___ rest!"
39. H. G. Well's novel about changing one's refractive index
42. "___ for Innocent" (novel featuring private investigator Kinsey Millhone)
43. Put or call
44. Italian saint
45. Black ink item
47. TV buying channel
48. Head off
49. Tang
51. Fizzle out
52. "The ___ ___ ___ ___," H. G. Well's alien invasion novel
60. Major League brothers' name

Solution on page 169

61. Consumed
62. Sharer's word
64. Overfill
65. Chain of hills
66. Cracker topping
67. "@#$%!," e.g.
68. Welles of "Citizen Kane"
69. Pizazz

Down

1. Some hosp. cases
2. Geometric fig.
3. Chinese nurse
4. Clerisy
5. Commuter's choice
6. Wrong
7. Olympics weapon
8. Circle meas.
9. Statesman Stevenson
10. Evangelist Billy
11. "Pieces of Me" singer McKenna
12. Start of an example
13. Miami's county
21. Beer barrel poker
22. Unusual partner?
25. Port of ancient Rome
26. Some soft drinks
27. Snake, to Medusa
28. Richard of The Stones
29. Place to find dates?
30. Bermuda or Vidalia
32. Anouk of film
33. Belle or Bart
34. Dept. that cleans up
36. Diamond honor

37. ___ Saud (former Saudi king)
40. "___ I can help it!"
41. Wrapper
46. Adequate
48. Go public with
50. Dactyl opening
51. "Funny Face" director Stanley
52. City on the Brazos
53. ___ breve
54. Cheer the home team
55. Rock musical
56. Passenger inquiries: Abbr.
57. "And away ___!"
58. Twin
59. Mlle. from Madrid
63. One of a D.C. 100

Sci Fi Novels at the Movies

Across

1. Obi-Wan portrayer
5. Lose one's cool
10. Word on a dollar
14. Champagne Tony of golf
15. Say "li'l," say
16. Enlist anew
17. Ruin
18. Attains status
19. Fellow
20. Margaret Atwood novel, film with Dunaway and Duvall
23. Colored part of the eye
24. Zero-star review
25. Film starring Will Smith loosely based on Asimov's work
28. Chanel fragrance for men
32. Summary
33. Winter air
34. The Monkees' "__ Believer"
36. Film critic Pauline
37. Back-country
38. Kind of school
39. Rwy. stop
40. Sudden moves
41. It joins the Rhone at Lyons
42. Acute suffering
44. "The War of the ___," novel made into a film
45. Web address
46. Body of an organism
47. Short story by Philip K. Dick, film starring Tom Cruise
54. Like a hippie's hair
55. Prayer starter
56. Place for pins
57. Book after Neh.
58. Lofty home
59. Unnamed ones
60. "Get lost!"
61. Fear greatly
62. Ticked

Down

1. "M*A*S*H" man
2. Judah's mother
3. "The New Colossus" poet Lazarus
4. Person who eats human flesh
5. Allow
6. Rose by any other name?
7. Not yet final, at law
8. Recognized
9. Reservoir for sewage
10. Some are vital
11. Film holder
12. Frank Herbert novel made into a film
13. Withdraw, with "out"
21. Go down
22. Mermaid feature
25. Vexes
26. Ranch in "Giant"
27. Neptune's realm
28. "Battlefield ___," novel made into a film
29. Foie ___
30. Alpine region of Austria and Italy
31. Improve, as text
33. Junkyard dogs
35. "Planet of the ___," novel made into a film
37. Locomotive track
38. Fort defenses
40. Former coin of Spain
41. A portion
43. Eager
44. Expressed
46. Neighbor of Israel
47. Dance recklessly
48. Keen on
49. "The Sopranos" actor Robert
50. Sped
51. Roman emperor after Galba
52. Sorry sort
53. "The ___ Machine," novel made into a film
54. "___ Miz"

Solution on page 169

Ray Bradbury

Across

1. Early pulpit
5. Diaper, in Britain
10. Track action
14. Bookbinding leather
15. Not __ in the world
16. Part of the Dept. of Labor
17. "The Martian ___," Ray Bradbury book
19. Other, to Pedro
20. Seaman
21. Oscar winner Burl
22. Sulu portrayer on "Star Trek"
24. Golf's Davis Love __
25. These, in Tours
26. Feminine pronoun
28. Hook
30. Like a moonscape
32. Year in Edward the Confessor's reign
33. Entanglement
35. A hand
36. Place that allows "eggs-tradition"?
37. "The ___ Man," Ray Bradbury book
40. Range: Abbr.
42. Cal. column
43. "Tasty!"
44. Sounds of delight
45. Agenda details
47. Pub purchase
51. Perforated
53. Pizzeria order
55. __ TURN (road sign)
56. Purge
57. Walk in water
58. Winnebagos, for short
59. Gone across a pool
60. "___ 451," Ray Bradbury novel
63. Heavenly instrument
64. Capital of Tibet
65. Daytona 500, for one
66. Surveys
67. "Breaking Away" director
68. Inuit conveyance

Down

1. Frigid
2. Angora fabric
3. Inner-city area
4. "Double Fantasy" singer
5. Green
6. Entree
7. Good buddies
8. Relative of ante-
9. The day before this day
10. Items burned in 60-Across
11. Honored
12. Coaster sensations
13. ___ Paulo, Brazil
18. Metallic element
23. Neighbor of La.
26. Rapunzel's abundance
27. Toned
29. Mice catchers
31. Jazz pianist Art
34. Flying insect
36. Literary captain
37. Not safe
38. Hut
39. Large soup dish
40. Atlas item
41. "Something Wicked ___ ___ Comes," Ray Bradbury novel
45. Hosp. section
46. Thin
48. Fantastic
49. Beginner
50. Checked for prints
52. Frolics
54. Inspirations
57. "Say again?"
59. "Thar ___ blows!"
61. Moment of realization
62. Many mins.

Solution on page 169

Jules Verne

Across

1. Alibi ___ (excuse makers)
5. Support
9. Filmdom's Rowlands
13. Finger ___
15. "Horton Hears ___"
16. Multicolored
17. In what place
18. Go lickety-split
19. Long in the tooth
20. "Twenty Thousand Leagues ___ ___ ___," Jules Verne novel
23. "Good" cholesterol, briefly
24. Treasury div.
25. Seconds: Abbr.
27. Chewy candy
30. Ass
32. E.g., e.g.
33. Gallows reprieve
35. Taxi, often
38. Mallorca, e.g.
39. Cast
41. Rancho hand?
42. Pooped
44. Singer Stuarti
45. Gave the once-over
46. They're in the act
48. Thick
50. "I __ reason why..."
51. Chield
52. Poseidon's realm
53. "Journey to ___ ___ ___ the Earth," Jules Verne novel
60. Captain in Jules Verne novel
62. Turnpike turn-off
63. Still in play
64. Feast of Esther month
65. Latvian
66. Chairman's hammer
67. "Peer ___"
68. Penultimate Greek letters
69. Place to trade

Down

1. Stevedore's org.
2. Actress Madeline
3. Squeezed (out)
4. Dry
5. Spa
6. ___ bit (slightly)
7. Cartoonist Addams
8. Seoul man
9. Transcript fig.
10. "Around the World in ___ ___," Jules Verne novel
11. Can't forgo
12. Extra: Abbr.
14. Printing flourish
21. Lovers' meeting
22. Quizzes
26. Appeared
27. One-sixteenth of a cup: Abbr.
28. Experienced seaman
29. Jules Verne home country
30. Mends
31. Court call
32. Sue Grafton's "___ for Alibi"
34. "Of ___ I Sing"
36. Working without ___
37. Land east of Eden
40. John Lennon hit
43. Carnival sight
47. Useless
49. Lapel label
50. Wretched
51. Some Balts
52. Sweater problem
54. Old mates
55. Credit card name
56. Jack of old oaters
57. 1972 Kentucky Derby winner __ Ridge
58. Above
59. Thick fabric
61. Morsel

Solution on page 169

2001 A Space Odyssey

Across

1. Boor's lack
5. Beeish
10. Barely move
14. Appointed time
15. "Baloney!"
16. Look
17. Big name on the autobahn
18. Arrived
19. Actress Charlotte et al.
20. "Oh my God! – ___ ___ ___ ___!," Bowman's last transmission in "2001"
23. Gen. Robert ___
24. Just manage, with "out"
25. Vestiges
28. Solid object that appears in "2001"
33. "Fiddler on the Roof" matchmaker
34. Shot in the dark
35. ___ Canals
36. "Pet" that's a plant
37. Beast of Borden
38. Like some vases
39. Computer in "2001"
40. Slippery as ___
41. Andy's "Taxi" role
42. Checks out
44. Inhabitant of Ionia
45. "Go jump in the loch!"
46. Got on
47. Director of "2001"
54. Cordial
55. Works
56. Drifting
57. Together, musically
58. Assign to, as blame
59. Retained
60. Contemptible one
61. Maker of Citation business jets -C
62. Very wide shoe spec

Down

1. Native of Thailand
2. August, in Arles
3. Things to chew on
4. Betting option
5. Fishes
6. Frank killed by 39-Across
7. "Sock ___ me!"
8. "No way!"
9. Words without sense
10. Golda Meir's land
11. In the neighborhood
12. Average marks
13. Letters at sea
21. Title beekeeper in a 1997 film
22. WBA stoppages
25. Moon crater where a 28-Across is found
26. Former tenement
27. Indigo-yielding shrubs
28. Sources of inspiration
29. Parisian peeper
30. Disciple's query
31. Sal Mineo movie of 1958
32. Navajo home
34. Delight
37. Wrapper
38. Narcotic plant
40. Islands off Hibernia
41. Leopold's partner
43. Glossy finish
44. Large lizard
46. Ohio rubber center
47. "The Sweetest Taboo" singer, 1985
48. Quiz answer
49. Certain Prot.
50. Urges
51. "Got it"
52. French chef's mushroom
53. Actress Winslet
54. Nursery cry

Solution on page 169

Dune

Across

1. Terza ___ (Italian verse form)
5. Play groups
10. Duke ___, father of 56-Across
14. Like Nash's lama
15. Alaskan tongue
16. "Put ___ on it!"
17. Chemistry Nobelist Hahn
18. Anything unoriginal
20. "Dune" author
22. "There but for the grace of God ___"
23. High school course
27. "Boola Boola" collegian
30. "Lady Mac," for one
33. Oedipus, e.g.
34. "Bene ___," secretive sisterhood in "Dune"
36. Salad leaf
38. Fairy-tale heavy
39. This instant
41. 1960s pitcher Blue Moon
42. Poker challenge
45. Greek dish
48. Witness
49. Aged
51. Man's nickname
52. The spice in "Dune"
54. Recolor
56. Main character in "Dune"
62. Road hugger
65. "Had enough?"
66. Coloratura piece
67. End
68. Find out
69. Feds
70. Stagnates, as a pond
71. Nickname for football coach Bill Parcells

Down

1. Upper covering of a house
2. Foreword: Abbr.
3. Prefix with physics
4. Beside
5. Money handler
6. Der ___: Adenauer
7. Soothsayer
8. Muslim headdress
9. Playing marble
10. Starbucks buy
11. Seat of White Pine County, Nev.
12. Apex
13. Canticle
19. Club publication
21. 1995 earthquake site
24. Kind of shower
25. Withdraw
26. Lumberjack
27. Conceit
28. Stowe character
29. Golda Meir's land
31. Tonic's partner
32. Mexican tribe
35. Endangered whale
37. Affairs
40. Blue state?
43. Yemen's capital
44. Inundates
46. Disrobe
47. Eye woe
50. Bird, once
53. Beelike
55. Black billiard ball
57. Hokkaido native
58. Cut down
59. "Mon ___!"
60. Author Hunter
61. Some transfusions
62. Tease
63. Escort's offer
64. Fall flat

Solution on page 169

Isaac Asimov

Across

1. Offenses
5. Desert region in S Israel
10. Slender
14. "I smell __!"
15. Tug's tow
16. Pitches in
17. "The ___ Series," Isaac Asimov's famous work
19. Managed care grps.
20. Situps strengthen them
21. Have a bawl
22. Courtroom event
24. Future fry
25. Blunder
26. Isaac Asimov story about a nursemaid robot
28. "Darn ___!"
30. Dependable
33. Book before Neh.
34. Gore and Green
36. Pres. of the U.S.
37. Fannie ___ (securities)
38. Chief robopsychologist in many Isaac Asimov stories
41. Mutual fund fee
43. Senate declaration
44. "Yikes!"
45. Beaver's handiwork
46. Words from Caesar
48. "Drying out" program
52. Rough design
54. L-P filler
56. Comedian Philips
57. ___ Laws of Robotics (written by Isaac Asimov)
58. Farm team
59. __ Cruces, New Mexico
60. Earl ___

61. Equal in value
64. Whodunit hero Wolfe
65. Above
66. Untie
67. Hammer part
68. Supporter of the arts?
69. James of "Thief"

Down

1. Adventurous expedition
2. Collection of Isaac Asimov stories and a Will Smith movie
3. Sickness at the stomach
4. R.R. stop
5. Piston, for one, briefly
6. Diners

7. Hold
8. Bigheadedness
9. Chamber of the heart
10. "Master"
11. Edible bean .
12. Worship as a god
13. Ed.'s piles
18. Lives
23. Curtain holder
27. EMTs' destinations
29. Tout
31. Philosopher William of
___
32. ___ Fail (Irish coronation stone)
35. "Smile!"
37. Emcee's need
38. "Ditto"
39. Educators' org.

40. Shakespearean setting
41. Mormon gp.
42. Yellow ribbon site
46. Rocks, to a bartender
47. "Galactic ___ Series," by Isaac Asimov
49. Treasure State capital
50. Actress Plummer
51. ___ University, where Isaac Asimov was a professor
53. Assess, as a dress
55. The "N" of U.S.N.A.
58. Dines
60. Econ. figure
62. Between sine and non
63. Jean-___ Godard

Solution on page 170

Robert A. Heinlein

Across

1. Clairvoyance, for short
4. River to the Rio Grande
9. Words to live by
14. Doo-wop's __ Na Na
15. Splash gently against
16. Scrub, NASA-style
17. Symbol for torque
18. Eleniak of "Baywatch"
19. Offspring
20. Solvent
22. Have status
24. "___ Troopers," Robert A. Heinlein novel
27. "___ in the Sky," Robert A. Heinlein novel
31. Guitarist Eddy
32. Active
33. Engine
36. Celestial bear
38. Songstress Fitzgerald
39. Blood-typing system
40. Building
43. Big ___
44. Amount to make do with
46. Piles
47. Looks ahead
49. Stratagem
51. Rate
53. "The Moon Is ___ ___ Mistress," Robert A. Heinlein novel
54. State where Robert A. Heinlein was born
58. Film box nos.
60. Like some salads
61. Reeves of "Speed"
64. Accumulate
67. Tee follower
68. Supersized
69. Pool problem
70. "Die Meistersinger" heroine
71. Subdued
72. Vast extents
73. Object in a courtroom

Down

1. Spaniard's "these"
2. Mine passage
3. Singer Abdul
4. Gratification
5. Singer Kitt
6. Inflation meas.
7. Symbol of might
8. "Double ___," Robert A. Heinlein novel
9. Rum cocktail
10. Notice
11. Lean-___ (sheds)
12. Capote, to friends
13. Native: Suffix
21. Church calendar
23. Insurance company with a spokesduck
25. Eskimo
26. Execute
28. Peach ___
29. Sitcom originally named "These Friends of Mine"
30. "___ Daughter" (1970 film)
33. Island south of Sicily
34. Voodoo
35. Teatro Costanzi premiere of 1900
37. Moses' mount
41. Russian country house
42. Serial parts
45. "Stranger in a ___ Land," Robert A. Heinlein novel
48. Lorelei Lee's creator
50. Put out
52. Woman's shoe
55. Doorkeeper
56. "Superman" actor Christopher
57. Think tank nuggets
59. Food fish
61. Airline to Amsterdam
62. It's bottled in Cannes
63. Workmanship
65. Violinist Bull
66. Census datum

Solution on page 170

The Hitchhiker's Guide to the Galaxy

Across

1. Breather?
5. Some writers work on it
9. ___ fide
13. "Pagliacci," e.g.
15. Frost
16. Grand ___
17. "Let's Make ___"
18. Santa ___, Calif.
19. WWW code
20. Alien friend of 10-Down
23. Step on it
24. Cut
25. Done for
27. James Garfield's middle name
30. Sheen
32. "Guilty," e.g.
33. NASDAQ debuts
35. ___ the line
38. "__ to differ"
39. "Most massively useful thing" according to "The Hitchhiker's Guide to the Galaxy"
41. Tiny divider
42. Postpone
44. "Felicity" star Russell
45. "Young Frankenstein" woman
46. Second
48. Mediterranean island
50. Long hard seat
51. Out-of-date: Abbr.
52. Metro area
53. Starship with Infinite Improbability Drive in "The Hitchhiker's Guide to the Galaxy"

60. "The Thin Man" role
62. Far from exciting
63. Cry from the bench
64. Sacred image: Var.
65. Beat by a nose
66. Isabella, por ejemplo
67. Libretto
68. Fly like an eagle
69. Nibble away

Down

1. Take it easy
2. High hair style
3. Literary adverb
4. Sheepskin holder
5. Termagant
6. [It's gone!]

7. Moderate
8. Spackle targets
9. Going rate: Abbr.
10. Englishman who escapes earth's destruction in "The Hitchhiker's Guide to the Galaxy"
11. Ceiling
12. Wheel connector
14. Part of many stars' names
21. Send in
22. "Soap" family name
26. Writing instrument
27. Goya's "Duchess of ___"
28. Zaphod ___, character in "The Hitchhiker's Guide to the Galaxy"
29. Loose overcoat
30. Bring down

31. Cyberspace traveler
32. Mine
34. Nudge
36. Kafka character
37. Gov. Bush's state
40. Between Heaven and Hell
43. Carve
47. Ancient city in S Egypt
49. In reference to
50. Penniless
51. None of the above
52. Pint or quart
54. Tough-guy actor Ray
55. Indian music
56. Actor Kinnear
57. Valhalla host
58. Tuneful Horne
59. No-win situation
61. Six-footer

Solution on page 170

Chapter 11: Drama

King Lear

Across

1. Resting places
5. Possibilities
8. Fit of resentment
12. Way out
13. Cold one
14. "Pagliacci" role
15. Quarrel
16. Avatar of Vishnu
17. Still in the game
18. Literary device used in "King Lear" to reveal inner thoughts
20. Bird of prey
21. Yogi
22. Marshy area
23. Round body
26. King Lear's eldest daughter
30. Hotfoot it
31. Not fair
34. Teamster's rig
35. Carroll girl
37. Slick stuff
38. Narnia lion
39. Like old recordings
40. Crime plotted by 26-Across against King Lear
42. Questionnaire datum
43. Timeless
45. Minded
47. Calendar box
48. Scout's mission
50. Arduous journey
52. Worthy of reverence
56. Republic in SW South America
57. First governor of Alaska
58. Wire nail
59. Moist
60. Marathon
61. Give temporarily
62. Plan
63. Formicary resident
64. Irascible

Down

1. First Lady of the 1940s
2. Really big show
3. Ring up
4. Conflict
5. Baghdad resident
6. Thighbone
7. Influence
8. Sanctity
9. Newton, e.g.
10. Number of acts in "King Lear"
11. Antagonist
13. Fragmented
14. Spoken for
19. Lash of old westerns
22. Supporting
23. Embarrassment
24. Kitchen light
25. "Die Lorelei" poet
26. Embellish richly
27. Track event
28. Pol's concern
29. Like notebook paper
32. Disgusting
33. Cause of inflation
36. King Lear's youngest daughter
38. Pergola
40. Kentucky Derby time
41. When mammals began
44. Unadorned
46. Make possible
48. King Lear's second daughter
49. Pass laws
50. Sound of impact
51. Cold coating
52. Miles of "Psycho"
53. Engendered
54. Singer k. d. ___
55. Current event?
56. X, to Xanthippe

Solution on page 170

A Streetcar Named Desire

Across

1. "Writing on the wall" word
5. Bid
10. Con game
14. Vocal music
15. Word after yes or no
16. Bandleader Puente
17. City setting for "A Streetcar Named Desire"
19. Accusatory words
20. Lows
21. V-E Day celebrants
23. Kofi of the UN
26. Insipid
29. Lay out
30. "___ Dancer" (Nureyev documentary)
31. Discrimination
32. Oil worker
34. Lennon's in-laws
36. Principal character in "A Streetcar Named Desire"
41. Starbuck's captain
42. Uncover
44. Kind of preview
48. It may be critical
50. "Cogito __ sum"
51. First name of "A Streetcar Named Desire" author
53. Shouts
54. St. Francis's home
55. Huxtable and Lovelace
57. HVAC measures
58. 1/100 of a meter
64. Sheltered, in a way
65. 1981 Literature Nobelist Canetti
66. Chooser's opening
67. Trueheart of the comics
68. Would-be suitor of 36-Across
69. Belle ___, plantation lost in "A Streetcar Named Desire"

Down

1. Bill Gates ISP
2. Fair-hiring abbr.
3. Tropical storm hdg.
4. "I" problem?
5. Skaggerrak fjord
6. Cinco de Mayo event
7. Lobster ___ Diavolo
8. Bard's nightfall
9. Convened again
10. Sister of 36-Across
11. Large towns
12. Swear
13. Sweet dessert
18. Popeil of infomercials
22. Doesn't bother
23. Shrinks' org.
24. Workers' rights org.
25. One of the major leagues: Abbr.
27. Low life?
28. Hourglass contents
30. Irritate
33. Reptiles
35. Willa Cather's "One of ___"
37. Radio operators
38. Supervisor
39. Yesterday, in Italy
40. Stuffing herb
43. _____ Alamos
44. "___ Mater" (hymn)
45. Snuggle
46. Comes afterward
47. Liqueur flavorers
49. Washington airport
52. Command to an attack dog
53. Web video gear
56. Signal receiver
59. Crimson foe
60. College basketball tourney, for short
61. Pipe joint
62. It may have a window: Abbr.
63. Cereal grass

Solution on page 170

Hamlet

Across

1. Hamlet, Prince of ___
8. Country where Hamlet was in school
15. Natural environment
16. Cheer
17. Surprise
18. East, in Ecuador
19. Pitcher Hershiser
20. Sloth, e.g.
21. Dalai Lama's city
24. Most precipitous
29. "Casablanca" role
30. Philippine island
33. Copenhageners
34. Stain
35. Located the source of
38. Neb. neighbor
39. ___ and Guildenstern, classmates of Hamlet's
42. Cold, to Conchita
44. Looks after
45. Reproductive cells
48. Stockpile
50. Plane reservation
51. 40 winks
52. Dead King Hamlet's brother
55. All in
57. Finished first
58. First of 13 popes
60. They have big bills
64. Hamlet's beloved
68. Where "Zaza" was filmed
69. Bishop's domain
70. Third day of the week
71. Values highly

Down

1. Some AL batters
2. Attack a sub?
3. David Stern is its commish
4. Some Surrealist works
5. Turns on
6. Asthmatic sound
7. TV music vendor
8. Form the late King Hamlet takes in the play
9. Bone-chilling
10. Came down
11. G.I. chow in Desert Storm
12. Acute tubular necrosis, in medicine
13. Bring in
14. Chemical suffix
21. What Leary tripped on
22. Cow chow
23. Paul Simon song
24. Favorable termination of endeavors
25. Days gone by
26. Touchdown site
27. Poseidon's realm
28. Sound of disapproval
31. "___ Tu": 1974 hit
32. Spoiler
36. Gaelic tongue
37. Information
40. Diamond Head's island
41. Eh
42. Radio regulator
43. "Too-ra-loo-ra-loo-___"
46. Ryder rental
47. Well put
49. The prince in "The Prince and the Pauper"
53. Michigan county or its seat
54. Take back, in a way
56. Chessman
58. Rich deposit
59. Certain Prot.
60. Sylvester, to Tweety
61. Sch. in Stillwater
62. Western tribesman
63. Trigonometry abbr.
65. Loser at Antietam
66. Ending for intellectual
67. JFK's U.N. ambassador

Solution on page 170

Dramatic Words

Across

1. Dramatic player
6. Palm Pilot, e.g.
9. Drama with singing
14. Lucky piece
15. Indonesia's ___ Islands
16. Dunn of "Saturday Night Live" and namesakes
17. "Look, Ma, no ___!"
18. Place for a VCR
19. Sorry souls
20. Suffix with lay
21. Pertaining to Australia
23. Bouquets
25. CPR performer
26. Classical greek drama genre
28. Drama with no set script, for short
31. Domicile
32. Indonesian resort island
34. First name in fashion
36. "___ rang?"
37. Round trip?
38. Old Spanish queen
39. On the way
41. Tempo
42. Thrum
44. Inane
46. Toyota model
47. Pocatello sch.
48. Book of the Bible
50. Iambic ___, Elizabethan drama verse
54. Big cut
57. Paradigm of sluggishness
58. Garage contents
59. Impertinence
60. Sen. Thurmond
61. Pliny's 154
62. With "out," barely beats
63. Atlantic lead-in
64. Potato bud
65. "Laughing" animal

Down

1. Workout woe
2. ___ room
3. Equivalent
4. Commanded
5. Realty ad abbr.
6. City west of Venice
7. Code subject
8. Polly, to Tom Sawyer
9. Cloverleaf part
10. Domesticated fowl collectively
11. "I kiss'd thee ___ kill'd thee": Othello
12. ___ avis
13. Part of NCAA
21. TV's "Judging ___"
22. Send, as money
24. Catullus composition
26. Low islands
27. Wind instruments
28. Nastase, of tennis
29. Charge too high a price
30. Locale
32. Thin fastener
33. Disney owns it
35. Heb. judge
37. Codeine source
40. Instruction
42. Cinque follower
43. Classical greek drama genre
45. Job follower
46. Gooey stuff
48. Europe's "boot"
49. Wait on
50. Head-turner
51. ___'acte: intermission
52. Japan's first capital
53. "Look!" to Livy
55. Cinematographer Nykvist
56. The Crystals' "___ Rebel"
59. Book before Esther: Abbr.

Solution on page 171

A Midsummer
Night's Dream

Across

1. Pre-euro German money
6. Lab heaters
11. Whimsical
14. Change
15. Biblical queendom
16. Woodsman's tool
17. __ Lama
18. Brad Pitt thriller
19. Beer made by Grant's and others: Abbr.
20. Weizman of Israel
21. "My gal" of song
22. Madrid Mmes.
23. 1988 Meg Ryan film
24. Expressed disapproval
27. Tour of duty
28. Come-___ (marketing ploys)
29. "A Theory of Semiotics" author
30. Thespian
32. Annual foursome
35. Worker's demand
36. ___-upon-Avon, Shakespeare's birthplace
38. Complete
40. Heavy coats
43. Unsettle
45. Application
46. Anti-smog org.
48. __ the hole
49. Shaped into a sphere
51. Sawbuck
52. Camp beds
53. Classic Pontiac
54. Oberon's jester in "A Midsummer Night's Dream"
55. Animal that 44-Down becomes

56. Wonderland cake words
58. "The Sound of Music" heroine
59. Kind of chart
60. Tourney type
61. Interior
62. W. Hemisphere grp.
63. Sunday songs
64. "The Gondoliers" girl

Down

1. Got by
2. Hippolyta is Queen of the ___ in "A Midsummer Night's Dream"
3. Free from confinement
4. Bump on a log
5. Reagan's antimissile program: Abbr.
6. Suffix with seer
7. This and this
8. State in the W United States
9. Biblical brother
10. Honshu honorific
11. Titania is Queen of the ___ in "A Midsummer Night's Dream"
12. Stretch
13. Brewers' supplies
22. Walk with long steps
24. Trial
25. Basket maker
26. Hawaiian coastal region
27. Began
31. Game stick

33. If nothing changes
34. "Rugrats" dad
37. Bungle
38. Mediterranean capital
39. Flies over the equator?
41. Accountant's stack
42. Distinct sort or kind
43. Repeated from the beginning
44. Most outgoing actor in the troupe in "A Midsummer Night's Dream"
47. Turkish capital
50. Marc Antony addressee
53. Indiana city of song
54. Sheet of glass
56. N.T. book
57. Dash lengths
58. Cambridge univ.

Solution on page 171

Opera

Across

1. They're not part of the body: Abbr.
4. ___ Tzu
8. Stage org.
12. They form bonds
15. Crown
16. Advance
17. Steer
18. Dover domestic
19. Opulence
20. State in SW United States
22. Goes postal
24. Wonder
25. Guilty of perjury
26. Words of an opera
30. Opera by Georges Bizet named after the main character
34. "___ Around": Beach Boys hit
35. Diana Ross musical, with "The"
36. Melbourne marsupial
37. With is well, comforting signal
38. Downright
41. Prefix denoting speed
42. Atari founder Bushnell
44. Doze (off)
45. Composition in verse
46. Author who wrote the play that the opera "Faust" is loosely based on
48. "Don ___," an opera with music by Mozart
50. Hint
52. Nov. runner
53. Swallows
56. Wounded
60. Gift tag word
61. 100 cents
63. Blood of the gods
64. Fill-in
65. Circular band
66. Wee
67. Try for a fly
68. F.C.C. concerns: Abbr.
69. Serpentine letter

Down

1. Hemingway moniker
2. Culinary directive
3. Arias, usually
4. Shelter grp.
5. Derisive laugh
6. Country of origin for "opera"
7. Noble
8. Rapid in tempo
9. Entre ___
10. It's hailed by city dwellers
11. Work without ___ (take risks)
13. Composer of the opera "The Magic Flute"
14. Vermont ski resort
21. Cereal box stat.
23. Serpentine
25. Medicated tablet
26. Chinese unit of weight
27. Nome dome home
28. Pretty girl
29. Great ___ (bird with a glossy blue-black head)
31. Wall builder
32. Burstyn or Barkin
33. Ruth's mother-in-law
38. Square
39. Lyon king
40. Parkinson's treatment
43. Try
45. Stately mansion
47. Logs
49. Throw up
51. Astronaut's wear
53. P.M. times
54. Kind of cut
55. Robin Cook thriller
56. Canines
57. Clarified butter
58. Millions of years
59. Prohibitionists
62. Three-min. period

Solution on page 171

Sam Shepard

Across

1. "Operation Solomon" airline
5. Botch
10. Shuttle site
14. Sampras of tennis
15. Professor Corey
16. A long way off
17. Think of it!
18. Clamor
19. Ices
20. "Curse of the ___ ___," Sam Shepard play
23. Eye bank donation
24. Delivery room doctors, for short
25. Comrade
28. U.S. 1 and others
31. Premature
33. Web address suffix
36. Sam Shepard play that won the 1979 Pulitzer Prize for Drama
39. "The God of ___," Sam Shepard play
41. Sonata movement
42. Not in favor
43. Lacking a visible stem
46. __ few rounds
47. Dickens's Barnaby
48. It used to be sufficient
49. Jackie's O
50. Winery sight
53. Cone on the plains
58. Sam Shepard play first produced in 1985, set in the American West
62. Insurable item
64. "Spider-Man 2" director
65. Stop up a hole
66. Northern arm of the Black Sea
67. Ancient Italian
68. Trillion: Prefix
69. Sign on
70. Comic actor Arnold
71. Scene of heavy W.W. I fighting

Down

1. Certain Prot.
2. Caused
3. On __ (carousing)
4. Discover
5. Very small painting
6. It's pumped in a gym
7. Gulp from a bottle
8. Hustle music
9. Sixteen oz.
10. Indochina country
11. Progeny
12. Buffoon
13. "___ Miniver"
21. Action word
22. "Just __!"
26. ___ the good
27. Croesus' kingdom
29. Bow-toting god
30. Because
32. Revelation response
33. Mitchell heroine
34. Come and go
35. Prizefighter
37. "I Dream of Jeannie" star
38. Idler
40. Car nut?
44. 1890s Veep ___ P. Morton
45. Affectedly dainty
51. Akron Class AA ball team
52. Wedding ritual
54. Vacant
55. Paperwork units
56. Habituate: Var.
57. Ventriloquist Bergen
59. "Fool for ___," Sam Shepard play
60. Paycheck abbr.
61. Govt. investigator
62. Satisfied sigh
63. Israeli submachine gun

Solution on page 171

Arthur Miller

Across

1. Cpl. or sgt.
4. Sister of Helios
10. Well-put
13. "Thought you'd never __"
14. Warmer, in a way
15. Earsplitting
17. Main character in 16-Down
19. Fr. miss
20. Assistant on the Hill
21. MilleMiglia is its frequent flier program
23. Composer Gustav
25. Beyond, in verse
26. Select, with "for"
27. Church singers
28. "Bel Canto" novelist Patchett
30. Mennonite sect
32. Future rev.'s school
33. Verse starter
34. "Mamma ___!"
35. Arthur Miller's second wife
41. Activate, as a bomb
42. Piece of work
43. Queen ___
45. African nation
48. Soup source
49. Jersey
51. Having four sharps
52. Liberal leader?
54. Novelist Lurie
55. "The ___," Arthur Miller play
58. "All My ___," Arthur Miller play
59. Diva ___ Te Kanawa
60. Disposal of sewage
64. "Out!"
65. The Wizard of Menlo Park
66. Run a tab
67. Bullfight cry
68. Literature Nobelist Gordimer
69. Secret gp.

Down

1. Slangy turndown
2. CBS forensic drama
3. State of USA
4. Tom of "Tomorrow"
5. Moray catcher
6. China's ___-tse
7. Funny Bombeck
8. Kevin formerly of "S.N.L."
9. TV comic Kovacs
10. "Summer and Smoke" heroine
11. Hoi __
12. Dutch export
16. "___ of a Salesman," Arthur Miller play
18. 1953 Leslie Caron role
22. Prepare for competition
23. Roast hosts, briefly
24. "Um, pardon me"
28. Whichever
29. Stealthy Easterner
31. Uglify
33. Einstein's birthplace
34. Hitmakers?
36. Bit of sunshine
37. Afghan's neighbor
38. Sun follower?
39. Something left out
40. Coin with 12 stars on it
44. Topological abbr.
45. Thrills
46. Physicist Fermi
47. Pertaining to a nerve
48. Rum drink
49. Everett in "Citizen Kane"
50. Help for the stumped
53. Barnaby Jones portrayer
54. __ Martin (classic car)
56. Name
57. City near Vance Air Force Base
61. Grammar bestseller "Woe ___"
62. Pained cries
63. PBS helper

Solution on page 171

Anton Chekhov

Across

1. Rhine tributary
5. First year of Cornelius's papacy
9. Raptor's weapon
14. Min. fraction
15. De-crease?
16. "__ Mio"
17. Chekhov's other career
19. "The ___ Sisters," Chekhov play
20. Research site
21. Ability
22. City council rep.
23. Fish covering
25. Chekhov's home country
28. "Oh, brother!"
29. "Son of Frankenstein" role
33. Ref. work
34. "Uncle ___," Chekhov play
36. Cape Town's home: Abbr.
37. Cologne cry
38. Inhabitant of Italy
40. Symbol of solidity
41. Dockworkers' org.
42. Informs
43. Appraise
45. Guns the engine
47. Directly
48. Evening meal
49. Sort out
51. U.N. observer grp.
52. "The ___ Orchard," Chekhov play
55. "The ___," Chekhov play about four theatrical characters
59. Grasps
60. Fag
62. Scope
63. Halley's sci.
64. Football positions
65. "I ___ vacation!"
66. Pitch
67. Soap maker's plate

Down

1. Date with a Dr.
2. "Off the Court" author
3. Actors Alejandro and Fernando
4. Rapturous delight
5. Harvest fly
6. Rugrat's bed
7. Mauna ___, HI
8. B&B
9. General Mills brand
10. Fashion designer Laura
11. Elders' teachings
12. "A Good Scent from a Strange Mountain" Pulitzer winner Robert ___ Butler
13. Depilatory brand
18. Unlawful
21. Roberts of "That '70s Show"
23. Shrunken
24. ___ Major (southern constellation)
25. Show again
26. Verbal white flag
27. Chilled soup
30. Small assemblage
31. Missouri river
32. Autumn toiler
34. Worth
35. Rawboned
39. Lingerie item
44. Orbital extremes
46. Vile
48. Pop singer married twice in 2004 news
50. Getting-off place: Abbr.
52. "The Chinese Parrot" hero
53. "__, James!"
54. Cuxhaven river
55. Friday et al.: Abbr.
56. The ___ Reader (magazine)
57. Former Ford models
58. With a discount of
60. Felix or Fritz
61. Prefix with propyl

Solution on page 171

Romeo and Juliet

Across

1. Des Moines hrs.
4. One of the Pillars of Islam
8. Burnoose wearers
13. Other, to Ortega
15. Three oceans touch it
16. E-mail option
17. Biblical kingdom
18. Job detail, briefly
19. 12-year-old, say
20. Tax
22. Romeo's family name
24. Juliet's family name
26. Physicist Niels
27. They're forbidden
29. Gnawing animal
33. African grassland
36. SeaWorld star
38. ER pronouncement
39. Oy!
40. Quartet member
41. Prepare for action
42. Siemens unit
43. Silent movie star?
44. Appears
45. Small firearm
47. Lazy woman?
49. Type of sec'y
51. Emerge
55. Juliet's age at the start of the play
59. Town where "Romeo and Juliet" is set
60. Some opera singers
61. Prosperity
63. Swear
64. Cord fiber
65. God of thunder
66. Director Riefenstahl
67. Working stiff
68. "Unimaginable as ___ in Heav'n": Milton
69. Oral surgeon's deg.

Down

1. Humorous
2. Leaf opening
3. "The Sound of Music" name
4. Hurry
5. Venomous snake
6. Carpe ___
7. John ___ Astor
8. "Romeo, Romeo, wherefore ___ ___ Romeo?"
9. Recompense for hardship
10. Take down ___: humble
11. Roquefort hue
12. Since, in a seasonal song
14. Teems
21. Place for a letter
23. Bellini heroine
25. "__ With Love"
28. Mall units
30. She plays Carmela on "The Sopranos"
31. Average
32. Small fry
33. Seductress
34. K-12, in education
35. Plain of Jars land
37. Vocally
40. Triple-meter dance, in France
41. Not limited to one class
43. Not friendly
44. Except for
46. Ankle bone
48. Harsh
50. "Choppers"
52. Adored
53. Without a break
54. Count who hopes to marry Juliet
55. Recipe amt.
56. It grows on you
57. "That __ five minutes ago!"
58. Okinawa port
62. Stewbum

Solution on page 172

Chapter 12: Award Winners

Pulitzer Prize for the Novel Before 1950

Across

1. "Time ___ a premium"
5. Benchmarks: Abbr.
9. Caulking material
14. Labels
15. State of USA
16. It's motto is "Dirigo"
17. "The Magnificent ___," winner 1919 Pulitzer Prize for the Novel
19. "The Temptation of St. Anthony" artist
20. Get it?
21. Whence the Magi, with "the"
22. Full of excitement
23. Waterfall
25. Mass __
28. Org.
29. Antagonist
30. Small merganser
31. Edith ___, author of "The Age of Innocence,"
34. Conductor ___-Pekka Salonen
35. Radiator sound
38. Second largest violin
39. Explosives
40. Ring master?
41. Swift black-spotted cat
43. Flows
45. Riddle-me-___
46. ___ Tarkington, author of 17-Across
50. Dignified conduct
52. Devoted fan of a band
54. Eleventh-hour
55. Eastern European
56. Poetically ajar
57. Strap
59. "The ___ ___," winner 1932 Pulitzer Prize for the Novel by Pearl S. Buck
61. Candidate for Supreme Court in the News
62. Topological shapes
63. Greek promenade
64. First computer programmer
65. Greek war goddess
66. MGM co-founder

Down

1. Mississippi source
2. Identical to
3. Superior of a convent
4. China's Lao__
5. 1960 hit by the Everly Brothers
6. Not these
7. Force
8. "___ yer old man!"
9. Greek alphabet ender
10. Baseball's Hank and Tommie
11. "All the ___ ___," winner 1947 Pulitzer Prize for the Novel
12. Young ___
13. Confronted
18. Sheriff's command
22. Playground retort
24. Intimidates
25. "A Confederacy of Dunces" author
26. Superlative suffix
27. First word of "Jabberwocky"
29. Army base near Petersburg, Va.
32. Build up
33. Shorten again, as pants
35. Reddish brown chalcedony
36. Pivot
37. Upton ___, 1943 Pulitzer Prize the Novel winner
39. 10 C-notes
42. In heaven
44. In order that
47. City north of Lisbon
48. Walk softly
49. Bray
51. Title of respect: Abbr.
52. Brilliance
53. Ham's medium
55. By and by
57. Laboratory
58. TV Tarzan Ron
59. Pioneer cell phone co.
60. Handy form of communication?: Abbr.

Solution on page 172

Pulitzer Prize for Fiction in the 1950s

Across

1. Stupid
5. Illustrations
8. Hall of Fame football coach Hank
13. Mayberry role
14. Coffin stand
15. Kind of glasses
16. Author of "A Fable," winner 1955 Pulitzer Prize for Fiction
19. Sun, e.g.
20. Gay Talese's "___ the Sons"
21. "What ___ care?"
22. Novel by A. B. Guthrie, Jr., winner 1950 Pulitzer Prize for Fiction
26. Gymnastics coach Karolyi
27. Where Harleys are mfd.
28. Succulent plant
29. Mediterranean seaport
30. Conrad ___, author of "The Town," winner 1951 Pulitzer Prize for Fiction
34. Hosp. diagnostics
36. Hawaiian medicine man
37. Followed
41. USPS pieces
43. Move forward
44. Milky gem
47. Small denomination
49. Rx writers
50. Prom wheels
51. Author of "The Caine Mutiny," winner 1952 Pulitzer Prize for Fiction
55. Actress Ruby
56. Big bag
57. Former USIA division
58. Author of "The Old Man and the Sea," winner 1953 Pulitzer Prize for Fiction
64. Dump into a Dumpster
65. Tach readings
66. The Buckeye State
67. Signs of sadness
68. Put to work
69. Average guy?

Down

1. Average name
2. A.P. competitor
3. Bag thickness
4. Not on deck
5. Ready follower
6. Do a pit job
7. Transverse beam
8. Man from U.N.C.L.E.
9. Toll rd.
10. Melt down, as fat
11. Anatomical ring
12. Robin's sweetie
14. Infant
17. S&L offering
18. Spoke
22. Istanbul native
23. Early Chinese dynasty
24. "___ Dawn I Die" (Cagney/Raft flick)
25. Civil ___
26. ___ nova
31. Form of greeting
32. Rock blaster
33. Hearing range
35. Storekeeper's stock: Abbr.
38. Important PC command
39. Light brown
40. Schoolroom sight
42. Transparent, modern-style
43. Money dispenser, briefly
44. Senior
45. Penetrate
46. Supreme Egyptian god
48. Heebie-jeebies
52. Hertz competitor
53. Alternative to smoking
54. Transport vehicle
56. Rx amts.
59. Hoop site
60. Toulouse title: Abbr.
61. First name?
62. Make public
63. Day, in Hebrew

Solution on page 172

Pulitzer Prize for Fiction in the 1960s

Across

1. Multitude
5. Crimson Tide, briefly
9. Part of Nasdaq: Abbr.
14. City on Fukien coast
15. Bidding site on the Net
16. Halt
17. Author of "To Kill a Mockingbird," winner 1961 Pulitzer Prize for Fiction
19. Bothered
20. A, And, The, e.g.
21. "___ and Consent," winner 1960 Pulitzer Prize for Fiction
22. Second-century date
23. Not relaxed
25. Keep possession of
28. U.K. foe of 1982
29. "House Made of ___," winner 1969 Pulitzer Prize for Fiction
33. Resell illegally
34. Languor
36. Yonder yacht
37. Part of many German names
38. "The Edge of ___," winner 1962 Pulitzer Prize for Fiction
40. Put in stitches
41. Work at
42. Advantages
43. Feminine suffixes
45. "Anna and the King" setting
47. Disfigure
48. Contemptibly small
49. The "E" in EGBDF
51. Writer Rand
52. Selected
55. Activist's activity
59. "The Keepers of the ___," winner 1965 Pulitzer Prize for Fiction
60. "The Confessions of ___ ___," winner 1968 Pulitzer Prize for Fiction
62. Put into words
63. Orrin Hatch's state
64. "Render therefore ___ Caesar..."
65. Lens
66. Monument Valley feature
67. Sail holder

Down

1. Gag reflex?
2. "Rubaiyat" writer
3. Breed
4. Average
5. Capital of Germany
6. Fit for the job
7. West of cinema
8. Affirmative vote
9. Chem lab array
10. Worked for
11. H.H. Munro's pen name
12. Suffix for abnormalities
13. Transfer
18. Overshadow
21. Cattle breed
23. Tanning place
24. Sea birds
25. Answers an invitation
26. Dangerous strain
27. Roberts of "That '70s Show"
30. Bus. aides
31. Caracole
32. Informative
34. Mystery writer's award
35. Poker phrase
39. Commercial makers
44. Sudden burst of temper
46. Pickles
48. Sister of Mary and Lazarus
50. Takes a turn?
52. Big swig
53. Lanford Wilson's "The ___ Baltimore"
54. "___ sight!"
55. Fund-raising grps.
56. Sicilian city
57. Goes down
58. Gait faster than a walk
60. Book before Deut.
61. Swallowed

Solution on page 172

Pulitzer Prize for Fiction in the 1970s

Across

1. Sportscaster Albert
5. Nor. neighbor
8. Song from Bob Dylan's "Desire"
12. Certain plaintiff, at law
13. Glimpsed
14. Grind
15. Gain altitude
16. Silver State sch.
17. Bacon product
18. "___ Gift," winner 1976 Pulitzer Prize for Fiction
20. More than just interested
21. Jittery
22. Morrison of the Doors
23. "The ___ Angels," winner 1975 Pulitzer Prize for Fiction
26. "Gravity's ___," denied 1974 prize by Pulitzer board
30. ___ Cologne (skunk of cartoons)
31. Bivalve mollusk
34. Whit
35. Memorize
37. Bean holder
38. Olympic skater Cohen
39. Tolstoy's Karenina
40. Evening
42. Brief time
43. Wallace ___, author of "Angle of Repose," winner 1972 Pulitzer Prize for Fiction
45. Woodland deities
47. Car wash option
48. Kama ___

50. Capital of the French department Calvados
52. James Alan ___, author of "Elbow Room," winner 1978 Pulitzer Prize for Fiction
56. Montezuma, for one
57. Deal with successfully
58. Oz visitor Dorothy
59. Sturdy
60. Takeoff artist
61. They may be split
62. Spring flower
63. Three times, in Rx's
64. Audition

Down

1. Go, to the dogs
2. Without ___ (broke)
3. 500 sheets
4. Consisting of words
5. Ships
6. Eudora ___, author of "The Optimist's Daughter," winner 1973 Pulitzer Prize for Fiction
7. Ltr. holders
8. Inability to sleep
9. Be rude to
10. "Well, well!"
11. Reserved
13. Sweltering
14. Bottled spirits
19. Two-run homer prerequisite
22. It holds the mayo
23. They're nuts
24. Birth cert., e.g.
25. Jungle vine
26. Some wines
27. Overbearing

28. Alternative
29. WWII women
32. Stud poker?
33. Oodles of ounces
36. Sneezing causes
38. It may be vacant
40. Gender
41. Purim honoree
44. 1980's White House name
46. One in the cross hairs
48. Rifle attachment
49. Stimulant
50. Emperor of Russia
51. Italian town
52. Exam for a doc-to-be
53. Playing with a full deck
54. Automotive pioneer
55. Robin's residence
56. Hawaiian tuna

Solution on page 173

Pulitzer Prize for Fiction in the 1980s

Across

1. Rope with running noose
6. Steak ___
11. D.J.'s stack
14. Catch some z's
15. Actress Massey
16. Weed whacker
17. Author of "The Color Purple," winner 1983 Pulitzer Prize for Fiction
19. Early evictee
20. It may be long or short
21. Actor Beatty et al.
22. Fin
24. Hon
26. Cohort of Chevy and Laraine
28. Author of "The Executioner's Song," winner 1980 Pulitzer Prize for Fiction
32. False front
35. Sound astonished
36. U.N. arm
37. First name of author of "Breathing Lessons," winner 1989 Pulitzer Prize for Fiction
38. Transmitter starter
40. Slithery fish
41. Gold Seal co.
42. "I don't think so"
43. Land measures
44. Novel by John Updike, winner 1982 Pulitzer Prize for Fiction
48. Greek column style
49. Spirits
53. Spanish diacritic
55. Author Silverstein
56. Soccer phenom Freddy
57. "...___ quit!"
58. Author of "A Summons to Memphis," winner 1987 Pulitzer Prize for Fiction
62. Word in most Commandments
63. Youngest of Chekhov's "Three Sisters"
64. Japanese porcelain
65. Hazardous for driving
66. Beethoven's last symphony
67. Billiard shot

Down

1. Future J.D.s' hurdles
2. Permit
3. Fishing net
4. Brief time
5. Sandal feature
6. Crown
7. Woes
8. Fine, informally
9. Tampa-to-Jacksonville dir.
10. Flap attached to a cap
11. Chivalrous man
12. "Lonesome ___," winner 1986 Pulitzer Prize for Fiction
13. Oracle
18. "Witness" director Peter
23. A mean Amin
25. "___ petit placidam sub libertate quietem" (motto of Massachusetts)
26. Growl
27. The Pointer Sisters' "___ Excited"
29. Chills
30. Fashion monthly
31. The supreme Supreme
32. Teri of "After Hours"
33. Donald, to Dewey
34. Lack of ability
38. "Don't look at me!"
39. Kind of proportions
40. Recording studio effect
42. Skittle
43. Proclaim with approval
45. Muscle beach sight
46. Gung-ho
47. "___ a Song Go Out of My Heart"
50. NFL cofounder George
51. Smells
52. Alison ___, author of "Foreign Affairs," winner 1985 Pulitzer Prize for Fiction
53. First name of author of "Beloved," winner 1988 Pulitzer Prize for Fiction
54. ___-Z (Camaro model)
55. Shipped
59. "___ tu" (Verdi aria)
60. Bronze metal
61. Singer Sumac

Solution on page 173

Pulitzer Prize for Fiction in the 1990s

Across

1. Stumble
5. Securely confined
9. Get rid of
14. "La Dolce Vita" composer
15. One way to stand by
16. Words of empathy
17. Touts' hangouts, briefly
18. Dark film genre
19. TV producer Spelling
20. Novel by E. Annie Proulx, winner 1994 Pulitzer Prize for Fiction
23. Left on a map
24. They may be lent or bent
25. Conditional release
28. Lao-tzu's system
32. "It's ___!"
33. Tribal emblem
36. It's heard in a herd
37. "A ___ Scent from a Strange Mountain," winner 1993 Pulitzer Prize for Fiction
38. "The ___," winner 1999 Pulitzer Prize for Fiction
39. Inner surface of the hand
40. Paintings
41. Like a chimney sweep
42. Chocolate alternative
43. Egypt's Lake ___
45. Refuses
46. Coffee dispensers
48. It's soothing
49. Novel by Richard Ford, winner Pulitzer and PEN/Faulkner in 1996
56. "Johnny B. ___": Berry hit
57. Gazed at
58. Prime time hour
59. Like days of yore
60. Visitor to Siam
61. "___ Little Tenderness"
62. Fowl pole?
63. Stem-to-stern strip
64. Dwarf, e.g.

Down

1. Easy gait
2. Philip ___, author of "American Pastoral," winner 1998 Pulitzer Prize for Fiction
3. "Let ___"
4. What phishers try to catch
5. Gary of "CSI: NY"
6. Embrace
7. Smart-alecky
8. High nest: Var.
9. Schematic
10. Kid's retort
11. Gross minus net
12. Cornfield pest
13. Roosters' mates
21. Alternative to high water
22. Basketball Hall of Famers Archibald and Thurmond
25. Heathen
26. Old marketplace
27. Mob scenes
29. Building supports
30. Where dos are done
31. "The ___ Kings Play Songs of Love," winner 1990 Pulitzer Prize for Fiction
33. Also
34. No longer hot
35. Sample
38. "Deed I Do" singer
39. Remittances
41. Snake
42. It may follow trig
44. Soft leathers
45. Flip-flop, e.g.
47. ___ preview
48. Designer Geoffrey
49. Frankenstein's assistant
50. ___ contendere
51. Extinct bird
52. Fraction of a newton
53. Grime
54. "Dragonwyck" author Seton
55. Wine buyer's concern

Solution on page 173

Pulitzer Prize for General Non-Fiction

Across

1. ___ buco (veal dish)
5. Army div.
10. Assign to a role
14. Birthday thought
15. Horse opera
16. Tutsi foe
17. "The Soul of a ___ ___," winner 1982 Pulitzer Prize for General Non-Fiction
19. Teen follower?
20. Early 12th-century date
21. "Yeah, right"
23. "Pilgrim at Tinker ___," winner 1975 Pulitzer Prize for General Non-Fiction
26. State in the SE United States
29. Just right
30. Haste, in Hanover
31. Pretend
32. Give away
34. Folkie Guthrie
36. "Guns, ___, ___ ___," winner 1998 Pulitzer Prize for General Non-Fiction
41. Boxing prize
42. Shoot for, with "to"
44. French farewell
48. "Was to be," in Latin
50. "___ out?"
51. Author of "The Dragons of Eden," winner 1978 Pulitzer Prize for General Non-Fiction
53. Grps.
54. Dress
55. Kind of palm
57. Wine: Prefix
58. "___ ___ ___: An Oral History of World War Two," winner 1985 Pulitzer Prize for General Non-Fiction
64. End of the road?
65. Pitcher Ryan
66. Word on a price tag
67. By way of, briefly
68. In the loop
69. Snick and ___

Down

1. "A League of Their ___"
2. You: Ger.
3. U-turn from NNE
4. Meter which measures electrical resistance
5. Places
6. Bounty stop of 1788
7. "Lord, is ___?": Matthew
8. Pitcher Robb ___
9. Refrigerant gas
10. Gliding dance step
11. "The Guns of ___," winner 1963 Pulitzer Prize for General Non-Fiction
12. Dorm room staple
13. Deep dish
18. When doubled, defensive fire
22. Spartan serfs
23. Municipal facility: Abbr.
24. Film director Nicolas
25. Gutter locale
27. Hyundai model
28. Hardly Joe Cool
30. "Or ___!"
33. Surprise attack
35. Future atty.'s exam
37. "Break ___!"
38. Serial segments
39. Oberhausen one
40. Writer Hubbard
43. Med. drama sites
44. Buttonhole
45. 4th letter of the Hebrew alphabet
46. Mangle user
47. Manolete nemesis
49. Patron Saint of Scandinavia
52. Prudential competitor
53. Erenow
56. Tip-top
59. Reporter's query
60. Guidonian note
61. Pasty-faced
62. Whiz
63. Line score letters

Solution on page 173

Pulitzer Prize for Drama in the 1980s

Across

1. Cartoonist Addams
5. Henry VIII's last wife
9. Banned pollutants
13. Place to roll?
15. Province
16. You, once
17. Pave over
18. Retired Senator Sam
19. Diva's song
20. "___ ___ Daisy," winner 1988 Pulitzer Prize for Drama
23. Prov. on Niagara Falls
24. Floors, briefly
25. In the red
27. __ Rice Burroughs
30. Third sign of the zodiac
32. Like an oxeye window
33. The O'Haras' home
35. Chest-thumping
38. St. Petersburg's river
39. "Crimes of the ___," winner 1981 Pulitzer Prize for Drama
41. "A Soldier's ___," winner 1982 Pulitzer Prize for Drama
42. "My Fair Lady" lady
44. ___ account (never)
45. Sushi supplies
46. Guard against assault
48. Bonkers
50. Saxony seaport
51. Kind of rally
52. Turkish chief
53. Wendy ___, playwright of 10-Down

60. Bay on Somersetshire coast
62. Outscore
63. Writer Jong
64. Tore
65. Limping
66. Precept
67. One of four Holy Roman emperors
68. Osman, for one
69. Classic sneakers

Down

1. Roster
2. Word form of "sacred"
3. Piedmont city
4. Serb or Croat
5. Sudden pains
6. Cuckoopint, for one
7. Italian artist Guido
8. Kidnapper's demand
9. Ed. group
10. "The Heidi ___," winner 1989 Pulitzer Prize for Drama
11. Existence
12. Rump
14. Actress Eleniak
21. Needle point?
22. Triathlon leg
26. Sulky
27. First name in stunts
28. Playwright of "Glengarry Glen Ross," winner 1984 Pulitzer Prize for Drama
29. Lustrous
30. Thou

31. Work for
32. I
34. Many millennia
36. Circle overhead?
37. Sounds of woe
40. Printer powder
43. Three or four
47. Make possible
49. Overturn
50. Memphis locale
51. 1976 Oscar winner Finch
52. Too
54. A-line line
55. Scandinavian native
56. "Star __"
57. Article in Die Zeit
58. Bumped off
59. D.C. baseballers
61. Tokyo, once

Solution on page 173

Pulitzer Prize for Drama in the 1990s

Across

1. Puts up, in a way
6. Blokes
11. Sweat shop?
14. End of ___
15. Lama's land
16. Tulsa sch.
17. Playwright of "Three Tall Women," winner 1994 Pulitzer Prize for Drama
19. B.S., e.g.
20. Ersatz
21. Feathers
22. "The Simpsons" storekeeper
23. Castro's country
25. Cole Porter's "___ Men"
27. Health resorts
28. Encourage
30. Go along with
32. "___ luck?"
33. Orchard unit
35. VCR insert
36. Playwright of "Lost in Yonkers," winner 1991 Pulitzer Prize for Drama
39. Sightsee
41. In
42. Middle grade
45. Kind of license
47. Acid neutralizers
49. Bookie's concern
50. Yogi's language
53. Winner 1996 Pulitzer Prize for Drama (playwright Jonathan Larson)
54. Prefix with angular
55. B'way postings
56. This, in Tijuana
58. Waiter's reward
59. Playwright of "Angels in America," winner 1993 Pulitzer Prize for Drama
63. Juan's wife
64. Kind of group, in chemistry
65. Relish
66. Civil War monogram
67. Bing Crosby's record label
68. Escalator feature

Down

1. "Some ___ meat and canna eat": Burns
2. So-so link
3. Paperboy
4. Kind of cracker
5. TV chef Moulton
6. Windy City transportation inits.
7. Poet Doolittle
8. Head monk
9. Little one
10. Anna of "Nana"
11. Picnic provision
12. Whip up
13. ___ Wilson, playwright of "The Piano Lesson," winner 1990 Pulitzer Prize for Drama
18. Composer Shostakovich
23. Tax preparer, for short
24. Coffeepot
26. Bread end
27. Read with a laser
29. Cheri of "SNL"
31. Inventory
34. Computer key
36. Bonkers
37. "___ no idea!"
38. Surroundings
39. "How I Learned ___ ___," winner 1998 Pulitzer Prize for Drama
40. Having an Oedipus complex
42. To make rid of
43. Article of Cologne
44. Attendance fig., often
45. Katie Holmes role in Dawson's Creek
46. Auto trim
48. Legendary king of Britain
51. Kind of column
52. "No Strings Attached" pop group
55. African village
57. NCO rank
60. Hawaiian acacia
61. Sched. guess
62. 16 1/2 feet

Solution on page 173

Hugo Awards

Across

1. "The Sweetheart of Sigma ___"
4. Pt. of a monogram
8. Unloads
13. Yearn
15. Griffin behind the "Wheel"
16. Stopped
17. Sermon ender
18. Tel ___, Israel
19. Some petty officers, for short
20. Science fiction novel by William Gibson that won the 1985 Hugo Award
23. Ascend
24. Archaeological object
29. "The buck stops here" monogram
30. Key to getting out of trouble?
33. Author of "The Gods Themselves," 1973 Hugo Award winner
34. "__ Brew": 1976 film
37. Almost forever
38. Author of "Rendezvous with Rama," 1974 Hugo Award winner
42. Classic cookie
43. Sagging
44. Ursula K. __ ___, winner of 1975 Hugo Award
47. Kid
48. Inflation meas.
51. Manhattan area
54. Pre-1917 autocrats
56. "___ ___ and the Goblet of Fire," winner of 2001 Hugo Award
59. Get in one's sights
63. Makes angry
64. Horace's handle
65. Stage play
66. November choice
67. Ceremony
68. Sylvan deity
69. Hockey's Lindros
70. D.C. type

Down

1. Grip
2. Monopoly buys
3. Feel in one's heart
4. Mosque official
5. Gulf of Finland feeder
6. Youngest of Chekhov's "Three Sisters"
7. Combo unit
8. Ruins
9. Classic card game
10. OR workers
11. White House souvenir
12. 1960's radical grp.
14. Microbe
21. Voodoo
22. Seventh in a series
25. Intensely ardent
26. Run ___ (go crazy)
27. Dairy Queen order
28. Remote targets
31. Good name for a cook
32. Orson Scott ___, winner of 1986 and 1987 Hugo Awards
34. Malt brew
35. A.T.M. maker
36. Caledonian
38. WATS part
39. Rules, for short
40. John of England
41. After "is," probably will
42. Hearty cheer
45. Beatty bomb of 1987
46. Long or Peeples
48. Treat for tabby
49. Magician's cry
50. Six-Day War side
52. Shot from a tee
53. Trial's partner
55. "Double ___," winner of 1956 Hugo Award
57. Hairy Himalayan
58. Min. fraction
59. Come-ons
60. Nest egg component
61. Padded surface
62. Actress Brenneman

Solution on page 174

Nobel Prize in Literature Before 1950

Across

1. City on Fukien coast
5. Switch position
8. Doings
14. Tennis score
15. Big D.C. lobby
16. Like a virgin?
17. Lofty lines
18. Stable snack
19. Job preceder
20. Winner of 1946 Nobel Prize in Literature, author of "Steppenwolf"
23. Suffix with drunk or tank
24. Windshield sticker
25. Gaffe
29. Captain for 40 days and nights
31. Actor Gibson
33. Words before profit or loss
34. Opening of the nose
38. No sound-alike
39. Winner of 1930 Nobel Prize in Literature, author of "Arrowsmith"
42. Rider's command
43. Former capital of Kazakhstan
44. Quote the raven
45. Sport ___
46. Rushes
49. Influences
51. Above
55. Daisy ___
57. Winner of 1936 Nobel Prize in Literature, author of "The Iceman Cometh"
60. Rectangle having equal sides
63. Scotland's longest river
64. Sons of, in Hebrew
65. "Pride and Prejudice" author
66. Portfolio part, in brief
67. San ___ (Riviera resort)
68. Ltr. opener
69. Room extension
70. Not name

Down

1. Wahine's welcome
2. Contemporary
3. Exaggerate
4. Polite reply from a ranch hand
5. All __ page
6. Cameroon coin
7. Earl "__" Hines
8. Party times
9. Ship
10. Organic compound
11. ___ degree
12. Inventor's monogram
13. 35mm camera
21. Concerned with a specific subject
22. Where Mark Twain is buried
26. Hindu princess
27. Native Oklahomans
28. Inexperienced
30. "Finnegans Wake" wife
32. "The Intimate ___" (1990 jazz album)
35. Louver feature
36. "Thy Neighbor's Wife" author
37. Outer limit
38. "The Bridge on the River ___"
39. George Bernard ___, winner of 1925 Nobel Prize in Literature
40. Part of the Corn Belt
41. Wharton's "___ Frome"
42. Places to go in London?
45. Person of great interest
47. "8 Mile" rapper
48. Deli buy
50. William Butler ___, winner of 1923 Nobel Prize in Literature
52. Free
53. First name of winner of 1938 Nobel Prize in Literature, author of "East Wind: West Wind"
54. Shade of blue
56. T. S. ___, winner of 1948 Nobel Prize in Literature
58. Washington and Wellington: Abbr.
59. Rain in Spain collector
60. Walton of Wal-Mart
61. Can. province
62. Liner letters

Solution on page 174

Nobel Prize in Literature After 1950

Across

1. Accompanied by
5. Gumbo vegetables
10. "How long has it __?"
14. Mediterranean port of Spain
15. Singer Bonnie
16. Female friend, in France
17. Winner of 1976 Nobel Prize in Literature, author of "The Adventures of Augie March"
19. "Your majesty"
20. Craggy ridge
21. Unenlightened
23. Mother ___
25. Wight or Man
26. Sequentially
32. Capt.'s superior
35. Neck and neck
36. Authoritative text
37. General Robert __
39. Anaheim player
42. 1988 N.L. Rookie of the Year Chris
43. Gentle as ___
45. Drs. Zira and Zaius, e.g.
47. Sydney is its cap.
48. Winner of 1993 Nobel Prize in Literature, author of "Song of Solomon"
52. Left
53. Vehicle with caterpillar treads
57. Winner of 1953 Nobel Prize in Literature and Prime Minister
62. The first Mrs. Trump
63. Hemingway sobriquet
64. "La Dolce Vita" actress
66. Mary Kay rival
67. Pola of silent films
68. Ringlet
69. Faxed
70. Clothesline alternative
71. Those, to Tomas

Down

1. Came to
2. "__ you!"
3. More factual
4. Summer top
5. Metal source
6. De __, Illinois
7. Irritate
8. Unaccented
9. Double curve, as in yarn
10. Isaac ___ Singer, winner of 1978 Nobel Prize in Literature
11. Discharge
12. The Emerald Isle
13. Essential
18. Hem in
22. Voluble
24. Three oceans touch it
27. Writer
28. Mystery writer's award
29. Abba
30. Some Harvard U. degrees
31. "Ouch!"
32. Vegetarian's no-no
33. Greeting in Grenoble
34. ___-Paul Sartre, declined 1964 Nobel Prize in Literature
38. Expatriate
40. Over: Prefix
41. Discounted by
44. College QB, often
46. Actress Braga
49. In stock
50. "Misery" director
51. Beginner
54. Albert ___, winner of 1957 Nobel Prize in Literature, author of "The Stranger"
55. S.A. cowboy
56. Asian weight units
57. Auditors
58. Experience
59. "Once ___ a time…"
60. Sluggish
61. Act the siren
65. White wine aperitif

Solution on page 174

National Book Awards Before 1980

Across

1. Shelter
7. Breakfast cereal
13. "The Complete Stories of Flannery ___," 1972 National Book Award winner
15. Thomas ___, 1974 National Book Award winner for "Gravity's Rainbow"
16. Way out
17. Groups
18. Leaves home?
19. Heed
21. Suffix with chlor-
22. Artist
24. Letters on a brandy bottle
27. "The nerve!"
28. Philip ___, 1960 National Book Award winner for "Goodbye, Columbus"
29. W.W. II agcy.
32. Dolly of "Hello, Dolly!"
33. Yolk of an egg
35. Freight
37. Super power
39. Minute Maid Park player
40. "From ___ ___ Eternity," 1952 National Book Award winner
42. Eye part
44. Finalize, with "up"
45. Horizontal bar of wood
46. Capable of being moved
48. Part of the bargain
49. Stupid
50. Engine speed, for short
53. Davis et al.
54. Garr of "Tootsie"
55. Function
58. Robert Devereux's crime
61. John ___, 1958 National Book Award winner for "The Wapshot Chronicle"
62. Somebody
63. Cultivated
64. Thornton ___, 1968 National Book Award winner for "The Eighth Day"

Down

1. Egypt's Mubarak
2. Behaved
3. From Bergen
4. Buzzing pest
5. Actress Sothern
6. Baseball's Maris, to pals
7. Puzzle
8. Family name at Indy
9. Keynes's subj.
10. Nasdaq unit: Abbr.
11. Sodom escapee
12. Power holders
14. Take over for
15. Fake jewelry
20. "___ Man," 1953 National Book Award winner by Ralph Ellison
22. Cockpit figure
23. "Wheel of Fortune" buy
24. Electrical units
25. Mom-and-pop enterprise
26. "Man!"
28. "Kidnapped" author's inits.
29. Earthy pigment
30. Joyous hymn
31. Right Guard rival
34. Softens
36. Salon stuff
38. Unwed fathers
41. Left out
43. French pronoun
47. Playful mammal
49. Bob's companion
50. Mend the lawn
51. Lying facedown
52. Clementine's father, e.g.
53. Composer Jacques
54. Old Chinese money
55. When D.S.T. ends
56. ___ Beta Kappa
57. Unagi, at a sushi bar
59. Dustup
60. Brit. record label

Solution on page 174

National Book Awards in the 1980s and 1990s

Across

1. ___ DeLillo, 1985 National Book Award winner
4. Slowly, in music
9. ___ Linda, CA
13. Dramatic opening?
14. Strand in winter, maybe
15. Norse war god
16. Dismounted
17. Sixty
19. "Sophie's ___," 1980 National Book Award winner (Hardcover)
21. E.L. ___, 1986 National Book Award winner
22. Nuns
24. V.P. under G.R.F.
25. Moira Kelly did her voice in "The Lion King"
27. First name in clowndom
32. Regarding, in memos
36. Sidewalk Santa, e.g.
38. Blazing stars
39. 1993 National Book Award winner by E. Annie Proulx
42. Quemoy neighbor
43. Anklebones
44. Ural River city
45. Pipsqueak
47. Overstuff
49. Long period
51. Author of "Cold Mountain," 1997 National Book Award winner
56. Planetoid
61. Of no use
62. Author of "The World According to Garp," 1980 National Book Award winner (Paperback)
64. Fed. travel monitor
65. Novelist Paton
66. Lofty roost
67. Greek goddess of the earth
68. Do a critic's job
69. Spoken for
70. Leak sound

Down

1. City on the Yamuna River
2. Stews
3. Untagged?
4. Intellectuals
5. Command level: Abbr.
6. Hardly a BMOC
7. Fasten, as a ribbon
8. Kind of garage
9. Bonkers
10. Aroma
11. Joan of art
12. From the top
13. Foul weather wear
18. Packing a punch
20. Long time: Abbr.
23. Wasn't vigilant
26. Oscars org.
28. Taboo
29. Swear as true
30. Cops enforce them
31. Education station
32. They're often pressed for cash
33. Sovereign
34. Four: Prefix
35. Bone prefix
37. Rice ___
40. Arm bones
41. Gaseous element
46. Not skilled in
48. Have
50. Skin care name
52. Criticizes sharply
53. Tiny bits
54. Pluralizers
55. Self-titled sitcom
56. Admitting a draft
57. Alone: Stage direction
58. "Take __!"
59. Feminizing suffix
60. Bogarde of film
63. Never, in Nuremberg

Solution on page 174

Chapter 13: Children's Books

Dr. Seuss

Across

1. Hot times abroad
5. Ship's company
9. Harsh
14. Kicked in
15. Russo of "In the Line of Fire"
16. Bird of prey
17. Dr. Seuss book about colorful food
20. Versace rival
21. Bad atmosphere
22. Snoot
24. Lord's Prayer start
25. Without premeditation
30. ___ Pepper
33. Fly catcher
34. Creature of habit?
35. Basketball Hall-of-Famer Harshman
36. Mtn. stats
37. Quarterback Favre
39. Mars, to the Greeks
40. Scream
41. Clumsy sort
42. Word in many university names
43. "Hop on ___," Dr. Seuss book
44. "The ___ ___ ___ ___," Dr. Seuss feline book
47. Sun. talk
48. Math rings
49. On
52. Tropical fruit
56. "One Fish Two Fish ___ ___ ___ ___," Dr. Seuss book
60. Theater awards since 1956
61. "Pardon..."

62. Stage opening
63. World's largest manufacturer of farm equipment
64. "___ small world!"
65. Tim of "WKRP in Cincinnati"

Down

1. Pudding ingredient
2. O'Hara's estate
3. Anon's partner
4. Come across as
5. Richard of TV's "The Real McCoys"
6. District
7. H.S. requirement
8. Guitarist Montgomery
9. Exceptional intellect
10. Fuzzbuster's detection
11. Short pans
12. Deception
13. Disaster relief org.
18. Foul
19. Quantity
23. Advantage
25. Acute
26. Salk's conquest
27. At the summit
28. Tree house?
29. In the open
30. Fergie, formally
31. Van Susteren of Fox News
32. GE product
35. Pal

37. College ___
38. Pied Piper follower
42. Glisten
44. Shade of red
45. Court figures
46. Psychological injury
47. Morley of "60 Minutes"
49. Texas shortstop, familiarly
50. Tony winner Neuwirth
51. Cartoon dog
53. Many miles off
54. "Well done!"
55. Italian wine city
57. "Bali ___"
58. Common preservative
59. Masked

Solution on page 175

The Little Engine That Could

Across

1. Beethoven's "Archduke ___"
5. Jots
10. Small salamanders
14. Rope fiber
15. La ___ (Milan opera house)
16. Sunscreen additive
17. Tidy up, in a way
18. Little Engine's motto going up
20. Pastor
22. Extreme
23. ___ Helens
24. Big do
26. Inuit
29. Little Engine's motto going down: "I ___ I could"
32. Thomas Jefferson, religiously
33. Pandemonium
34. "So that's it!"
36. Kind of warfare
37. Window covering
38. Resign
39. Ike's command
40. Fair-haired
41. Fencing action
42. Intimidate
44. Boil
45. Personal appearance
46. Hot Pontiacs
47. Obviously surprised
50. Little Engine's obstacle to overcome
54. Pleasingly formed
57. Turned on by
58. Stink ending
59. Montmartre dearest
60. Wallet wad
61. Little Engine's destination
62. 16th century Italian poet
63. Moniker

Down

1. 1969 Oates novel
2. Italian naturalist Francesco
3. Poker player's declaration
4. Value taught in "The Little Engine That Could"
5. "No kidding?"
6. Group of eight
7. Himalayan goat
8. "Aladdin" prince
9. ___ Jose
10. Novel ending
11. It's true
12. It gives skiers a lift
13. Mideast capital
19. Monetary unit of Turkey
21. Mo.-end document
24. Lend ___ (help)
25. Little Engine's cargo along with toys
26. Margin
27. Look after
28. Bolshoi rival
29. Biblically yours
30. Stomping ground
31. Femoral region
33. Toy that flagged down the Little Engine
35. To ___: exactly
37. Blue-gray
38. Interrogative sentence
40. Lasting a short time
41. "Exodus" author Uris
43. Hire
44. Workroom
46. Gadabouts
47. "Never Wave at ___": 1952 film
48. Spice Girl Halliwell
49. Greatly
50. Tussaud, et al.
51. Sigmund's daughter
52. Couple
53. Button, to Frosty
55. When DST ends
56. Volga, formerly

Solution on page 175

The Wizard of Oz

Across

1. Go off
6. Don Adam's detective
11. __-Magnon
14. Philanthropist
15. Desert havens
16. Vintner's prefix
17. Composition of Dorothy's path in "The Wizard of Oz"
19. Suffix with form
20. Some choir members
21. Union agreements?
22. Scandal sheet
23. Dorothy's dog in "The Wizard of Oz"
25. Piston, for one, briefly
27. Actress Winslet
28. Cutting tooth
30. Peril
32. Slangy denial
33. French articles
35. Marsh plant
36. Brainless character in "The Wizard of Oz"
39. Pitcher's boo-boo
41. Present day?
42. "Think" sloganeer
45. Nonsense
47. "1984" setting
49. Get ___ deal
50. Rice-___
53. Feel sorry for
54. All-Star reliever Robb
55. Self-satisfied
56. Last of a Latin trio
58. Benchmark: Abbr.
59. Wizard's location in "The Wizard of Oz"
63. ___ Z
64. Gives up
65. Percentage
66. __ Marino
67. Lock of hair
68. Specialized angler

Down

1. Popular ice cream maker
2. Future school?
3. Open
4. Hoi __
5. Meadowlands gait
6. Bawl
7. "The Sound of Music" heroine
8. Actor's whisper
9. Catalog
10. Disapproving sounds
11. Trait the lion wants in "The Wizard of Oz"
12. Associated
13. Military catapult
18. A Ryder
23. Woodman's element in "The Wizard of Oz"
24. Out __ limb
26. ___ Rabbit
27. Was familiar with
29. Draws into mouth
31. Resulted (from)
34. Census datum
36. Lento
37. "Let's go!"
38. Pertaining to the races
39. Priest's square cap
40. Forsake
42. First
43. Short time
44. Indy 500 month
45. Dorothy's state in "The Wizard of Oz"
46. Pound
48. Geronimo, for one
51. Paris's ___ Rivoli
52. Cruel dudes
55. Certain subdivision
57. Retailer's gds.
60. Balaam's beast
61. It's past due
62. "___ out!" (ump's call)

Solution on page 175

Harry Potter

Across

1. Dressed
5. Barney's nickname for his boss, the sheriff
9. Ancient region near the Dead Sea
13. Slow movement
14. Body of honeybees
15. Entice
16. Entre ___ (confidentially)
17. Windex targets
18. "___ Angel": West movie
19. "Harry Potter" author
21. "The ___ Incident" (1943 Fonda film)
22. Nonclerical group
23. Olympic sprinting champion Devers
24. Warhol genre
27. Noyes or Nobel
29. Ocelot features
30. First name of Harry Potter's father
32. Barrier
34. Filly's father
35. Pig language?
36. Like old recordings
37. Egyptian boy king
38. Backed
39. ___ Island, Fla.
40. A person without magical abilities in "Harry Potter" books
42. Calling
43. "The Music Man" city
44. Committee head
46. Animals
48. Ballgame played by Harry Potter

52. Chilled
53. Murder by suffocation
54. Crow's-nest cry
55. "Titanic" heroine
56. Fastener for Rosie
57. Irving hero
58. Wide-mouthed pitcher
59. Sidewalk stand drinks
60. Prefix with -morph

Down

1. "And" or "or": Abbr.
2. "Over there!"
3. Côte d'___
4. Uninhabited
5. Be ready for
6. Fran Drescher TV role
7. Diver Louganis
8. German river
9. Potion
10. Headmaster at Harry Potter's school
11. Yes-___ question
12. Copy cats?
14. Alley challenge
20. Conflicts
21. Buffoons
23. Narrow valley
24. Attention getter
25. Kind of den
26. Inhabitant of Portugal
27. Within
28. Move rhythmically
30. Green hue
31. Partook of
33. Othello, e.g.

35. First name of Harry Potter's mother
36. Wedding
38. Site of the Taj Mahal
39. Female servant
41. Male goose
42. Army trainee
44. Bend
45. Ups
46. Last word in the fourth "Harry Potter" book
47. Have ___ (freak out)
48. One pound sterling
49. Comparison word
50. Part of a parachute
51. Shot in the arm
53. Swimsuit top

Solution on page 175

The Hardy Boys

Across

1. IRA part
5. Stadium stats
9. Play makers?
13. Adriatic wind
14. Vader of "Star Wars"
15. Attire for Galahad
16. Pace
17. Hells Canyon state
18. London greeting
19. Father's job in "The Hardy Boys"
21. Sound
22. Gregarious: Comb. form
23. Middle eastern dry streambed
24. Change
27. Has a feeling
29. "Now!" in Nicaragua
30. Ashes, e.g.
32. Pitcher Fernandez
34. "Holy ___!"
35. Elder Hardy boy
36. Clarified butter
37. Conductor __-Pekka Salonen
38. Noise
39. Rimes of country music
40. High waisted style of 19th century dress
42. Kingdom in N Europe
43. City near Provo, Utah
44. Where the heart is
46. Bit of parsley
48. Collaborate
52. Like puppies
53. La ___, Calif.
54. Plastic ingredient
55. Book after Joel
56. Cantilevered window
57. Mysophobiac's fear
58. Bluster
59. Env. contents
60. "The moan of doves in immemorial ___": Tennyson

Down

1. Opening run
2. "Unforgettable" singer
3. Lit ___ (college course, familiarly)
4. Hand woven pictorial design
5. Pie cuts, essentially
6. Applause
7. "__ Jury" (Spillane novel)
8. HBO rival
9. Makes right
10. Girlfriend of 35-Across
11. Finish the bathroom
12. Place for mail
14. Abandon
20. Chewed stimulant
21. Author Fleming and others
23. TV Guide span
24. What "tauto-" means
25. "___ Line Is It Anyway?"
26. Girlfriend of 53-Down
27. Put in the mail
28. Tuscany cathedral city
30. Straight
31. Amscrayed
33. Forswear
35. Configuration
36. The Hardy boys' aunt
38. Victory: Ger.
39. Give the slip to
41. One doing clerical work
42. Katmandu's land
44. Baby's woe
45. Swiss features
46. Cut line
47. Mountain lion
48. Chex choice
49. Seed coating
50. Six years, for a senator
51. Chows down
53. Younger Hardy boy

Solution on page 175

Nancy Drew

Across

1. Court matter
4. Deadens
9. Gazillions
14. Ordinal suffix
15. Worried
16. Training group
17. "There but for the grace of God ___"
18. "Cheers" waitress
19. Court call
20. Nancy Drew's hometown
23. Cricket teams, e.g.
24. System of social perfection
28. Hatcher of "Desperate Housewives"
29. Gull relative
32. Sleeps briefly
33. ___ degree
36. Harbor sights
38. Suffix for boy
39. Drew housekeeper
42. Debt memo
44. Take notice of
45. Desire
46. Nancy Drew's dog
48. Jack Benny catchword
50. Starch used in puddings
54. Mintage
56. Confident
59. Pseudonym of the "Nancy Drew" authors
62. Tribunal
65. "My Cousin Vinny" Oscar winner
66. Carol contraction
67. Like lemon juice
68. Grenoble's department
69. Experiences
70. Code subject
71. Thrills
72. Cookbook phrase

Down

1. Sense of loss
2. Star in Quebec
3. Tremble
4. Button material
5. Beehive Stater
6. Least
7. Neighbor of Java
8. Antlered animal
9. Polar explorer
10. Nancy Drew's dad
11. Sum (up)
12. Rapper Dr. ___
13. Sun. delivery
21. Patti LuPone role
22. Ravenous
25. Physical suffering
26. Taping meas.
27. Hard lumber
30. Antiknock fluid
31. Floor covering
34. "___ moment"
35. Reply
37. Cash boy
39. Extremely popular
40. Oaf
41. Result
42. Part of T.G.I.F.
43. Alley ___, of the comics
47. Happens
49. Nonexperts
51. 1986 self-titled R&B album
52. Cordial
53. West Texas city
55. Poetic feet
57. Dummy Mortimer
58. Heavens above
60. Mayberry tosspot
61. Come in second
62. Craze
63. PC reader
64. Mr. ___ (old whodunit game)

Solution on page 175

Winnie the Pooh

Across

1. Capitol cap
5. Inquires
9. Cancel
14. Springsteen's "___ Fire"
15. Up ___ good
16. City near Venice
17. Mideast royal name
18. Upon
19. Michelangelo masterwork
20. "___ Robin," one of Winnie-the-Pooh's best friends
23. Easter's beginning
24. Present day hero?
25. Rasping instruments
27. Pou __: vantage point
30. Winnie-the-Pooh creator
34. Light ax
39. Portion of time
40. Quatrain rhyme scheme
41. Consecrate
43. "Baseball Tonight" airer
44. Revlon rival
46. Chinese restaurant offering
48. Bay State symbol
50. Pop the question
51. Spook
53. Sign up for
58. "This __ bust!"
61. ___ ___ Wood, where Winnie-the-Pooh lives
64. Find the answer
66. Get copy ready
67. Imply
68. Not our
69. Part of the Hindu trinity
70. "If all __ fails..."
71. Winnie-the-Pooh's favorite food
72. Afternoon affairs
73. Did in

Down

1. Some are slipped
2. Missouri River metropolis
3. Lament
4. Break up, informally
5. Rat-___
6. "And ___ bed"
7. Big name in book publishing
8. Actress Loren
9. Paramount
10. 401, to Marcus
11. Nothing for Nicole
12. "Do ___ others..."
13. Winnie-the-Pooh animal type
21. Pane holder
22. Goes by
26. Seductress
28. Picture
29. Winnie-the-Pooh's wise friend
31. Santa checks it twice
32. "I don't think so"
33. Novelist O'Brien
34. Narrative
35. Coin of ancient Greece
36. Old-time schoolteacher
37. Helps in a heist
38. Small cask
42. Overseas title: Abbr.
45. Bow and arrow skill
47. __ out (barely managed)
49. English poet Dowson
52. "Frasier" dog
54. Celebrities
55. Immune response orchestrator
56. Do blackboard duty
57. Keep getting Mad?
58. Panama, e.g.: Abbr.
59. Artsy Manhattan locale
60. Architect William Van ___
62. 1972 Kentucky Derby winner __ Ridge
63. Letters from the Corinthians
65. Compete (for)

Solution on page 176

Make Way for Ducklings

Across

1. Enterprise counselor
5. Entre ___
9. Flip response?
14. Benjamin Disraeli, e.g.
15. Bridge hand
16. Year, to Yves
17. "Make Way for Ducklings" author
19. Dorothy, to Em
20. "Make Way for Ducklings" food from policeman Michael
21. "Make Way for Ducklings" city
22. French summer
23. PC messages
25. 7-Up competitor
28. Stylish, in the 60's
29. Water swirl
33. Cow catcher
34. Blender setting
36. Hot blood
37. Walk-___: bit parts
38. "Make Way for Ducklings" family name and duck type
40. Carrere of "Wayne's World"
41. Get on in years
42. Match
43. Articulate
45. Sermon's basis
47. Check fig.
48. Transversely
49. Jewish teacher
51. Hollywood's West
52. Second-largest nation
55. Stronghold
59. Roman fountain
60. "Make Way for Ducklings" medal won
62. Metal pin
63. Furthermore
64. Heavy metal
65. Sea mammals
66. Aid in a scam
67. Ballpark figs.

Down

1. Office fill-in
2. Derby
3. Black-and-white predator
4. Ailment
5. Snapple rival
6. Acorn sources
7. Consumption
8. It's a mess
9. Le Duc Tho's city
10. Maroon
11. Turn ___ profit
12. Art ___ (retro style)
13. Taken in
18. End result
21. Justice Ruth ___ Ginsburg
23. Imitate
24. Fable finale
25. Rest on the surface of a liquid
26. Where the buffalo roam
27. "The Private Lives of Elizabeth and ___" (Bette Davis film)
30. "Likewise"
31. Hangs on a clothesline
32. A dog's age
34. Exactly
35. School
39. Jordan's only seaport
44. Molasses
46. Go places
48. Surrounded by
50. Touches up
52. Hubs: Abbr.
53. Indy driver Luyendyk
54. St. Petersburg's river
55. Tip-off
56. Executes
57. Washington in Paris, e.g.
58. Old Fords
60. Tax preparer, for short
61. Priestly garb

Solution on page 176

Charlotte's Web

Across

1. 8th month of the Jewish calendar
5. Pedal pushers
9. Big name in nonstick cookware
13. Pews' place
14. Carriage
15. City on the Truckee River
16. AC or DC
17. ___-Detoo ("Star Wars" droid)
18. Dilettante's delights
19. Mr. ___, farmer in "Charlotte's Web"
21. Buggy places?
22. Smallest
23. Robin Cook thriller
24. Many emigrants have one
27. Maybelline mishaps
29. Foolish
30. Sows
32. Amazement
34. Grounded birds
35. Devotee
36. U.K. honors
37. Sun Yat-___
38. Directed
39. Car parker
40. Hit
42. Meet, as expectations
43. Harvard rival
44. White garment
46. Uses a sieve
48. Rat in "Charlotte's Web"
52. Japheth's father
53. Tippy craft
54. "Coriolanus" setting
55. Boo-boo, in totspeak
56. Sheriff Lobo portrayer
57. Scratches (out)
58. Roseanne, once
59. Maleska's predecessor
60. Hollows

Down

1. "Mockingbird" singer Foxx
2. Manchurian border river
3. ___ plaisir
4. Careless
5. Develops
6. Bother
7. Coll. major
8. However, briefly
9. Psychological injury
10. Full name of Wilbur's savior in "Charlotte's Web"
11. Advance amount
12. Something that is lost
14. Diamond weight
20. Counting-out word
21. Executes
23. USN rank
24. Countless years
25. Shows up
26. Showcase for Wilbur in "Charlotte's Web"
27. Germ
28. Fragrant
30. "___ Pig," spun in Charlotte's web
31. Genesis name
33. Gem State motto word
35. Similar to
36. Overcame
38. Is sick
39. Perfume holder
41. Preference word
42. Boxing ring boundaries
44. Red head
45. In with
46. Snoot
47. "The Music Man" setting
48. Bit of filming
49. Drag
50. The groundhog seeing its shadow, say
51. Untouchables chief
53. Cornfield sound

Solution on page 176

THE EVERYTHING LITERARY CROSSWORDS BOOK • **139**

Little House on the Prairie

Across

1. Eurasian duck
5. Licentious revelry
9. Guam's capital
14. Billion follower
15. Actress Zadora et al.
16. Follow
17. Recklessly daring
19. Oncle's wife
20. ___, amas, amat
21. "Back ___ hour" (shop sign)
22. Flammable material
23. Laura ___ ___, "Little House on the Prairie" author
26. Mini-whirlpool
27. Bucket of bolts
28. Farm bird
30. Manipulator
32. ___ of the Apostles
36. ___ Darya (Aral Sea feeder)
37. U.S. region where "Little House on the Prairie" is set
40. Be in arrears
41. Skip a turn
43. Disappearing phone feature
44. Emasculate
46. Big tournament
48. Support
49. Played father on TV show "Little House on the Prairie"
54. Disavowal
55. "___ Russia $1200" (Bob Hope book)
56. __ de guerre
58. "Alive" setting
59. Older sister's affliction in "Little House on the Prairie"
61. Poker Flat chronicler
62. Hard to come by
63. Blood type, briefly
64. Court postponements
65. Served past
66. Wing: Prefix

Down

1. Emmy-winning Thompson
2. Home of the Dolphins
3. Mistaken
4. Minute
5. For all to see
6. Competitor
7. Profits
8. Fashion monogram
9. The Scourge of God
10. Old-timer
11. "Cold Case Files" carrier
12. Fertilizer ingredient
13. K.C. Royal, e.g.
18. Crown
22. Stadium sections
24. Mdse.
25. Cart part
28. Gender ___
29. Medical suffix
30. City near Venice
31. Popular low-fares flier: abbr.
33. Ingredient
34. Airline monogram
35. Cambodian coin
38. Something to shoot for
39. Rotated
42. Organized group
45. Affirmative action
47. Moon stages
48. Borrowed against
49. ___ Work (road sign)
50. Vedic thunder god
51. Sachet scent
52. Orleans's river
53. Long time follower
54. Morse bits
57. Religious title: Abbr.
59. Lingerie item
60. Alphabet trio

Solution on page 176

Aesop's Fables

Across

1. Shots, for short
5. Japanese food fishes
9. Put in prison
14. Basketball Hall-of-Famer Harshman
15. In the know about
16. Composer Grofe
17. "The Boy Who ___ ___," Aesop Fable
19. Aesop's position in society
20. Palillo of "Welcome Back, Kotter"
21. Vegas opening
23. Soul singer Redding
24. Bonkers
27. Coal bucket
29. Receive by succession
32. A.B.A. member: Abbr.
33. Cage's "Leaving Las Vegas" co-star
34. Snuggle
37. "The Ant and the ___," Aesop Fable
41. Put in stitches?
42. Miner's aid
45. Radiator part
47. Barbary Coast country
49. Product originally named Fruit Smack
52. It happens
53. "The Tortoise and the ___," Aesop Fable
54. State-of-the-art
56. Spanish article
57. "In that thou laid'st __...": Shak.
59. "The ___ ___ Laid the Golden Eggs," Aesop Fable
64. English poet
65. French peak
66. Curse
67. Arm
68. Dirty Harry's employer: Abbr.
69. Religious practice

Down

1. Gremlin producer
2. Make a dent in
3. Dr.'s order
4. Supervisor
5. "The ___ Mouse and the Country Mouse," Aesop Fable
6. Four seasons in Madrid
7. "__ have to do"
8. Chesterfields
9. Failing grades
10. Giant Hall of Famer
11. Spoiled rotten
12. Brand with ibuprofen
13. Ebbets Field shortstop
18. It may get into a jamb
22. Surgical knife
24. Actor Asther of old films
25. The Wildcats of the Atlantic 10 Conf.
26. Ruffian
28. Lone Star State sch.
30. Hormone of the pancreas
31. Audition
35. Moo __ pork
36. When tripled, a WWII film
38. Java is in it
39. Lift
40. Exceptional
43. Hr. fraction
44. Like some answers
45. Horse pen
46. Chemical used as an emollient
48. Spliced item
49. Uniform hue
50. Like some cereals
51. Painter of ballerinas
55. "The ___ in Sheep's Clothing," Aesop Fable
56. Took advantage of
58. S.F. hours
60. Across the street from: Abbr.
61. "Bali ___"
62. Sprint competitor
63. Frequent title starter

Solution on page 176

The Hobbit

Across

1. "___ la vista, baby!"
6. Average marks
10. St. Louis gridders
14. Fall blooming daisylike flowers
15. Silicate stone
16. Opera singer Pinza
17. "Nothing ___!"
18. Thessaly peak
19. Take a header
20. "The Hobbit" author
22. Miscellany
23. Execute perfectly
24. Large soup dish
26. ___ Andy ("Show Boat" role)
30. Kitty's comment
32. Main antagonist in "The Hobbit"
33. Former Secty of the Navy who headed NASA
35. Muse count
37. Bilbo ___ in "The Hobbit"
39. Wizard in "The Hobbit"
44. Rose part
46. Language
47. Middle-___ where "The Hobbit" takes place
51. Lucie's brother
53. Like the Kalahari
54. Continuously
56. Main church section
58. Bridge coup
59. "The Lord ___ ___ ___," novel began as a sequel to "The Hobbit"
65. Cohesive notes?
66. Sci-fi princess
67. Best possible
68. "What are the ___?"
69. "Believe ___ not!"
70. Mild cheese
71. Spiffy
72. Agent Scully
73. Berlin avenue

Down

1. Trip to Mecca
2. Hebrew lyre
3. Tend to the batter
4. Jamboree shelter
5. Inert elemental gas
6. Biscuit
7. Fifth letter of the Greek alphabet
8. Go gingerly
9. Italics feature
10. Form again
11. Georgia state wildflower
12. Surroundings
13. Farewell
21. Sing the blues
25. "___ HOOKS"
26. Corn site
27. Wanted poster abbr.
28. Mrs. Al Bundy
29. Not pos.
31. Hairpiece
34. Suspicious
36. Indigenous
38. But, to Brutus
40. Genetic identifier
41. Farmer's field: Abbr.
42. Him, to Henri
43. Disobeyed a zoo sign?
45. Refer briefly to
47. "For Your Eyes Only" singer
48. Refer indirectly
49. Republic in central Africa
50. Least wild
52. 1943 Bogart film
55. Dependable
57. "All My Children" villainess
60. Salty cheese
61. "American ___" (Fox TV hit)
62. Dickens girl
63. Kotter of "Welcome Back, Kotter"
64. Roy Rogers's real surname

Solution on page 176

Chapter 14: International

Mexican Literature

Across

1. Word after date or time
6. Court grp.
10. Capital of Manche
14. Dog tag datum
15. Straight up
16. Chain with many links?
17. Novel written by 26-Across, translated to "The Underdogs"
19. Lion King's queen
20. Salem-to-Boise dir.
21. Fretted fiddle
22. Montreal university
24. Bryn ___ College
25. Engage in logrolling
26. First of the novelists of the Mexican Revolution
31. Polite
32. Played for a sap
33. Unfold, in verse
35. "Lucky Jim" author
36. Coming after
38. Slumber party guest
39. "Shop ___ you drop"
40. "Ronzoni __ buoni": old ad slogan
41. "Able was __ saw Elba"
42. Mexican author of "Gringo Viejo"
46. Philbin cohort Kelly
47. Palmtop organizers: Abbr.
48. Respiration
51. Business letter abbr.
52. With a needle: Prefix
55. At the drop of ___
56. First Mexican to receive the Nobel Prize in Literature
59. Arid
60. "Over there!"
61. "If I Had a Hammer" singer Lopez
62. Believed
63. Emmy winner Falco
64. "The Second Coming" poet

Down

1. Flat fish
2. Noah count?
3. "As I Lay Dying" father
4. Smaller than lge.
5. Triumph
6. Not yet delivered
7. Close, as an envelope
8. Atlantic City casino, with "the"
9. Medicinal application spray
10. Solitary
11. Ethnic cuisine
12. Hang in the hammock
13. Gem for some Libras
18. Sony acquisition of 2002
23. Gunk
24. Hosp. diagnostics
25. Contemptible
26. Copycat
27. Kansas City college
28. Words before sight and mind
29. France's longest river
30. ___-ski
31. Hipster
34. "Boola Boola" collegian
36. Means of evasion
37. Looped handle
38. Understands
40. Opening
41. Silliness
43. Violent, perhaps
44. Mental grasp
45. 1999 Ron Howard film
48. Shindig
49. First South Korean president
50. Rank above viscount
51. Yours, to Yves
52. Pacific capital
53. Insincere talk
54. Israeli arms
57. Trawler's catch
58. Paydirt

Solution on page 177

Irish Literature

Across

1. Minimal
6. Actress Pitts
10. Field yield
14. Middle of an F major chord
15. Dublin's land
16. Geraldine Chaplin's mother
17. Hayseed
18. Rolaids rival
19. Comply
20. The W.B. in W. B. Yeats, Irish literary figure
23. Saucepot cover
24. In due time
25. Inhabitant of Japan
30. Irish dialect
34. "I guessed it!"
35. Davis of Hollywood
37. Autocrats
38. Recently: Abbr.
40. Irish author of "Gulliver's Travels"
42. Cutter or clipper
43. Checked out
45. Did a doggie trick
47. Form of evidence, these days
48. Blissful
50. Inhabitant of Canada
52. Eliel Saarinen's son
54. Bar stock
55. Irish minimalist playwright
61. Roller coaster cry
62. Awful
63. To one side
65. Yield, as interest
66. Novelist Goncharov
67. "Aladdin" character
68. Pinhead
69. Column next to the ones
70. Rye disease

Down

1. Put down
2. Sufficient, old-style
3. Golfer Isao
4. "A Streetcar Named Desire" woman
5. Effective
6. Sixth letter of the Greek alphabet
7. Cuckoopint, for one
8. Lion, in Swahili
9. Deserving more credit
10. Self-possession
11. Court covering
12. Lulu
13. Salary
21. Nice notions
22. Precisely
25. Irish author of "Ulysses"
26. Leading
27. Deputised group
28. Embroiders
29. Computer of 1946
31. __-dah
32. Russian skater Rodnina
33. House shower
36. Shaving lotion brand
39. Apartment
41. Old Greek garb
44. "Mon ___!"
46. Parcel
49. Charging need
51. More profound
53. Oil source
55. George Bernard ___, Irish playwright
56. Ethereal: Prefix
57. Muffin choice
58. Poetic dusks
59. Sharp flavor
60. Peter, Paul and Mary, e.g.
61. Marked by drinking
64. Asian occasion

Solution on page 177

Charles Dickens

Across

1. J.F.K. advisory
4. Ushers
11. HBO rival
14. "__ won't be afraid": "Stand By Me" lyric
15. Strong
16. Aquatic shocker
17. Dictatorial
19. Opposite SSW
20. "___ Twist," Charles Dickens novel
21. Capital of Ontario
23. Indian bread
24. Era in Great Britain when Dickens wrote
26. Annoyance
28. Ho Chi __
29. Soundless communication: Abbr.
30. Hesitant sounds
31. Type of rug
32. One of TV's Ewings
34. Dicken's holiday story
40. Business mag
41. It may be due
42. A baa maid
43. NYSE listings
45. Jr.'s exam
46. Egg holders: Abbr.
47. Duenna
50. "When We Were Kings" subject
51. The act of uniting again
52. Horse in a Mary O'Hara book
55. Schubert's "The __ King"
56. "David ___," Charles Dickens novel
59. First-rate
60. Rampaging
61. "China Beach" locale
62. Your, to Yves
63. Greek
64. Heavy wts.

Down

1. Inner: Prefix
2. Gimlet or screwdriver
3. Abate
4. Sheets and stuff
5. Cabinet dept.
6. Had fare
7. __ Bingle (Crosby moniker)
8. Pilfer
9. "A house ___ a home"
10. The "N" of U.N.C.F.
11. Court battle?
12. Pertaining to the mind
13. Jones of the Miracle Mets
18. Dr. Pavlov
22. Advertising suffix
24. ___ Cong
25. Topsy-turvy
26. Unimpressive brain size
27. Semicircle
28. Richie's mom, to Fonzie
31. Department of eastern France
32. "Hey, you!"
33. Charade
35. Gone up
36. Some batteries
37. Reserved
38. Fess (up to)
39. Moonves of CBS
43. Browbeat
44. Seeds-to-be
45. Foreign correspondent?
46. Roman 152
47. "___ Expectations," Charles Dickens novel
48. Canon competitor
49. Who "ever loved you more than I," in song
50. Actress Woodard
52. Humorist Lebowitz
53. Grand Dragon's group
54. USN bigwigs
57. Jim Bakker's ministry, briefly
58. Bigfoot's designation?

Solution on page 177

James Joyce

Across

1. Bat maker's tool
6. "Finnegans ___," Joyce novel
10. Little rascals
14. Nocturnal hunter
15. Ornamental jug
16. Anti-piracy org.
17. Third-stringer
18. Vigorous
20. Joyce short story directed as a movie by John Huston
22. Rang out
23. 1040EZ issuer
24. Ibsen's Gabler
25. Child
29. Treasure guardian
33. Prefix with science
34. Q-Tip target
35. Jumble
36. Young ___ (tykes)
37. R-V connection
38. The Tigers, on scoreboards
39. "Forgot About ___" (1999 rap song)
40. Barbara and Jenna, to Jeb
42. Toots
43. Golda of Israel
44. Swamp thing
45. Mishaps
47. Nightclub employee
49. Astronomical altar
50. Flemish painter
52. Joyce novel with the character Leopold Bloom
56. Collection of short stories by James Joyce

58. Swindle
59. "___ where wide the golden sunlight flows": Gilder
60. Children's author Blyton
61. "___ Ben Jonson!"
62. Okla., once
63. Nintendo rival
64. Animate

Down

1. At sea
2. Enemy leader?
3. Drain
4. Erich Weiss's stage name
5. Sportscaster Dick
6. Do a gardening job

7. Barley beard
8. Prison warden
9. Made a boo-boo
10. James Joyce's home country
11. Arachnid
12. Discharged a debt
13. Plate appearance that doesn't count as an AB
19. Ingenious article
21. Column in a ledger
24. Old what's-___-name
25. "A Portrait of the Artist as a ___ Man," Joyce novel
26. ___ vincit amor
27. Not yet hard
28. ___ lepton (physics particle)
30. Like days of yore

31. Have coming
32. Watchful ones
35. Lowly
37. Composer Prokofiev
38. Doctor
41. Person who mends shoes
42. Strong acid, chemically
43. Part of a score
45. Sleuth Lupin
46. Floor duster
48. Laura of "ER"
50. Subterfuge
51. Over, to Otto
52. Food stamp org.
53. Prelude to a duel
54. Neutral tone
55. Short distance
56. Multiplication symbol
57. Apparatus

Solution on page 177

French Literature

Across

1. TV Guide listings
6. No angel
10. Lustful god
14. Free to attack
15. Give a new look to
16. Zola novel
17. _____ acid
18. ___ effort
19. Anatomical passage
20. French literary figure who wrote "The Hunchback of Notre-Dame"
22. Paving stone
23. NASA craft
24. Lead-tin alloy
26. Big zero
30. 9-5 carmaker
32. French "father of science fiction"
33. With no assurance of profit
35. Actress Bonet
37. French poet who wrote "Illuminations"
39. Kind of illusion
44. Plow puller
46. Take off
47. Yogi was behind it
51. West Coast wine region
53. Implored
54. Eye's image receiver
56. "Wayne's World" name
58. Bears: Sp.
59. French novelist and feminist who wrote "Indiana"
65. Elbow-wrist connection
66. Cape Town cash
67. External
68. "As ___ on TV"
69. Game designer Rubik
70. Cardio medication
71. Whitehall whitewall
72. Pizazz
73. Condescend

Down

1. Serb, e.g.
2. Half: Prefix
3. Auricular
4. Have a yen for
5. Pub perch
6. Rodeo bull
7. Option
8. Ouida's "___ of Flanders"
9. Pamplona runners
10. Maroon
11. Violent, perhaps
12. Early afternoon time
13. French existentialist novelist
21. Crash boat mission
25. Shaped like Humpty Dumpty
26. Neither's partner
27. What a "Wheel of Fortune" contestant might buy
28. Mil. honor
29. PD alert
31. Life story, briefly
34. Put away
36. Leaped
38. Dapper one
40. Prank puller
41. Newspaper div.
42. Bygone greeting
43. Blazed a trail
45. Virgin Mary
47. French literary figure who wrote "In Search of Lost Time"
48. Stahl of "60 Minutes"
49. Yom Kippur celebrant
50. Herbal beverage
52. Forgiveness
55. Coincide
57. Ages and ages
60. British nobleman
61. Something to follow
62. Quintillionth: Prefix
63. Literary detective Wolfe
64. Globule

Solution on page 177

Rudyard Kipling

Across

1. To be, in Bordeaux
5. Computer image extension
9. Appends
13. City in West Yorkshire
15. Haste, in Hanover
16. Tight hold
17. Rudyard Kipling's birth country
18. Capital of Italia
19. Tenant's payment
20. Rudyard Kipling's origin tales for kids
23. "___ you serious?"
24. Part of p.c.
25. France's Oscar
28. Healthful
31. Pertaining to Sweden
33. Palindromist's preposition
34. Simile's middle
35. Conservative leader
36. "The Man Who ___ ___ ___," by Rudyard Kipling
40. The __-i-noor diamond
42. Suffix with cash
43. Uncle: Scot.
44. OK, in a way
47. Proposed
51. They have flat tops
52. Braz. neighbor
53. Motor add-on
54. Book of tales by Rudyard Kipling including "Rikki-Tikki-Tavi"
59. Frank server
61. Jorge of '70s-'80s baseball
62. Ten to one, for one
63. Face up to
64. Puffed up
65. Sanctified
66. Japanese sandal
67. Afflictions
68. Brain wave

Down

1. Hebrew prophet
2. Professor's goal
3. Biblical divider
4. Polish language
5. British island
6. Tchaikovsky's first name
7. A Muppet
8. Paraphernalia
9. Concurred
10. Salad sauce
11. "You're a better man than I am, Gunga ___!," Rudyard Kipling
12. Boston or Galveston, e.g. (abbr.)
14. KLM rival
21. Hamlet's love
22. Hard water
26. Peer Gynt's mother
27. Letter after pi
29. DiCaprio, to fans
30. Capote nickname
31. Opposite NNW
32. Sleepless
34. Like pocket dicts.
36. Wind-broken horse
37. Costa __ Sol
38. Global currency org.
39. By birth
40. Rudyard Kipling novel
41. Solitary
45. Bounty's destination
46. Expert ending
47. Keyboard instruments
48. Firmly implanted
49. Kay Thompson creation
50. Sitting Bull, e.g.
52. Pending
55. Rock's Bon ___
56. Russia's ___ Mountains
57. Tarzan creator's monogram
58. Neighbor of Java
59. Noncombat area, for short
60. Fair-hiring letters

Solution on page 177

Robert Louis Stevenson

Across

1. Philosopher Hoffer
5. Molecule builders
10. Sound of a leak
14. WB sitcom about the Hart family
15. Something to talk about
16. Bishop of Rome
17. Bagel topper
18. Singer Lopez
19. Highway
20. Robert Louis Stevenson adventure novel
23. Trade
24. Spread
25. "Strange Case of Dr Jekyll and ___ ___," by Robert Louis Stevenson
28. Robert Louis Stevenson's birth country
33. Discontinue
34. Brings up
35. Pigeon English?
36. Surrounded
37. Discovers
38. Transportation to N.Y.C.
39. Epilogue
40. Shut
41. Duck
42. Step up
44. Got up
45. Apex
46. Draws on
47. Famous character in 20-Across
54. Nil
55. Abreast (of)
56. Compatriot
57. Golfer Aoki
58. Spreadsheet elements
59. Mars rovers' org.
60. One of the Ivies
61. Cap sites
62. Hebrew for "delight"

Down

1. Once, long ago
2. Stern
3. Suffix with flex
4. Activator
5. Harmonize
6. Yankee manager
7. 60's TV boy
8. Prefix for small
9. Cutting instrument for paper
10. Spread out awkwardly
11. Any day now
12. W.W. I plane
13. But, to Brutus
21. A or B, on a record
22. Plenty
25. Fibber of radio
26. Bridle parts
27. Capital of Cuba?
28. Have a feeling
29. Suffix with motor
30. Litmus reddeners
31. Oslo's land, on stamps
32. Actress Mamie Van __
34. Prison uprising
37. Pancake
38. Noted fictional reporter
40. Thick-soled shoe
41. Half of sechs
43. When there's darkness, in a Koestler title
44. Put a value on
46. "I give up!"
47. ___ majeste
48. Algerian seaport
49. Make the first statement of a case
50. In good shape
51. ___ Tepes (Dracula)
52. "What ___?"
53. Tom Clancy hero
54. CITY STATE __

Solution on page 178

Russian Literature

Across

1. English channel, with "the"
5. Indy 500 sound
10. Missive: Abbr.
13. Bronte heroine
14. Prudential rival
15. Peacock tail features
17. Russian novelist who wrote 19-Across
19. "___ Karenina," Russian novel
20. Mature
21. Severe experience
23. Shoebox marking
24. They're tender
26. Applications
28. By means of
29. "___ far, far better thing..."
33. Lean
34. Russian author of "The Artamonov Business"
36. Pronoun
37. Large sailing vessel
38. "___ Como Va" (1971 Santana hit)
39. "Crime and ___," Russian novel
41. Hydrocarbon suffixes
42. SeaWorld attraction
43. Ultimate ending
44. Prohibitionists
45. Wharves
47. Hide _____ hair
48. North American elk
51. Graduating class
55. Peek-__
56. Russian author of 39-Across
59. Pizza Quick Sauce maker
60. Printer company
61. Tiny bit
62. Afros, e.g.
63. Harvests
64. Lacking

Down

1. Lux. neighbor
2. Ogler
3. Slangy suffix
4. Among
5. Worth
6. Poll answerer: Abbr.
7. Mel
8. Experimental artist Yoko
9. City leader
10. Results in
11. Newcastle-upon-___, England
12. Actress Sofer
16. "My Gal ___"
18. Mint stack
22. Run the show
24. Neuter
25. It's no Occident
26. "Okay"
27. Tuscany town
28. Religious pilgrim
30. O. Henry specialty
31. Some terriers
32. They may have it
33. Dosage amts.
34. Start of a Chinese game
35. Verbal jewel
37. Astronaut's wear
40. Irreligious
41. A coming
44. Cooked
46. Duck with soft down
47. Vacancy signs, e.g.
48. "___ and Peace," Russian novel
49. Make ___ call (misjudge)
50. ___ stick
51. "Quit it!"
52. Bone head?
53. Bygone theaters
54. British actress Sylvia
57. Ajar, in poems
58. Medicare's org.

Solution on page 178

The Art of War

Across

1. Honeybunch
5. Bear
10. Comic Marty Allen's greeting, "Hello ___!"
14. Ivy League member
15. Shady spot
16. "Bearded" bloom
17. Spanish pronoun
18. North Sea tributary
19. Film dog
20. "Know your ___ and know yourself," from "The Art of War"
22. "The Art of War" author
24. Make __ for: support
25. Mex. Mrs.
26. Cut over
29. Caesar's lucky number?
30. Terre Haute sch.
33. Like Pindar's works
34. Yoga posture
36. Austrian article
37. "One hundred victories in one hundred battles is not the most skillful. Seizing the enemy ___ ___ is the most skillful," from "The Art of War"
41. USPS limbo
42. Wedding
43. Stockings
44. Thumbs-up
45. "Amscray!"
46. American rival
48. Active ingredient in marijuana
49. Actor with seven Emmys
51. A score
54. Master of any art
57. Llama land
58. "The Art of War" country of origin
60. Head lines, for short?
62. Work with yarn
63. Queues
64. Dumbo's wings
65. Jeanne d'Arc et al.: Abbr.
66. EGBDF part
67. D'back, e.g.

Down

1. Recolor
2. Cushiness
3. An Arkin
4. Investigate
5. Dr. Seuss character
6. Forest
7. Misuse
8. Rebuffs
9. Salad sauce
10. Rigg or Ross
11. Start with while
12. Big name in luxury
13. Son of Rebekah
21. AT&T rival
23. Dickensian clerk Heep
26. Rough and disorderly
27. Roman official
28. Singers Gobbi and Schipa
29. Word in a Carly Simon title
30. Utterly stupid person
31. Clear thinking
32. Exhorted
34. Going strong
35. Bay Area airport letters
38. Zero
39. Vehicle with one wheel
40. "The Art of War" chapter count
46. Insecure
47. ___ Ziyyona, Isr.
48. Some bolt holders
49. Nitrogen compound
50. More judicious
51. Toll rds.
52. Hit the road
53. Lake near Niagara Falls
55. More than lifelike
56. Barbarous person
59. Presumed cause of AIDS
61. Abbr. on old maps

Solution on page 178

Answers

Chapter 1: Romance

Jane Austen

A	A	R	P		P	E	T	A			E	M	M	A
T	H	E	O		A	R	I	D		P	A	E	A	N
M	A	N	S	F	I	E	L	D			L	T	G	E	N
			T	E	N	N	E	S	S	E	E			
I	H	O	P	E	S	O			H	A	R	B	O	R
T	O	P	O			W	A	K	E		S	A	B	E
A	D	O	N	A	I		B	A	I	T		B	S	A
	S	E	N	S	I	B	I	L	I	T	Y			
I	O	S		I	T	N	O		A	M	U	L	E	T
S	P	U	N		H	T	T	P			R	O	D	E
O	S	M	I	U	M			O	R	L	A	N	D	O
		C	H	I	E	F	T	A	I	N				
V	I	D	E	O		P	R	E	J	U	D	I	C	E
H	A	R	S	H		P	E	N	A		O	N	L	Y
S	M	U	T			S	E	T	H		T	O	R	E

Bridget Jones's Diary

N	O	L	A		P	A	N	I	C		F	E	E	S
O	N	E	D		E	L	U	D	E		E	N	V	Y
V	E	A	L		L	A	D	E	N		I	C	E	D
E	D	G	E	O	F	R	E	A	S	O	N			
N	A	U	R	U			S	U	B	S	I	S	T	
A	Y	E		T	H	O	N		S	I	T	C	O	M
		A	R	A	F	A	T			E	O	N	S	
	H	E	L	E	N	F	I	E	L	D	I	N	G	
F	A	V	A		S	A	L	M	O	N				
T	H	E	B	E	S		D	E	N	G		G	E	L
C	A	R	A	C	A	S			M	A	R	C	O	
		S	U	B	T	E	R	R	A	N	E	A	N	
S	T	A	T		R	O	M	E	O		N	E	R	D
L	O	S	E		E	A	M	E	S		E	N	T	O
Y	E	A	R		S	T	A	L	E		S	E	E	N

Wuthering Heights

S	U	M	S		E	R	I	S		O	M	A	R	S
P	R	E	C	E	D	E	N	T		L	O	C	A	L
E	L	L	I	S	B	E	L	L		I	M	A	G	O
C	S	A		S	E	L	A		A	V	E	N	U	E
	N	L	E	R	S		P	N	I	N				
P	A	C	I	N	G		T	O	G	E	T	H	E	R
A	S	H	O	E		S	H	I	R	R		E	A	U
L	Y	O	N		R	A	I	N	Y		T	A	G	S
E	L	L		D	I	D	N	T		S	I	T	E	S
D	A	Y	B	R	E	A	K		J	E	T	H	R	O
			L	I	L	T		T	O	P	I	C		
R	E	H	A	B	S		G	I	S	T		L	T	D
A	B	O	M	B		C	A	T	H	E	R	I	N	E
N	O	B	E	L		B	E	A	U	T	I	F	U	L
A	N	O	D	E		C	A	N	A		A	F	T	A

Danielle Steel

Nora Roberts

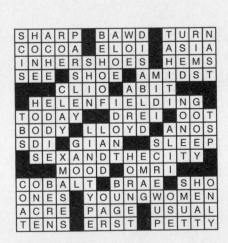

Chick Lit

Romantic Novels at the Movies

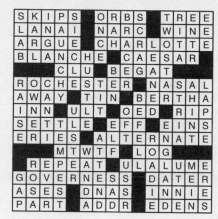

Jane Eyre

The Scarlet Letter

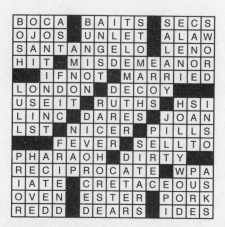

Jackie Collins

Chapter 2: Mystery

Raymond Chandler

```
A S A P . S A C S . S S R S
D A W E S . U T A H . H I F I
O C H E R . M E R E . O D D S
P H I L I P M A R L O W E . .
T E L . A I M . . V E S P A .
S T E W A R T . S H O R T L Y
. . A B A . L O O . . E Y E .
. . T H E B I G S L E E P . .
C H O . L E E . L A W . . . .
D E G R E E S . P A R E N T S
C R E E K . S O N . . E A T .
. . T H E B L U E D A H L I A
H E H E . R A P T . B E L L I
U V E A . E V E R . S L I E R
B E R T . W A R Y . M E D S .
```

Dashiell Hammett

```
C A B S . A S T O R . M A S H
H U L A . W H O L E . A L L Y
I T E M . H A R D B O I L E D
C O W S L I P . . S L I D E .
. . P I L E D . A C E . . . .
S C R A P E . E D W A R D S .
L O A D S . L A Y E R . O H O
A N N E . B O R E D . T O O N
M I C . T O W E R . L O R R E
. C H A R L E S . F I R S T S
. . B U T . T E R S E . . . .
S P L A T . . R O T A T E S .
T H E T H I N M A N . D A Z E
A I D E . C O A S T . O K R A
G L A D . C R I E S . R E A L
```

Sherlock Holmes

```
S I M B A . H A T E . W A L T
U V E A S . A M E N . A M O R
M A G N I F Y I N G . T A R A
O N A D A R E . D R A S T I C
. . . N E S S . P L A I N . .
C H E E S E . P L A I N . . .
R O A M . S A I N T . A D A .
A S T U D Y I N S C A R L E T
M T S . A U D I T . B E A M .
. . . T Y P E S . I C I C L E
B A S R A . H A D A . . . . .
A G A I N S T . G I R A F F E
K I L T . I R E N E A D L E R
E L M O . C U R E . T I E I N
R E I N . K E Y S . S T E N S
```

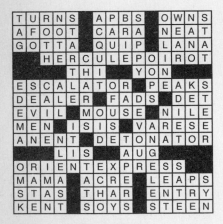

Agatha Christie

```
T U R N S . A P B S . O W N S
A F O O T . C A R A . N E A T
G O T T A . Q U I P . L A N A
. . H E R C U L E P O I R O T
. . T H I . . Y O N . . . . .
E S C A L A T O R . P E A K S
D E A L E R . F A D S . D E T
E V I L . M O U S E . N I L E
M E N . I S I S . V A R E S E
A N E N T . D E T O N A T O R
. . L I S . . A U G . . . . .
O R I E N T E X P R E S S . .
M A M A . A C R E . L E A P S
S T A S . T H A R . E N T R Y
K E N T . S O Y S . S T E E N
```

P. D. James

```
R E C . R A S A . D A R E S
A R L O . A B E D . E V E N T
N O E L . R E N O . B A D L Y
A D A M D A L G L I E S H . .
T E R E S A . P R E . E S P .
. . C O V E R H E R F A C E .
L A B . S I S I . S I D E S .
E R R S . S T A B S . T E N K
T R A I L . T B A R . D E Y .
B E S P E C T A C L E D . . .
E T S . O U I . T S E T S E .
. . E X P E R T W I T N E S S
P A R M A . A M E N . S A G S
B R I E R . D E L E . E R T E
S P E N D . E N D S . S S S .
```

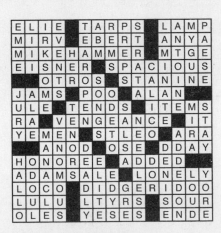

Mickey Spillane

```
E L I E . T A R P S . L A M P
M I R V . E B E R T . A N Y A
M I K E H A M M E R . M T G E
E I S N E R . S P A C I O U S
. . O T R O S . S T A N I N E
J A M S . P O O . A L A N . .
U L E . T E N D S . I T E M S
R A . V E N G E A N C E . I T
Y E M E N . S T L E O . A R A
. A N O D . O S E . D D A Y .
H O N O R E E . A D D E D . .
A D A M S A L E . L O N E L Y
L O C O . D I D G E R I D O O
L U L U . L T Y R S . S O U R
O L E S . Y E S E S . E N D E
```

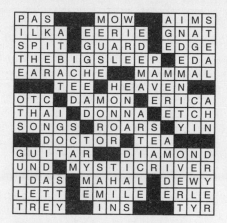

Mystery Novels at the Movies

Edgar Allan Poe

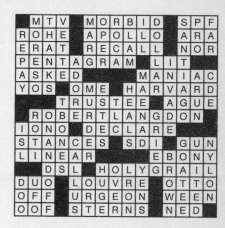

The Da Vinci Code

Chapter 3: Poetry

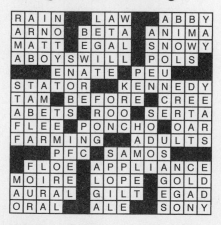

Robert Frost

Poetic Words

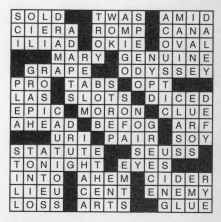

Homer

Howl

```
RESH  HALF  ASEAT
ESTA  AGAR  NEVER
ETAL  NOTE  AMERE
FERLINGHETTI
SERENA   HUH  ROT
     THIS  FEMALE
LOEB  BESTMINDS
ALLEN LIE   ANGEL
VOLAUVENT   TERA
IGETIT   ESPN
NYS  SEA   ABROAD
   SANFRANCISCO
ASIAN  TINA  DCON
MUSIC  EDAM  GAIN
TRADE  REDA  ERNA
```

Howl

Roses Are Red

```
 BAM  ISBN  DEPT
CUBA  TARO  ALOHA
HEAD  SLED  BREAD
ONSET MASS  OTTO
POE   HOOK  HOY
   FERN  TOO  GYM
THREAD KEEP  OOO
WOOD   BED   UNDO
IRS  MIEN  SPREAD
NAY  PRY   BURN
   USA  MOVE  ISH
ACTS  QUAD  SPREE
DREAD SHED  LEAD
MARGE EDGE  ONLY
 BIEN DIAL  WES
```

Roses Are Red

Violets Are Blue

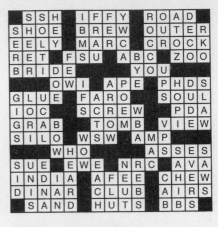

```
 SSH  IFFY  ROAD
SHOE  BREW  OUTER
EELY  MARC  CROCK
RET FSU  ABC  ZOO
BRIDE       YOU
   OWI  APE  PHDS
GLUE  FARO  SOUL
IOC   SCREW  PDA
GRAB  TOMB  VIEW
SILO  WSW   AMP
   WHO     ASSES
SUE EWE  NRC  AVA
INDIA  AFEE  CHEW
DINAR  CLUB  AIRS
 SAND  HUTS  BBS
```

Violets Are Blue

T. S. Eliot

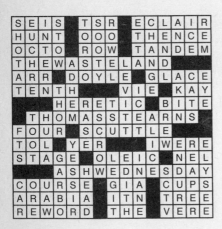

```
SEIS  TSR   ECLAIR
HUNT  OOO   THENCE
OCTO  ROW   TANDEM
THEWASTELAND
ARR DOYLE  GLACE
TENTH  VIE  KAY
   HERETIC  BITE
 THOMASSTEARNS
FOUR  SCUTTLE
TOL  YER   IWERE
STAGE OLEIC  NEL
  ASHWEDNESDAY
COURSE GIA  CUPS
ARABIA ITN  TREE
REWORD THE  VERE
```

T. S. Eliot

The Raven

```
LAVS  CUSP  OCCUR
ERIN  ISLE  POPPA
ELSA  NEAT  EPOCH
WEAKANDWEARY
ANGELA  RNA  ULU
YEE OBTAIN  EPOS
   EMAIL   EXTRA
 EDGARALLANPOE
FLOOR   AIMTO
TSOS COHEIR  SHE
DER  FUR  CASHIN
 CAMEATAPPING
ALIBI GLOB  ANDI
RESET OPAL  STEN
MYRRH NODE  MORE
```

The Raven

Walt Whitman

```
ASH  CDS   AGENTS
STA  PACA  SERUMS
CIVILWAR   ANEMIA
ORAN  GRAS  EWE
TUNAS  FREEVERSE
PATHOS RNA  OAK
  RIM  III  RULE
 LEAVESOFGRASS
HELP  LPN   MAD
AVE   SEE   EASIER
MYCAPTAIN   PASEO
  TUE  KNEE  NCOS
SEINES  DRUMTAPS
SCOTCH OGRE  PEI
HONSHU  YON  ENE
```

Walt Whitman

Chapter 4: Novels

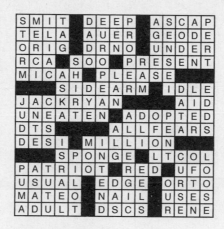

William Faulkner

Tom Clancy

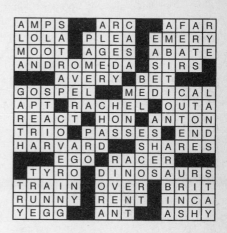

Michael Crichton

Stephen King

John Grisham

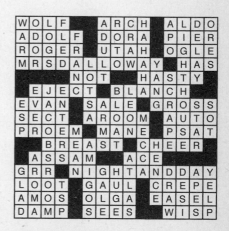

Virgina Woolf

Ayn Rand

John Updike

Gone with the Wind

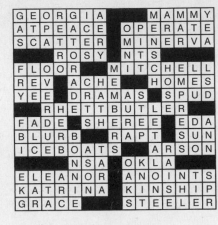

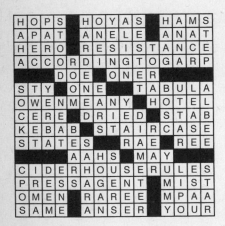

John Irving

Henry Miller

Banned Novels

Chapter 5: Classics

Moby-Dick

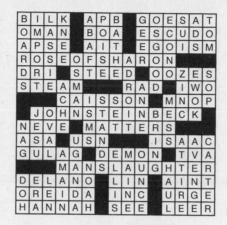

The Grapes of Wrath

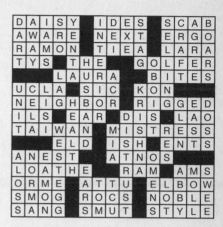

The Great Gatsby

The Catcher in the Rye

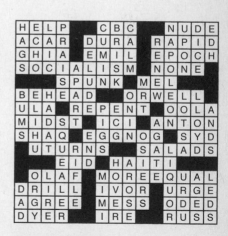

Lord of the Flies

Animal Farm

The Three Musketeers

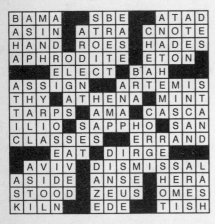

```
A P S I S   P A R I S   I N A
C O C K Y   I T A L Y   M I R
T R I E S   A H M E D   P E A
U T E S     O R S   C A L M
A H N   A C T S O   R O S S I
L O C   S O I   D R E S S E S
  S E A S A L T   A L I E N
      D A R T A G N A N
  N E V I S   N E S T E G G
L O R E L E I   R O E   A A A
E V E N S   S A M M S   L S D
S E C T   K O D     R I C O
B L T   D U M A S   C O L O R
O T O   E D E M A   A L E N E
S Y R   B U R S T   L L O Y D
```

A Tale of Two Cities

```
C A M E   C I R C A   D O R A
A L E X   A C O R N   O M E N
L O O P   R A B A T   N O E S
I T W A S T H E B E S T O F
    N O O N     L U G
L O N D O N   P R O P O S E D
A L I E N   T A U P E   I B O
R I N D   S I R E E   S T O P
A V E   L U R I D   S T O L E
M E R C E D E S   D A R N A Y
    R O D     S O R E
I H A V E E V E R K N O W N
G O O D   N E I L S   G D A Y
A W O L   L E V E E   T A R S
S A K E   Y E A S T   H Y D E
```

To Kill a Mockingbird

```
M E C C A   O F G A B   A C A
E M A I L   N I E C E   T L C
T O M R O B I N S O N   T I T
    I C E E   C T R S   I M O
B A L L   A S H E N   S C A R
O N L E A V E   S C O U T
O D E   L E E J   R I S E
    H A R P E R L E E
A M O R   M O E T   D E M
L E M M E   S H E A R E D
B A D E   N A D I R   D I L L
F B I   A E R O   E L E V
L A C   G R E G O R Y P E C K
A M A   A G A I N   S T R I A
T A L   L Y R E S   E S S A Y
```

Greek Mythology

```
B A M A   S B E     A T A D
A S I N   A T R A   C N O T E
H A N D   R O E S   H A D E S
A P H R O D I T E   E T O N
    E L E C T   B A H
A S S I G N   A R T E M I S
T H Y   A T H E N A   M I N T
T A R P S   A M A   C A S C A
I L I O   S A P P H O   S A N
C L A S S E S   E R R A N D
    E A T   D I R G E
  A V I V   D I S M I S S A L
A S I D E   A N S E   H E R A
S T O O D   Z E U S   O M E S
K I L N   E D E     T I S H
```

Roman Mythology

```
P O O P   A M A J   C E R E S
A R C O   T A B U   E X A C T
N A C L   W R E N   L E T H E
A L U I   O R E O S   M E O W
M E R C U R Y   E M P
    I N K   J U P I T E R
L A R E S   K U N T A   A S H
I S I S   C E N T S   S R T A
D O C   E A R T O   V E N U S
  F O R T U N A   V A L
      A C S   M I N E R V A
O M I T   E M I T S   C O O L
V E S T A   A L I I   T O I T
E M I L Y   R E D O   E N C E
R O N E E   S T A N   D E E R
```

The Prince

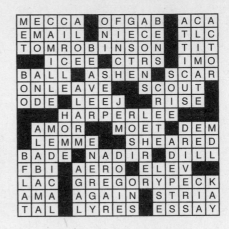

```
C L U B   M A J S   B O S C S
I A N A   P O U T   U N P O T
G R A D U A L L Y   S W O R E
    A N A   E R A   A O N E
P O I L U   P O W E R F U L
E N T O M B S   E N D S
T E E N   A P O L L O
  M A C H I A V E L L I
    M A N T I S   O B O E
    A T O M   I S O B A R S
O R D I N A R Y   F O R C E
R A N T   S E E   F I T
I T A L Y   A L L A T O N C E
E S T E E   D L I I   M E I R
L O E S S   Y S E R   Y E A R
```

Chapter 6: Biography & Memoirs

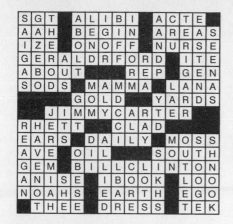

Presidential Autobiographies

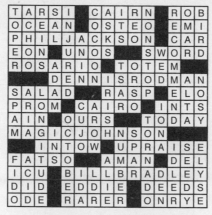

Basketball Biographies

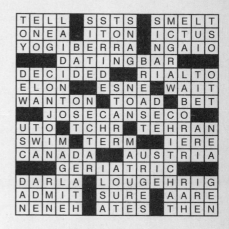

Baseball Biographies

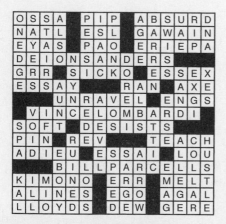

Football Biographies

Tennis Biographies

Boxing Biographies

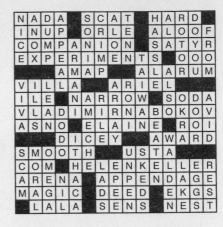

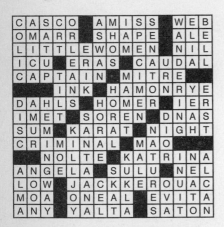

Golf Biographies

```
B A A L   B E T H   F L U T E
A B B A   I R A E   L E G E R
N E A R K I L L   O T H E R
J A C K N I C K L A U S
O R I S O N   O U R   N A M
    V I E W   D I V I N E
P E A L   D A V I S L O V E
A L C O A   E L S   H A B I T
N I C K F A L D O   D E L A
S T R I F E   O P T S
Y E A   I O N   E L A I N E
    A R N O L D P A L M E R
D R E A M   T A K E   L A H R
H O R A E   E R N E   A G R O
S T E A D   S A Y S   N E U R
```

Biographies at the Movies

```
A C T A   S A W   B O M B
C O E D   S P R Y   A O L E R
I D E A   C O G S   F R I D A
D A N G E R O U S   I N N S
    I L E N E   A R F
C A R O L E   E T E R N A L
A B E   E N T I R E   E U R O
R E I G N   H O I   S E R B O
N A N O   B A C K U P   S O S
E M E R S O N   S E V E R E
    I C Y   S C A L E
  P O L O   B E A U T I F U L
D E A L T   A I T S   L A R A
S P R A T   I N C A   E D D Y
T E S S   N E H   D E U S
```

Famous Autobiographies

```
N A D A   S C A T   H A R D
I N U P   O R L E   A L O O F
C O M P A N I O N   S A T Y R
E X P E R I M E N T S   O O O
    A M A P   A L A R U M
V I L L A   A R I E L
I L E   N A R R O W   S O D A
V L A D I M I R N A B O K O V
A S N O   E L A I N E   R O I
    D I C E Y   A W A R D
S M O O T H   U S T A
C O M   H E L E N K E L L E R
A R E N A   A P P E N D A G E
M A G I C   D E E D   E K G S
  L A L A   S E N S   N E S T
```

Autobiographical Novels

```
C A S C O   A M I S S   W E B
O M A R R   S H A P E   A L E
L I T T L E W O M E N   N I L
I C U   E R A S   C A U D A L
C A P T A I N   M I T R E
    I N K   H A M O N R Y E
D A H L S   H O M E R   I E R
I M E T   S O R E N   D N A S
S U M   K A R A T   N I G H T
C R I M I N A L   M A O
    N O L T E   K A T R I N A
A N G E L A   S U L U   N E L
L O W   J A C K K E R O U A C
M O A   O N E A L   E V I T A
A N Y   Y A L T A   S A T O N
```

Chapter 7: Best Sellers

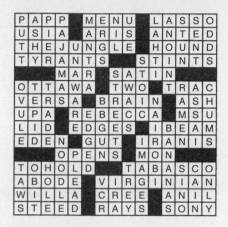

Bestselling Novels in the 1900s

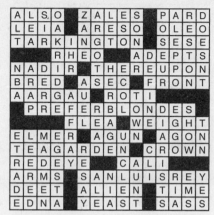

Bestselling Novels in the 1920s

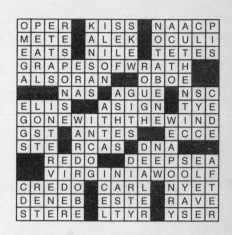

Bestselling Novels in the 1930s

Bestselling Novels in the 1940s

Bestselling Novels in the 1950s

Bestselling Novels in the 1960s

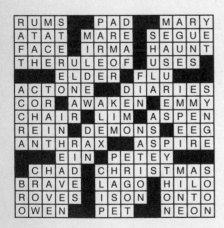

Bestselling Novels in the 1970s

Bestselling Novels in the 1980s

Bestselling Novels in the 1990s

Bestselling Novels in the 2000s

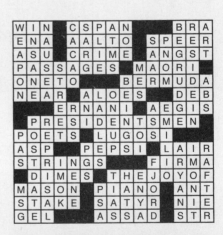

Bestselling Nonfiction in the 1960s

Bestselling Nonfiction in the 1970s

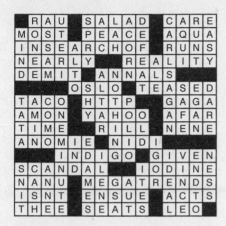

Bestselling Nonfiction in the 1980s

Bestselling Nonfiction in the 1990s

Chapter 8: Fairy Tales

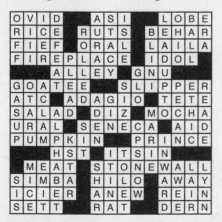

Cinderella

Snow White

Hans Christian Andersen

Three Little Pigs

```
LAP  CANS  AMAZE
ALAD LISA  MEDIC
PERE ARES  ERATO
STICKS CHINCHIN
EASIEST ATIE
 BAYOU  STREEP
WOMEN ENVOY SMU
OPEL BRICK ASIF
LAM BIRTH ADOLF
FLORAL YIELD
 EBBS PLURALS
BLOWYOUR OMELET
AEGIS SOUP STAR
TERRI APSE SODA
SKEET NEED SSW
```

Pinocchio

```
APPLE SPAS BAGS
CLAIM TUSH OVEN
MARIONETTE NOSE
ENT TARTAR SITE
 FIRE LEADER
CARLOCOLLODI
CLEAN LUCY EWE
COST TRACK MRED
PUT RUIN FAIRY
 PERFORMANCES
CANAAN EENY
AMAT ARFARF OFF
FISH WOODCARVER
ECTO ABRI ROUTE
SAYS YEAN EMMET
```

Beauty and the Beast

```
SCALP MIMI APE
UPLOAD ANON MAN
PRINCE MERCHANT
 DESSERT ODER
DEPOSIT TADPOLE
EVEN ROM LAP
BAD VERA NEVER
ADAGE MOL CRANE
RELAX ROSE PTA
 REC IBM COED
AGENDAS BIZARRE
HUGE BABYLON
MARRIAGE ENIGMA
EVE KNEE DENIES
DAT EATS DEATH
```

Charles Perrault

```
GNAW WHAT BRAT
ROME WHILE RIFE
ANYA YODEL ODAS
FOLKTALES SKIRT
 NOTES BEEN
ACCEPT ORANGS
BLISS CUBAN HUE
BINS PARIS COIL
END OASIS BOOTS
 GEORGE DUNDEE
 RUBE VAULT
POETS LITTLERED
LULL COSEC MAYA
UCLA IRISH PREY
SHAW RITT TESS
```

Fairyland Creatures

```
ISAAC ELF GATS
TESSA ASIA OSSO
AVAIL RTEI BTEN
LEPRECHAUN LETA
 BOAT THIRST
SARI RTES ENNEA
DRAGON SIGN
SPENCER MERMAID
 ARAB MYSTIC
TROLL WASI TONI
EARLAP LUNG
NINA IMAGINABLE
SLAM XENA ONLAY
EATA INCR MAUDE
STES EDE EPEES
```

Grimm's Fairy Tales

```
SAMI TSAR BAKED
ULAN ETNA EDINA
CINE TRON AITCH
HANSELANDGRETEL
 CREW RECU
BETRAY TUXEDO
ORNOT THUMB RED
SNOW ERASE WIFE
OST IMAGE DONOT
MTETNA NOOSES
 OHIO SEND
RUMPELSTILTSKIN
ONAIR TAGS MOBY
VINCI ISNO ABEE
EXIST ASSN NEXT
```

Chapter 9: Satire

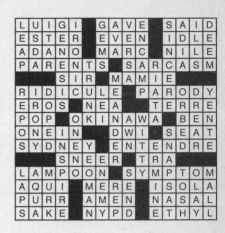

Lewis Carroll

Mark Twain

Satire Words

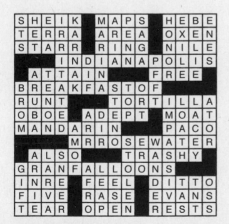

Kurt Vonnegut

Joseph Heller

Dark Satire

```
P D A S   O G E E   A K E L A
E R S T   D O M E   L E V E L
S O Y A   E V I L   L E A V E
T W O G E N T L E M E N
O N U S E S   D A Y   U A L
    L E S T   T W I N G E
  S A M   T H E T A M I N G
L A N A I   D R Y   Y A T E S
O F W I N D S O R   M E S
S E A N C E   B E T A
T S R   U M P   O L I V I A
    A B O U T N O T H I N G
M A R L A   R A C K   E S T A
F A U L T   S L A T   A T E M
R U S S E   E E R O   R A R E
```

Shakespeare Comedies

```
P I N T   S A N T A   M E S A
I T O O   E X C E L   Y V E S
N E W O R L E A N S   R E M Y
S M I L E D   A D O A N N I E
    E G O S       B A T
E T A   E M U L A T E   U M A
L I N E N   N A D A   C A I B
I G N A T I U S J R E I L L Y
S E A T   U N T O   N I L E S
A R B   A M U S I N G   Y R S
        E A R   N O R I
P U L I T Z E R   B A R E S T
H E L D   A N E M O M E T E R
A L E A   N O T E D   N O T O
T E E N   E S S A Y   E N I D
```

A Confederacy of Dunces

```
S T R O P   M S E C   A B A S
U H U R A   A C R O   P A N E
C A D E T   S H O E   O R N E
K N I G H T H O O D   G O L F
        S O I L   S C E N E I
P E R P   S E A S   R E S E T
J E E V E S   R A C E
S E T T L E D   W O O S T E R
        I D E E   U N A B L E
A R I S E   S N A P   D A M P
C A S T L E   G L O M
T I L E   M E L A N C H O L Y
I S A N   I M A S   G E N O A
V I N O   L I N K   E L C I D
E N D S   E R D A   E L E N A
```

P. G. Wodehouse

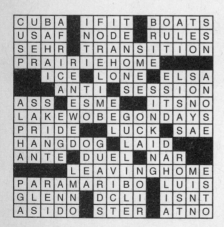

```
C U B A   I F I T   B O A T S
U S A F   N O D E   R U L E S
S E H R   T R A N S I T I O N
P R A I R I E H O M E
    I C E   L O N E   E L S A
      A N T I   S E S S I O N
A S S   E S M E   I T S N O
L A K E W O B E G O N D A Y S
P R I D E   L U C K   S A E
H A N G D O G   L A I D
A N T E   D U E L   N A R
    L E A V I N G H O M E
P A R A M A R I B O   L U I S
G L E N N   D C L I   I S N T
A S I D O   S T E R   A T N O
```

Garrison Keillor

```
B O O B   C L O G   A S K S
A M M O   H O A R Y   S E E K
R A I N   O L S E N   S P R Y
I N T H E P I T S   C U T I E
    O V E N S   S A M I
R A M M E D   S P E E C H
C H O I R   A G A I N   T O W
M E T E   P L A N T   P A R A
P A H   G R E G G   C A N S T
D E N N I S   B A S K E T
  R E A M   G N A T S
P S H A W   T R A N S P O R T
H O O T   C R A N E   O D O R
I D O L   D I S C S   R E M O
L A D Y   C O P E   T R A Y
```

Erma Bombeck

Chapter 10: Science Fiction

H. G. Wells

```
ORAL  THEDA  GLAD
DEMI  RAPID  ROSA
SCAT  AREAL  ARID
 THETIMEMACHINE
  RAN      IRA
ONTAP  KOO  UMASS
SERT  MEANIE  ITA
THEINVISIBLEMAN
IIS  OPTION  NERI
ASSET  HSN  AVERT
   NIP    DIE
 WAROFTHEWORLDS
ALOU  EATEN  OURS
CLOG  RIDGE  PATE
OATH  ORSON  ELAN
```

Sci Fi Novels at the Movies

```
ALEC  PANIC  ORDO
LEMA  ELIDE  REUP
DAMN  RISES  GENT
AHANDMAIDSTALE
   IRIS   PAN
IROBOT  EGOISTE
RECAP  CAROL  IMA
KAEL  RURAL  PREP
STA  DARTS  SAONE
 ANGUISH  WORLDS
  URL    SOMA
 MINORITYREPORT
LONG  OLORD  ETUI
ESTH  AERIE  THEM
SHOO  DREAD  SORE
```

Ray Bradbury

```
AMBO  NAPPY  BETS
ROAN  ACARE  OSHA
CHRONICLES  OTRO
TAR  IVES  TAKEI
III  CES  HERSELF
CROOK  STARK  MLI
   WEB  AID  NEST
 ILLUSTRATED
MTNS  THU  YUM
AHS  ITEMS  ROUND
PIERCED  PIE  NOU
 SCOUR  WADE  RVS
SWUM  FAHRENHEIT
HARP  LHASA  RACE
EYES  YATES  SLED
```

Jules Verne

```
IKES  BACK  GENA
LAKES  AWHO  PIED
WHERE  TEAR  AGED
UNDERTHESEA  HDL
   IRS   ASSTS
 TAFFY  DONKEY
ABBR  STAY  SEDAN
ISLA  THREW  MANO
SPENT  ENZO  EYED
 SCENES  MIDST
 SEENO   LAD
SEA  THECENTEROF
NEMO  EXIT  ALIVE
ADAR  LETT  GAVEL
GYNT  PSIS  MART
```

2001 A Space Odyssey

```
TACT  APIAN  INCH
HOUR  NOTSO  SEEM
AUDI  GOTIN  RAES
ITSFULLOFSTARS
  ELEE   EKE
TRACES  MONOLITH
YENTE  GUESS  SOO
CHIA  ELSIE  MING
HAL  ANEEL  LATKA
OBSERVES  IONIAN
  NAE   AGED
 STANLEYKUBRICK
WARM  OPERA  ASEA
ADUE  PINON  KEPT
HEEL  ESSNA  EEEE
```

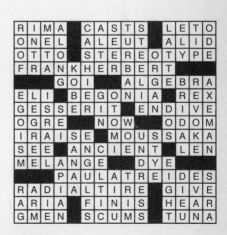

Dune

```
RIMA  CASTS  LETO
ONEL  ALEUT  ALID
OTTO  STEREOTYPE
FRANKHERBERT
   GOI  ALGEBRA
ELI  BEGONIA  REX
GESSERIT  ENDIVE
OGRE  NOW  ODOM
IRAISE  MOUSSAKA
SEE  ANCIENT  LEN
MELANGE   DYE
 PAULATREIDES
RADIALTIRE  GIVE
ARIA  FINIS  HEAR
GMEN  SCUMS  TUNA
```

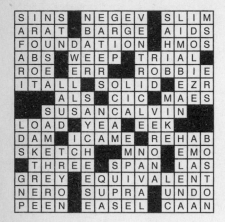

Isaac Asimov

Robert A. Heinlein

The Hitchhiker's Guide to the Galaxy

Chapter 11: Drama

King Lear

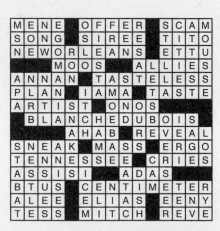

A Streetcar Named Desire

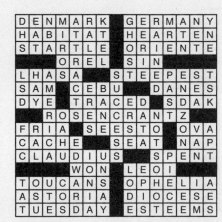

Hamlet

Dramatic Words

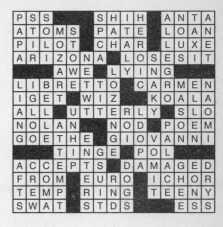

A Midsummer Night's Dream

Opera

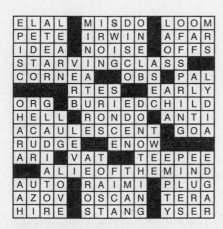

Sam Shepard

Arthur Miller

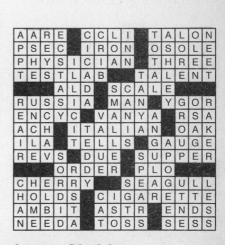

Anton Chekhov

Romeo and Juliet

Chapter 12: Award Winners

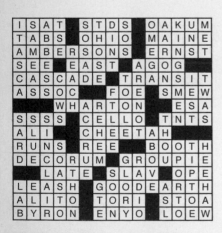

Pulitzer Prize for the Novel Before 1950

Pulitzer Prize for Fiction in the 1950s

Pulitzer Prize for Fiction in the 1960s

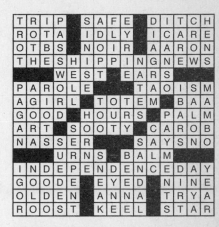

Pulitzer Prize for Fiction in the 1970s

Pulitzer Prize for Fiction in the 1980s

Pulitzer Prize for Fiction in the 1990s

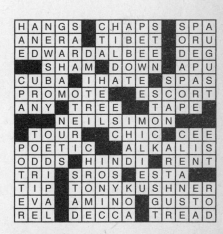

Pulitzer Prize for General Non-Fiction

Pulitzer Prize for Drama in the 1980s

Pulitzer Prize for Drama in the 1990s

Hugo Awards

Nobel Prize in Literature Before 1950

Nobel Prize in Literature After 1950

National Book Awards Before 1980

National Book Awards in the 1980s and 1990s

Chapter 13: Children's Books

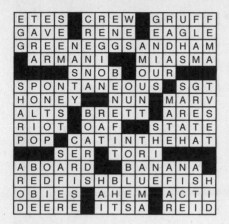

Dr. Seuss

The Little Engine That Could

The Wizard of Oz

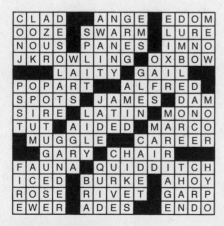

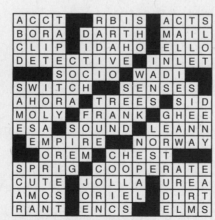

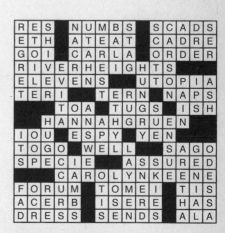

Harry Potter

The Hardy Boys

Nancy Drew

Winnie the Pooh

Make Way for Ducklings

Charlotte's Web

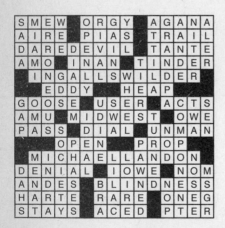

Little House on the Prairie

Aesop's Fables

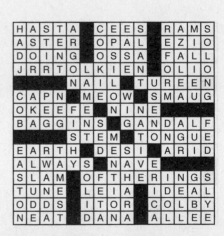

The Hobbit

Chapter 14: International

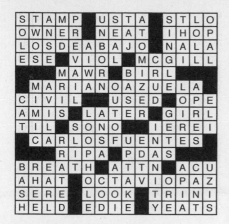

Mexican Literature

Irish Literature

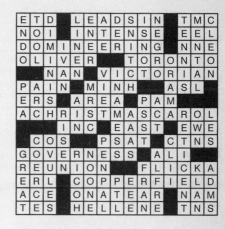

Charles Dickens

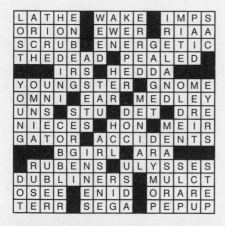

James Joyce

French Literature

Rudyard Kipling

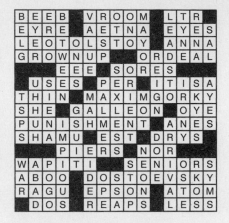

Robert Louis Stevenson

Russian Literature

The Art of War

THE EVERYTHING SERIES!

BUSINESS & PERSONAL FINANCE

Everything® Accounting Book
Everything® Budgeting Book
Everything® Business Planning Book
Everything® Coaching and Mentoring Book, 2nd Ed.
Everything® Fundraising Book
Everything® Get Out of Debt Book
Everything® Grant Writing Book
Everything® Guide to Foreclosures
Everything® Guide to Personal Finance for Single Mothers
Everything® Home-Based Business Book, 2nd Ed.
Everything® Homebuying Book, 2nd Ed.
Everything® Homeselling Book, 2nd Ed.
Everything® Improve Your Credit Book
Everything® Investing Book, 2nd Ed.
Everything® Landlording Book
Everything® Leadership Book
Everything® Managing People Book, 2nd Ed.
Everything® Negotiating Book
Everything® Online Auctions Book
Everything® Online Business Book
Everything® Personal Finance Book
Everything® Personal Finance in Your 20s and 30s Book
Everything® Project Management Book
Everything® Real Estate Investing Book
Everything® Retirement Planning Book
Everything® Robert's Rules Book, $7.95
Everything® Selling Book
Everything® Start Your Own Business Book, 2nd Ed.
Everything® Wills & Estate Planning Book

COOKING

Everything® Barbecue Cookbook
Everything® Bartender's Book, 2nd Ed., $9.95
Everything® Calorie Counting Cookbook
Everything® Cheese Book
Everything® Chinese Cookbook
Everything® Classic Recipes Book
Everything® Cocktail Parties & Drinks Book
Everything® College Cookbook
Everything® Cooking for Baby and Toddler Book
Everything® Cooking for Two Cookbook
Everything® Diabetes Cookbook
Everything® Easy Gourmet Cookbook
Everything® Fondue Cookbook
Everything® Fondue Party Book
Everything® Gluten-Free Cookbook
Everything® Glycemic Index Cookbook
Everything® Grilling Cookbook
Everything® Healthy Meals in Minutes Cookbook
Everything® Holiday Cookbook

Everything® Indian Cookbook
Everything® Italian Cookbook
Everything® Low-Carb Cookbook
Everything® Low-Cholesterol Cookbook
Everything® Low-Fat High-Flavor Cookbook
Everything® Low-Salt Cookbook
Everything® Meals for a Month Cookbook
Everything® Mediterranean Cookbook
Everything® Mexican Cookbook
Everything® No Trans Fat Cookbook
Everything® One-Pot Cookbook
Everything® Pizza Cookbook
Everything® Quick and Easy 30-Minute,
　　　　5-Ingredient Cookbook
Everything® Quick Meals Cookbook
Everything® Slow Cooker Cookbook
Everything® Slow Cooking for a Crowd Cookbook
Everything® Soup Cookbook
Everything® Stir-Fry Cookbook
Everything® Sugar-Free Cookbook
Everything® Tapas and Small Plates Cookbook
Everything® Tex-Mex Cookbook
Everything® Thai Cookbook
Everything® Vegetarian Cookbook
Everything® Wild Game Cookbook
Everything® Wine Book, 2nd Ed.

GAMES

Everything® 15-Minute Sudoku Book, $9.95
Everything® 30-Minute Sudoku Book, $9.95
Everything® Bible Crosswords Book, $9.95
Everything® Blackjack Strategy Book
Everything® Brain Strain Book, $9.95
Everything® Bridge Book
Everything® Card Games Book
Everything® Card Tricks Book, $9.95
Everything® Casino Gambling Book, 2nd Ed.
Everything® Chess Basics Book
Everything® Craps Strategy Book
Everything® Crossword and Puzzle Book
Everything® Crossword Challenge Book
Everything® Crosswords for the Beach Book, $9.95
Everything® Cryptic Crosswords Book, $9.95
Everything® Cryptograms Book, $9.95
Everything® Easy Crosswords Book
Everything® Easy Kakuro Book, $9.95
Everything® Easy Large-Print Crosswords Book
Everything® Games Book, 2nd Ed.
Everything® Giant Sudoku Book, $9.95
Everything® Kakuro Challenge Book, $9.95
Everything® Large-Print Crossword Challenge Book
Everything® Large-Print Crosswords Book
Everything® Lateral Thinking Puzzles Book, $9.95

Everything® Literary Crosswords Book, $9.95
Everything® Mazes Book
Everything® Memory Booster Puzzles Book, $9.95
Everything® Movie Crosswords Book, $9.95
Everything® Music Crosswords Book, $9.95
Everything® Online Poker Book, $12.95
Everything® Pencil Puzzles Book, $9.95
Everything® Poker Strategy Book
Everything® Pool & Billiards Book
Everything® Puzzles for Commuters Book, $9.95
Everything® Sports Crosswords Book, $9.95
Everything® Test Your IQ Book, $9.95
Everything® Texas Hold 'Em Book, $9.95
Everything® Travel Crosswords Book, $9.95
Everything® TV Crosswords Book, $9.95
Everything® Word Games Challenge Book
Everything® Word Scramble Book
Everything® Word Search Book

HEALTH

Everything® Alzheimer's Book
Everything® Diabetes Book
Everything® Health Guide to Adult Bipolar Disorder
Everything® Health Guide to Arthritis
Everything® Health Guide to Controlling Anxiety
Everything® Health Guide to Fibromyalgia
Everything® Health Guide to Menopause
Everything® Health Guide to OCD
Everything® Health Guide to PMS
Everything® Health Guide to Postpartum Care
Everything® Health Guide to Thyroid Disease
Everything® Hypnosis Book
Everything® Low Cholesterol Book
Everything® Nutrition Book
Everything® Reflexology Book
Everything® Stress Management Book

HISTORY

Everything® American Government Book
Everything® American History Book, 2nd Ed.
Everything® Civil War Book
Everything® Freemasons Book
Everything® Irish History & Heritage Book
Everything® Middle East Book
Everything® World War II Book, 2nd Ed.

HOBBIES

Everything® Candlemaking Book
Everything® Cartooning Book
Everything® Coin Collecting Book
Everything® Drawing Book

Everything® Family Tree Book, 2nd Ed.
Everything® Knitting Book
Everything® Knots Book
Everything® Photography Book
Everything® Quilting Book
Everything® Sewing Book
Everything® Soapmaking Book, 2nd Ed.
Everything® Woodworking Book

HOME IMPROVEMENT

Everything® Feng Shui Book
Everything® Feng Shui Decluttering Book, $9.95
Everything® Fix-It Book
Everything® Green Living Book
Everything® Home Decorating Book
Everything® Home Storage Solutions Book
Everything® Homebuilding Book
Everything® Organize Your Home Book, 2nd Ed.

KIDS' BOOKS

All titles are $7.95
Everything® Kids' Animal Puzzle & Activity Book
Everything® Kids' Baseball Book, 4th Ed.
Everything® Kids' Bible Trivia Book
Everything® Kids' Bugs Book
Everything® Kids' Cars and Trucks Puzzle and Activity Book
Everything® Kids' Christmas Puzzle & Activity Book
Everything® Kids' Cookbook
Everything® Kids' Crazy Puzzles Book
Everything® Kids' Dinosaurs Book
Everything® Kids' Environment Book
Everything® Kids' Fairies Puzzle and Activity Book
Everything® Kids' First Spanish Puzzle and Activity Book
Everything® Kids' Gross Cookbook
Everything® Kids' Gross Hidden Pictures Book
Everything® Kids' Gross Jokes Book
Everything® Kids' Gross Mazes Book
Everything® Kids' Gross Puzzle & Activity Book
Everything® Kids' Halloween Puzzle & Activity Book
Everything® Kids' Hidden Pictures Book
Everything® Kids' Horses Book
Everything® Kids' Joke Book
Everything® Kids' Knock Knock Book
Everything® Kids' Learning Spanish Book
Everything® Kids' Magical Science Experiments Book
Everything® Kids' Math Puzzles Book
Everything® Kids' Mazes Book
Everything® Kids' Money Book
Everything® Kids' Nature Book
Everything® Kids' Pirates Puzzle and Activity Book
Everything® Kids' Presidents Book
Everything® Kids' Princess Puzzle and Activity Book
Everything® Kids' Puzzle Book
Everything® Kids' Racecars Puzzle and Activity Book
Everything® Kids' Riddles & Brain Teasers Book
Everything® Kids' Science Experiments Book
Everything® Kids' Sharks Book

Everything® Kids' Soccer Book
Everything® Kids' Spies Puzzle and Activity Book
Everything® Kids' States Book
Everything® Kids' Travel Activity Book

KIDS' STORY BOOKS

Everything® Fairy Tales Book

LANGUAGE

Everything® Conversational Japanese Book with CD, $19.95
Everything® French Grammar Book
Everything® French Phrase Book, $9.95
Everything® French Verb Book, $9.95
Everything® German Practice Book with CD, $19.95
Everything® Inglés Book
Everything® Intermediate Spanish Book with CD, $19.95
Everything® Italian Practice Book with CD, $19.95
Everything® Learning Brazilian Portuguese Book with CD, $19.95
Everything® Learning French Book with CD, 2nd Ed., $19.95
Everything® Learning German Book
Everything® Learning Italian Book
Everything® Learning Latin Book
Everything® Learning Russian Book with CD, $19.95
Everything® Learning Spanish Book with CD, 2nd Ed., $19.95
Everything® Russian Practice Book with CD, $19.95
Everything® Sign Language Book
Everything® Spanish Grammar Book
Everything® Spanish Phrase Book, $9.95
Everything® Spanish Practice Book with CD, $19.95
Everything® Spanish Verb Book, $9.95
Everything® Speaking Mandarin Chinese Book with CD, $19.95

MUSIC

Everything® Drums Book with CD, $19.95
Everything® Guitar Book with CD, 2nd Ed., $19.95
Everything® Guitar Chords Book with CD, $19.95
Everything® Home Recording Book
Everything® Music Theory Book with CD, $19.95
Everything® Reading Music Book with CD, $19.95
Everything® Rock & Blues Guitar Book with CD, $19.95
Everything® Rock and Blues Piano Book with CD, $19.95
Everything® Songwriting Book

NEW AGE

Everything® Astrology Book, 2nd Ed.
Everything® Birthday Personology Book
Everything® Dreams Book, 2nd Ed.
Everything® Love Signs Book, $9.95
Everything® Love Spells Book, $9.95
Everything® Numerology Book
Everything® Paganism Book
Everything® Palmistry Book
Everything® Psychic Book
Everything® Reiki Book
Everything® Sex Signs Book, $9.95

Everything® Spells & Charms Book, 2nd Ed.
Everything® Tarot Book, 2nd Ed.
Everything® Toltec Wisdom Book
Everything® Wicca and Witchcraft Book

PARENTING

Everything® Baby Names Book, 2nd Ed.
Everything® Baby Shower Book, 2nd Ed.
Everything® Baby's First Year Book
Everything® Birthing Book
Everything® Breastfeeding Book
Everything® Father-to-Be Book
Everything® Father's First Year Book
Everything® Get Ready for Baby Book, 2nd Ed.
Everything® Get Your Baby to Sleep Book, $9.95
Everything® Getting Pregnant Book
Everything® Guide to Pregnancy Over 35
Everything® Guide to Raising a One-Year-Old
Everything® Guide to Raising a Two-Year-Old
Everything® Guide to Raising Adolescent Boys
Everything® Guide to Raising Adolescent Girls
Everything® Homeschooling Book
Everything® Mother's First Year Book
Everything® Parent's Guide to Childhood Illnesses
Everything® Parent's Guide to Children and Divorce
Everything® Parent's Guide to Children with ADD/ADHD
Everything® Parent's Guide to Children with Asperger's Syndrome
Everything® Parent's Guide to Children with Autism
Everything® Parent's Guide to Children with Bipolar Disorder
Everything® Parent's Guide to Children with Depression
Everything® Parent's Guide to Children with Dyslexia
Everything® Parent's Guide to Children with Juvenile Diabetes
Everything® Parent's Guide to Positive Discipline
Everything® Parent's Guide to Raising a Successful Child
Everything® Parent's Guide to Raising Boys
Everything® Parent's Guide to Raising Girls
Everything® Parent's Guide to Raising Siblings
Everything® Parent's Guide to Sensory Integration Disorder
Everything® Parent's Guide to Tantrums
Everything® Parent's Guide to the Strong-Willed Child
Everything® Parenting a Teenager Book
Everything® Potty Training Book, $9.95
Everything® Pregnancy Book, 3rd Ed.
Everything® Pregnancy Fitness Book
Everything® Pregnancy Nutrition Book
Everything® Pregnancy Organizer, 2nd Ed., $16.95
Everything® Toddler Activities Book
Everything® Toddler Book
Everything® Tween Book
Everything® Twins, Triplets, and More Book

PETS

Everything® Aquarium Book
Everything® Boxer Book
Everything® Cat Book, 2nd Ed.
Everything® Chihuahua Book

Everything® Cooking for Dogs Book
Everything® Dachshund Book
Everything® Dog Book
Everything® Dog Health Book
Everything® Dog Obedience Book
Everything® Dog Owner's Organizer, $16.95
Everything® Dog Training and Tricks Book
Everything® German Shepherd Book
Everything® Golden Retriever Book
Everything® Horse Book
Everything® Horse Care Book
Everything® Horseback Riding Book
Everything® Labrador Retriever Book
Everything® Poodle Book
Everything® Pug Book
Everything® Puppy Book
Everything® Rottweiler Book
Everything® Small Dogs Book
Everything® Tropical Fish Book
Everything® Yorkshire Terrier Book

REFERENCE

Everything® American Presidents Book
Everything® Blogging Book
Everything® Build Your Vocabulary Book
Everything® Car Care Book
Everything® Classical Mythology Book
Everything® Da Vinci Book
Everything® Divorce Book
Everything® Einstein Book
Everything® Enneagram Book
Everything® Etiquette Book, 2nd Ed.
Everything® Guide to Edgar Allan Poe
Everything® Inventions and Patents Book
Everything® Mafia Book
Everything® Martin Luther King Jr. Book
Everything® Philosophy Book
Everything® Pirates Book
Everything® Psychology Book

RELIGION

Everything® Angels Book
Everything® Bible Book
Everything® Bible Study Book with CD, $19.95
Everything® Buddhism Book
Everything® Catholicism Book
Everything® Christianity Book
Everything® Gnostic Gospels Book
Everything® History of the Bible Book
Everything® Jesus Book
Everything® Jewish History & Heritage Book
Everything® Judaism Book
Everything® Kabbalah Book
Everything® Koran Book

Everything® Mary Book
Everything® Mary Magdalene Book
Everything® Prayer Book
Everything® Saints Book, 2nd Ed.
Everything® Torah Book
Everything® Understanding Islam Book
Everything® Women of the Bible Book
Everything® World's Religions Book
Everything® Zen Book

SCHOOL & CAREERS

Everything® Alternative Careers Book
Everything® Career Tests Book
Everything® College Major Test Book
Everything® College Survival Book, 2nd Ed.
Everything® Cover Letter Book, 2nd Ed.
Everything® Filmmaking Book
Everything® Get-a-Job Book, 2nd Ed.
Everything® Guide to Being a Paralegal
Everything® Guide to Being a Personal Trainer
Everything® Guide to Being a Real Estate Agent
Everything® Guide to Being a Sales Rep
Everything® Guide to Being an Event Planner
Everything® Guide to Careers in Health Care
Everything® Guide to Careers in Law Enforcement
Everything® Guide to Government Jobs
Everything® Guide to Starting and Running a Catering Business
Everything® Guide to Starting and Running a Restaurant
Everything® Job Interview Book
Everything® New Nurse Book
Everything® New Teacher Book
Everything® Paying for College Book
Everything® Practice Interview Book
Everything® Resume Book, 2nd Ed.
Everything® Study Book

SELF-HELP

Everything® Body Language Book
Everything® Dating Book, 2nd Ed.
Everything® Great Sex Book
Everything® Self-Esteem Book
Everything® Tantric Sex Book

SPORTS & FITNESS

Everything® Easy Fitness Book
Everything® Krav Maga for Fitness Book
Everything® Running Book

TRAVEL

Everything® Family Guide to Coastal Florida
Everything® Family Guide to Cruise Vacations
Everything® Family Guide to Hawaii
Everything® Family Guide to Las Vegas, 2nd Ed.
Everything® Family Guide to Mexico
Everything® Family Guide to New York City, 2nd Ed.
Everything® Family Guide to RV Travel & Campgrounds
Everything® Family Guide to the Caribbean
Everything® Family Guide to the Disneyland® Resort, California Adventure®, Universal Studios®, and the Anaheim Area, 2nd Ed.
Everything® Family Guide to the Walt Disney World Resort®, Universal Studios®, and Greater Orlando, 5th Ed.
Everything® Family Guide to Timeshares
Everything® Family Guide to Washington D.C., 2nd Ed.

WEDDINGS

Everything® Bachelorette Party Book, $9.95
Everything® Bridesmaid Book, $9.95
Everything® Destination Wedding Book
Everything® Elopement Book, $9.95
Everything® Father of the Bride Book, $9.95
Everything® Groom Book, $9.95
Everything® Mother of the Bride Book, $9.95
Everything® Outdoor Wedding Book
Everything® Wedding Book, 3rd Ed.
Everything® Wedding Checklist, $9.95
Everything® Wedding Etiquette Book, $9.95
Everything® Wedding Organizer, 2nd Ed., $16.95
Everything® Wedding Shower Book, $9.95
Everything® Wedding Vows Book, $9.95
Everything® Wedding Workout Book
Everything® Weddings on a Budget Book, 2nd Ed., $9.95

WRITING

Everything® Creative Writing Book
Everything® Get Published Book, 2nd Ed.
Everything® Grammar and Style Book
Everything® Guide to Magazine Writing
Everything® Guide to Writing a Book Proposal
Everything® Guide to Writing a Novel
Everything® Guide to Writing Children's Books
Everything® Guide to Writing Copy
Everything® Guide to Writing Graphic Novels
Everything® Guide to Writing Research Papers
Everything® Screenwriting Book
Everything® Writing Poetry Book
Everything® Writing Well Book